REINVENTING
METAL

Copyright © 2013 by Neil Daniels

All rights reserved. No part of this book may be reproduced in any form, without written permission, except by a newspaper or magazine reviewer who wishes to quote brief passages in connection with a review.

Published in 2013 by Backbeat Books
An Imprint of Hal Leonard Corporation
7777 West Bluemound Road
Milwaukee, WI 53213

Trade Book Division Editorial Offices
33 Plymouth St., Montclair, NJ 07042

Printed in the United States of America

Library of Congress Cataloging-in-Publication Data is available upon request.

ISBN 978-1-48034-103-6

www.backbeatbooks.com

REINVENTING METAL

The True Story of Pantera and the Tragically Short Life of Dimebag Darrell

AN UNAUTHORIZED BIOGRAPHY

NEIL DANIELS

Backbeat Books

An Imprint of Hal Leonard Corporation

To Darrell Lance Abbott,
also known as Dimebag Darrell,
R.I.P.
(August 20, 1966–December 8, 2004)

CONTENTS

Foreword by Jeff Waters — ix

Acknowledgments — xiii

Introduction — xv

PART ONE
THE GLAM METAL YEARS

1 At Hell's Gates: The Birth of the Panther — 3

2 Rock Out: The Making of *Metal Magic* — 15

3 Heavy Metal Rules: Pantera Unleashes *Projects in the Jungle* — 23

4 Onward We Rock: The Release of *I Am the Night* — 31

5 Rock the World: Phil Anselmo, *Power Metal*, and the Dawn of a New Era — 53

PART TWO
SOUTHERN COWBOYS FROM HELL

6 At the Cemetery Gates: Finding a Label — 73

7 Psychos from the South: The Release of *Cowboys from Hell* — 81

8 Demons Be Driven: The Release of *Vulgar Display of Power* — 103

9 Strength Beyond Strength: The Release of *Far Beyond Driven* — 115

Contents

10 Five Minutes Alone: Communication Breakdown and Band Tension — 123

PART THREE
THE GREAT SOUTHERN TRENDKILLERS

11 Underground in America: The Release of *The Great Southern Trendkill* — 135

12 Hell's Wrath: Band Life Ain't Easy — 141

13 Southern Shredders: Ozzfest, *Official Live*, and Some Much-Needed Downtime — 149

14 Goddamn Electric: Pantera Hit the Studio for *Reinventing the Steel* — 159

15 Immortally Insane: Pantera on Tour — 169

16 We'll Grind That Axe for a Long Time: The Inevitable Breakup of the Band — 179

Epilogue: A Decade of Domination—The Tragic Death of Dimebag Darrell and the Enduring Legacy of the Panther — 187

Afterword by Brian Slagel — 211

Discography — 213

Sources — 223

Index — 233

FOREWORD

WHEN I FIRST MET PANTERA, my band Annihilator had released *Alice in Hell*, which was considered an international hit record. Then we did our second album (*Never, Neverland*) and it was an even bigger success. We did a worldwide headlining tour for all of 1990 and were just finishing up when Judas Priest asked us to be their special guest on their mega-album *Painkiller*. I'd heard that Glenn Tipton chose Annihilator for the tour and Rob Halford picked the opening act. Glenn liked our record, which was amazing for me, as I was their number-one fan as a teen.

Rob's pick was a new band called Pantera. He said he thought they were going to be huge, famous, amazing, and groundbreaking. I don't think a lot of people listened to him—we didn't! None of the people on tour—not even the fans that were at these shows—had any idea what was going on. There was actually a bit of a negative reaction to Pantera. We shared a tour bus with them and, despite the clear cultural differences, we all got along, for the most part, in the name of metal, and having an amazing time supporting one of our favorite bands.

Foreword

Back in '91, a singer with a shaven head, tattoos, and baggy shorts, jumping around like a monkey and putting his middle finger in the air, was *not* what a European traditional heavy metal fan base was looking for onstage. Phil Anselmo looked more like a punk rocker; a Henry Rollins/punk rocker–type guy. It was absolutely something that was not around in heavy metal. If you can believe this, there were shows where they would get booed, and they were even happy to get off the tour halfway through. There were actually shows where they would walk offstage early, as the crowd was sometimes not happy with the aggressive attitude being shown to them by Phil, Rex Brown, and Diamond (as he was known then) Darrell Abbott. They were really good but we didn't clue in to just what these guys were about to do; nor did the fans or a lot of the press. Rob Halford got it, though. He got it way before the tour started. He saw another legend coming up.

I would meet them at their shows in Vancouver for years to come. The most memorable was on the *Reinventing the Steel* tour. I'd followed them in the '90s through music video channels, and of course everybody was wearing Pantera T-shirts. I knew they were a big band, but I didn't really get it until I saw that last tour. Kerry King or Tom Araya (from Slayer) had me on their guest list, but to be safe I got Phil Anselmo to put me on his, too. Early in the afternoon, I hung with the band and crew, talked about old times, and spent the rest of the day with Phil. I just assumed it was a double bill, or that Pantera were a special guest. I'm standing on Kerry's side of the stage, watching Slayer. The kids are going crazy. It was an awesome reaction, as always, for Slayer. I thought, How the fuck does Pantera follow that? How do you follow what I just saw from Slayer? Jesus Christ! And what happens next? Pantera came out with a slick light show, a bigger stage show, bigger explosions, pyro, flames, massive, powerful riffs, grooves, and sounds.

Foreword

And then I realized: Oh my God, they're the fucking headliners! That blew my mind—Pantera were even bigger than I thought they were! I was like, Jeff, you idiot, you're still getting it wrong after all these years. It was amazing to see full hockey arenas, with two bands of this caliber, playing in these venues. This was an era where traditional heavy music was literally banished to the underground by labels, press, the industry . . . unless you were playing a new kind of metal.

Pantera were an inspiration to musicians, fans, and bands like mine—bands that were simply trying to hang in and survive the roughest decade in real metal music. On a personal note, they left me with a great lesson that many young (and older) bands can learn from: No matter what you think of a band or a musician, *never* pass judgment on what you *think* is their potential . . . or else they might surprise you and make you look like a total idiot.

Jeff Waters
Annihilator
annihilatormetal.com

ACKNOWLEDGMENTS

Thanks to the following rockers and metalheads for making this book possible and for their ongoing support: Buddy Blaze, Steve Blaze, John Dittmar, Bernard Doe, Damon Duperre, Marc Ferrari, Joe Giron, Terry Glaze, Donny Hart, Gary Hetrick, Kenny King, Steve Kleinberg, Lenise Lopez, Bernadette Malavarca, Joel McIver, Jason McMaster, Mörat, Rick Mythiasin, Jamie Nelson, Walter O'Brien, Derek Oliver, Dave Peacock, Rick Perry, Martin Popoff, Karla Pronschinske, Paul Rees, Derek Shulman, Brian Slagel, Stuart Taylor, Kyle Thomas, Walter Trachsler, John Tucker, Mary Vandenburg, Jeff Waters, Jerry Warden, Frank White, and Neil Zlozower.

Thank you again to the following people for allowing me to interview them for the purposes of this book: Buddy Blaze, Steve Blaze, John Dittmar, Bernard Doe, Damon Duperre, Marc Ferrari, Joe Giron, Terry Glaze, Donny Hart, Gary Hetrick, Kenny King, Steve Kleinberg, Lenise Lopez, Jason McMaster, Mörat, Rick Mythiasin, Walter O'Brien, Dave Peacock, Rick Perry, Paul Rees, Derek Shulman, Brian Slagel, Stuart Taylor,

Acknowledgments

Kyle Thomas, Walter Trachsler, Jeff Waters, Jerry Warden, and Neil Zlozower.

Thank you again to the following people for allowing me to quote from their work for the purposes of this book: Chris Akin, Jason Arnopp, Vik Bansal, Bobby Black, Tony Bonyata, Nick Bowcott, Rich Catino, Spence D, Colin Devenish, Robyn Doreian, Patrick E. Douglas, Cameron Edney, Dave Everley, D. X. Ferris, Janiss Garza, Brandon Geist, Chris Gill, Mike Gitter, Joshua Gropp, Kenny Herzog, Shannon Joy, Jeff Kerby, Christopher Krovatin, Elliot Levin, Brandon Marshall, Keith McDonald, Therese McKeon, Metal George, Metal Odyssey, Gerri Miller, Mörat, H. P. Newquist, Justin M. Norton, Jeff Perlah, Rafi, Ramsey Ramirez, Steven Rosen, Amy Sciarretto, Roger Scott, Debbie Seagle, Lisa Sharken, Joshua Sindell, Skwer, Tazz Stander, Brad Tolinski, Jason Wellwood, David Lee Wilson, Ian Winwood, and James Zahn.

Apologies if I have missed any names—it was not intentional! Honest.

Visit neildaniels.com and neildanielsbooks.wordpress.com for details on my other books.

INTRODUCTION

WITH TWENTY MILLION ALBUMS SOLD and an enduring legacy, Pantera's influence on modern metal is assured. Their story is a tragic and complicated one, however, not only because of the murder of guitarist Dimebag Darrell Abbott, on December 8, 2004, but also because of the bad blood and hostility that continues to exist between the three surviving members.

Reinventing Metal is the first biography to tackle the story of one of the most innovative and influential metal bands of the past twenty years. It's a story that begins in Arlington, Texas, in the early '80s, at a time when American metal was just coming to fruition in the form of Californian thrash-metal bands like Metallica, Exodus, and Slayer, and New Yorkers like Anthrax.

In the beginning, Pantera were part of the glam-metal scene, but as 1986 dawned and thrash-metal bands began to make their mark, Pantera became something far more aggressive. With the arrival of a new front man from New Orleans, the no-bullshit Phil Anselmo, a new era began. Pantera's major-label breakthrough, *Cowboys from Hell*, and its mesmerizing follow-up,

Introduction

Vulgar Display of Power, are still regarded as among the greatest metal albums in popular music history.

Despite the reverence bestowed upon them, however, the band had a relatively short life span. From 1983 to 2000 they released only nine studio albums, the first four of which have been permanently deleted by a band that was never interested in trading on past glories (hence the song "Yesterday Don't Mean Shit"). Yet Pantera's impact on metal is still keenly felt more than a decade after their bitter, highly publicized split.

There have been notable spin-off bands, including the successful Down and Superjoint Ritual projects, led by singer Phil Anselmo, and Damageplan, formed by the late guitarist Dimebag Darrell and his elder brother, Vinnie Abbott. But they will forever be overshadowed by Pantera, who were one of only a handful of American metal bands to fill arenas around the world in the '90s (a famously difficult period for metal following the rise and eventual disintegration of the pompous, metal-hating Seattle grunge scene).

Pantera had an enormous influence on nu metal, groove metal, metalcore, and grindcore, and also earned the respect of the bands that inspired them in the first place, such as Black Sabbath, Kiss, Van Halen, and Metallica. There will never be a reunion—there could never be without the driving force of Dimebag Darrell—but with the various reissues and compilations to have seen the light of day since the band's split, there remains a constant thirst for all things Pantera.

Despite the success Pantera achieved, however, there has to date been only one related biography, *Black Tooth Grin: The High Life, Good Times, and Tragic End of Dimebag Darrell Abbott* by Zac Crain (2009). The other Dimebag-related book is *A Vulgar Display of Power: Courage and Carnage at the Alrosa Villa* by Chris Armold, which was published in 2007. The latter is an interesting read, although perhaps in bad taste considering its focus on Dimebag's murder. Dimebag Darrell's family

Introduction

released an official pictorial book, *He Came to Rock*, in 2008. But those books deal with Dimebag; *Reinventing Metal* is a book about the band.

This biography was written without the cooperation of the band, but I did speak to numerous people associated with them: friends who grew up with the Abbott brothers in Arlington, former roadies, and even former band members from the early years, as well as record company personnel from the *Cowboys from Hell* period onward. They know the story of Pantera as well as anyone else does.

There remains a tight veil around the band, and I did meet some resistance in writing this book, but it needed to be written. Such is the level of security around Pantera that once word began to spread about my attempts to interview those associated with the band's past or present, a number of potential interviewees dropped out, not wanting to sever ties with or potentially upset the band. One unnamed interviewee even went so far as to retract his interview after a very enjoyable transatlantic phone conversation; others simply refused to reply to my correspondence and reportedly warned off others from speaking to me. Rex Brown and Phil Anselmo have since announced their own autobiographies, but this book tells the band's story from all sides.

Pantera really were a unique band, innovative and dangerous. *Reinventing Metal* will tell you why.

Neil Daniels
September 2012
neildaniels.com

PART ONE

THE GLAM METAL YEARS

1

AT HELL'S GATES: THE BIRTH OF THE PANTHER

Kiss Alive. It made me wanna play music!
—Vinnie Paul to Ramsey Ramirez of Magx Online, 2010

WHEN PANTERA STARTED LIFE IN 1981 they were a very different band, fronted not by the iconic Phil Anselmo but by a Texan singer named Donny Hart. They were called Pantera's Metal Magic, and they sounded as fanciful and frivolous as the name suggests. The initial lineup consisted of eleventh grader Vince Abbott (Vinnie Paul Abbott) on drums and his younger brother, Darrell, on guitar, plus bassist Tommy Bradford, guitarist Terry Glaze (who was in the same class at Arlington High School as Vinnie), and the aforementioned Hart on vocals.

They were just a bunch of kids playing around, getting their feet wet, copying their rock star heroes. Hart owned a PA system and had previously played in a band with his high school buddy Bradford. Vinnie had been in bands too. Bradford was the quiet, Charlie Watts member of the band; he and Hart would attempt to play some of their favorite songs, including complicated epics like Led Zeppelin's "Stairway to Heaven." When Glaze moved into the neighborhood, the three budding musicians became friends. Things were falling into place.

Although Vinnie was fairly quiet growing up, he was an extremely proficient drummer. He was also somewhat cunning. When Bradford, Hart, and Glaze said they wanted to play with him, Vinnie told them he would only join if he could bring his kid brother along too. Vinnie was an excellent musician, but the others weren't really interested in Darrell. Vinnie, on the other hand, didn't think very much of Hart. The compromise was that both could stay in the band.

The six-piece lineup of Pantera's Metal Magic made their live debut in the drama hall of Vinnie's school, James Bowie High School. It was something of a novelty for the other kids at the school to have classmates who could actually play rock music, as Donny Hart remembers:

"I can vividly recall one particular moment. I can't remember what song it was on but out of the corner of my eye could see something flying past me, and that's Darrell doing a knee-slide. I think we did three concerts [in total]. I went to Sam Houston High School, and in my second year of high school we did concerts there, too, just as we did at James Bowie High School, and then in between those two we did a concert at a community center that was more like a party. We just handed out flyers and spread word of mouth and we had so many kids show up that the cops came and shut us down."

The core of the band was undoubtedly the Abbott brothers. Before he became known as Diamond Darrell, the younger Abbott was born Darrell Lance Abbott on August 20, 1966, in Ennis, Texas, to parents Carolyn and Jerry. Jerry was known locally as a country musician and producer. Darrell got into music relatively late compared to other famed guitarists. The story goes that one Christmas, Jerry asked him if he wanted a BMX bike or a guitar; Darrell chose the bike. However, after discovering first Black Sabbath and then Kiss, he asked his old man if he could trade in the BMX for a Hondo Les Paul, which he played through a small Pignose amp. Darrell's fate was sealed. "Initially, I just used the guitar as a prop," he later told *Guitar World*'s Brad Tolinski. "I'd pose with it in front of a mirror in my Kiss makeup when I was skipping school."

Before long Darrell had mastered the lead riff to Deep Purple's hard rock monster "Smoke on the Water." Jerry showed his son how to play barre chords, while Darrell soon discovered the Electro-Harmonix Big Muff Pi fuzz and feedback distortion. But the impact of Kiss guitarist Ace Frehley cannot be overstated. Darrell would dress up as Frehley, complete with the Kiss makeup, and stand in front of the mirror with his fake starburst orange-pink Les Paul guitar, posing as his rock idol, imagining himself as an extrovert rock star.

One of Darrell's childhood buddies was Gary Hetrick, who was also a cousin of Rita Haney, Darrell's future on/off girlfriend. "He was the biggest Kiss fan," Hetrick recalls. "We used to walk up to this little store called U-Totem when the Kiss cards came out. We bought Kiss cards there and would open them on the back steps of Short Elementary School. We used to go to a drugstore and . . . get all the magazines like *Sixteen*, and they were always just covered with Kiss posters. We tried to get every new poster we could find."

Little did Darrell know that, many years later, at the height of their popularity, Pantera would end up opening for their shock-rock heroes. When he met Frehley as an adult, he asked the Kiss guitarist to autograph his chest; such was Darrell's dedication to the band that he then had the autograph tattooed so it could never be washed off.

After Frehley, Darrell's biggest influence was undoubtedly the eccentric Dutch-born American shredder Eddie Van Halen, whose band Van Halen released their self-titled studio debut in 1978. He also loved the music of British rock band Def Leppard—particularly their first album, *On Through the Night*, which made greater use of the twin-guitar sound than did latter-day Leppard albums—and was a big fan of Angus Young of AC/DC and Michael Schenker, the German guitarist formally of Scorpions and the British band UFO.

Initially, Darrell's influences were not particularly wide-ranging in that he did not stray outside of popular music. He wasn't into jazz or classical; in fact, the only remotely classical influence he had was Randy Rhoads of Quiet Riot and the Blizzard of Ozz. There were also local influences, like Bugs Henderson and Jimmy Wallis, and of course ZZ Top's Billy Gibbons, a fellow Texan, was another major source of inspiration. The band's gritty, hard-nosed blues-rock would provide a template for Pantera, who retained some touches of the blues—a genre lost on many other metal bands—even in their later years. (It is almost obligatory for Texans to like ZZ Top's music in the same way that New Jerseyites tend to love the music of Bruce Springsteen.)

Darrell's tastes broadened over time. He also enjoyed the music of a number of blues artists and country singers, such as Merle Haggard and David Allan Coe, and would develop a fierce appreciation for the soul/funk-influenced hard-rock band King's X. He learned quite early on—through his father—that great musicians have eclectic tastes and influences in music. It's unlikely that he would have turned out to be such a great player if he had only ever listened to Ace Frehley.

As well as showing Darrell various different chord shapes, Jerry also taught his son to play a number of songs, including the J. J. Cale classic "Cocaine," subsequently made famous by Eric Clapton. He also showed his son how to tune a guitar. Aside from that, Darrell was almost totally self-taught, and did not take guitar lessons. The last thing he wanted to do was to go home and learn a riff from a chord sheet. He listened to the music and learned by ear. The process was one of trial and error.

Darrell's parents divorced when he was in his teens. Jerry Abbott moved into a trailer park down in Arlington, Texas, and worked at a studio called Pantego Sound. Darrell started to hang out there as a teenager, and soon got to know the business and the technology behind the making of records. He wanted to see what his dad did at work. Jerry would even pay him a few dollars here and there for helping out. But Darrell never abused his dad's hospitality, and always asked if it was okay for him to spend a bit of time at the studio. "When you're a little kid, you have nerve," he later told *Guitar World*'s Brad Tolinski. "I'd walk right up to whoever was recording and say, 'Hey, dude, what's the lick of the week?' I'd be strappin' them dudes up, and getting them to show me their shit."

Darrell soon made a name for himself in local talent contests, and during one such show at the Agora Ballroom in Dallas he won a maroon-colored Dean ML electric guitar. The guitar would have an interesting future, and one that is certainly worth retelling.

A few years later, age sixteen, Darrell wanted a car—specifically a yellow Pontiac Firebird, *the* car of choice for American teens during the '80s. He needed to raise about $600 to buy one. He had barely used the maroon ML since he won it; he hated it, in fact, and it had practically lived under his bed until he swapped it for his buddy Walter Trachsler's Hondo, which looked like Eddie Van Halen's guitar. But now he wanted it back.

Darrell showed the guitar to his friend Buddy Blaze, who was in his early twenties at the time and already had a collection of six or seven guitars. Blaze actually had an ML of his own on order from Dean Zelinsky in a different color; he wanted Darrell's guitar, but he didn't want to buy it from him. "Don't sell your trophies," he told the overexcited teen. "One day it will be something to show the kids and be proud of."

Some time later, the singer in Buddy Blaze's band walked into a rehearsal with a maroon Dean ML that he'd just bought from their mutual friend, Darrell, for $500. Blaze didn't want him to play the guitar in public so he gave the singer his Kramer guitar, fitted with a Floyd Rose tremolo, to use instead. Blaze himself played the ML for about a month, but only at rehearsals, never in public. He painted it candy-apple blue with some crappy paint and left it for about a year before he added a Floyd Rose, changed the bridge pickups, and made a few further adjustments to improve the sound. It still wasn't flashy enough for him, however. Blaze liked the way the guitar sounded but wanted to change the look of it some more:

"This is the real truth about the inspiration for the paint job: Eddie Ojeda from Twisted Sister was in all these videos with this cartoon lightning bolt guitar, and I thought, Man, that's kinda cool, but how come nobody's ever done a real lighting storm? I got together with this guy named Craig Patchin in Dallas and we went through a bunch of encyclopedias. We were looking at pictures of lightning storms and things like that. I told Craig what I didn't like and what I did like about it and he took a stab at it. I painted the guitar a base coat blue and Craig [added] the lightning finish. I picked the hardware. I was a machinist. I picked the Floyd and took it to the shop and ground the saddles to pick the radius of the pickup board and did that black and chrome thing. Basically, that became the 'Dean from Hell.' I played it for a couple of years like that. I would show it at guitar shows and things like that. Darrell came up to me one day and he said, 'Hey dude, make me a copy of that guitar.' He goes, 'I love that thing. Can you make me a copy of it?' I go, 'Sure, no problem.'"

In the meantime, Blaze had begun making guitars for Vivian Campbell of Whitesnake, and in 1987 had moved over to Kramer Guitars, where he launched the NightSwan. He was about to move to New Jersey from Dallas and was far too busy to make a copy of the Dean ML for Darrell. The last thing he did before leaving was go to Darrell's house to give him the ML guitar. Darrell told him there was no way he could take the guitar—what if he scratched it? Blaze said he could borrow it for a few months. A few weeks later, Darrell called him to say he wanted to add a Lawrence pickup to the guitar, and then called back a few weeks after that to say he wanted to keep the instrument: He just had to have it.

Blaze: "I said, 'Darrell, do you remember when you tried to sell me that guitar that you won?' He goes, 'Yeah.' I said, 'Well, that's that guitar. Do you remember when I said never sell your trophies?' He said, 'Yeah.' And I said, 'Well, you're lucky that it ended up in my hands. . . . It was always yours—just keep it.' He was like, 'You're fuckin' kiddin' me, man. How much? I've got this Flying V, I'll send it to you.' And I go, 'Whatever, Darrell.' He said, 'Do you like sneakers? What size do you wear?' He sent me a pair of python sneakers [made from] snakeskin and made me this god-awful cheap pair of sunglasses. I still have those, too: He put my name on them with lightning bolts. . . .

"It truly was my favorite guitar. I re-carved it. I set the Floyd on it properly. It took a lot of work but the proof is in the pudding. Darrell recorded everything with that guitar, and God knows how many shows he played with it. I never sold the guitar back to Darrell. . . . We were brothers."

Darrell had no idea that the 'Dean from Hell' would become as iconic as Eric Clapton's Blackie Stratocaster, Eddie Van Halen's Frankenstrat, and Jimi Hendrix's Flying V. But then, the guitar wasn't the only thing he won in talent shows as a teenager. In fact, it has been said he was barred from entering some contests because his playing was so good that it was obvious he was going to walk out of the venue with the top prize.

Back then, the two things Darrell loved the most were his guitar and his yellow Firebird, which sat parked outside the family home. It sat there for a long time, in fact, on account of all the speeding tickets he received, which he would stick to his bedroom wall next to posters of Ace Frehley.

Darrell's friend Gary Hetrick witnessed to some of the other formative moments in the guitarist's teenage years. Older brother Vinnie would sometimes rub people up the wrong way, but Darrell wasn't like that. Everybody knew who he was on account of his burgeoning reputation as a guitar player, and he was very popular with the girls in Arlington. But his first love was always music, as Hetrick recalls:

"It took him a long time to lose his virginity, and once that happened he wasn't bangin' chicks every night. He wasn't a real ladies' dude. He was more an observer of people, and he was real private, too. Every fucking night people would knock on his door or ring his door[bell] wanting to talk with him. My job was to go and answer the door like the gatekeeper and I would tell people he's practicing. Even if he was in there watching TV; no, he's practicing. I ran people off a lot."

Darrell's closest relationship, however, was with his brother. Vincent Paul Abbott was born on March 11, 1964. His friends called him Vince, but in later years he preferred to go by the name Vinnie Paul. Growing up together in a musical house, the Abbott brothers shared mutual influences, although Vinnie's heroes were largely drummers: Neil Peart of the Canadian progressive-rock band Rush and Peter Criss of Kiss; Alex Van Halen and Tommy Aldridge, John Bonham and Keith Moon. He also enjoyed painting and building models.

Darrell later recounted Vinnie's introduction to the drums in an interview with *Guitar World*'s Brad Tolinski: "One day Vinnie came home from school with a fuckin' tuba. My old man said, 'Son, you won't be able to make a penny playing that thing. Take it back right now and tell them that you're going to play drums!'"

Like the Van Halen brothers, Eddie and Alex, Darrell and Vinnie Abbott had a tight friendship based on mutual respect and admiration. There was an abundance of chemistry between them, and it seemed inevitable that the brothers would eventually form some kind of musical union. They learned a lot from each other, and had the same goal—to be rock stars. While Darrell would become the key musician in Pantera, Vinnie played a fundamental role in teaching his brother about timing, and how important it is to get it right. Once, when they were practicing Boston's AOR hit "More Than a Feeling," Vinnie pointed out that Darrell had missed a chord and insisted they learn the song properly.

Each of the Abbotts brought something different to the table: Vinnie, his strict business sense and blue-collar ethic, Darrell, his street smarts and energy. They respected each other's differences from the start and learned how to work together. Vinnie played the typical elder brother at times to keep Darrell in line, and they had their fair share of teenage arguments and fights, but they knew they were fortunate to have each other. The fact that Vinnie could play the drums as well as he did back then was a source of pride for Darrell, and vice versa. They had a sort of silent communication and each knew intuitively what the other was thinking, which would sometimes make life difficult for the rest of Pantera in the future.

One day, when Vinnie was listening to his precious collection of 45s in his room, Darrell came in with his guitar and amp and asked his older brother if he wanted to jam. Vinnie asked him what he wanted to play, and Darrell said he knew "Smoke on the Water." They played the opening lead riff for hours, building upon their immediate, instinctive chemistry. It was in the blood.

Pantera's Metal Magic would often rehearse at the Abbott household, which soon came to resemble a practice room with a kitchen. The boys' mom, Carolyn, was like a second mother to many of their friends. She'd come home from work and cook dinner before she retired to her bedroom while her boys and their friends played rock music all night. She let them have as much freedom as they wanted and rarely told them to turn down the volume. Sometimes things got out of hand, however, and Jerry would have to step in and tell them to behave.

"I remember [once] their dad threw us all out," says Stuart Taylor, a budding photographer (and, back then, a homeless drug addict) who lived with the Abbotts for a time. "It was one time after a concert.... Pantera had a band hotline and people would prank call [it] all the time. The phone rings, Darrell answers it, and somebody hung up on him, so when the phone rings again, Rex [Brown] goes, 'I'll handle this.' He gets the phone, he picks up, and goes, 'Hey, you son of a bitch and motherfucker, don't be fuckin' callin' here—Oh shit! It's Darrell's dad!' He yelled at Rex and Darrell on the phone . . . and told everyone to get their crap out of the house."

Nonetheless, Jerry spent a lot of time with the band and would often invite them down to Pantego Sound. He was coaching his boys in the hope that one day they would become professional rock stars. If success did arrive at some point in the future, he figured, there might be some fiscal remuneration. They were an investment. Even back then, the intention was always to make an album. Jerry was extremely supportive and eager to help; anything his boys were part of, he was interested in—not that they realized how good they had it at the time. Years later, after he had left the band, Donny Hart looked back and realized what a big perk it was for Pantera's Metal Magic to have access to Jerry and Pantego Sound.

Hart wrote some lyrics for the band, but much of their material was written by Terry Glaze, who would also collaborate with Vinnie and Tommy Bradford. They'd try to fit in jamming and songwriting sessions after school and at weekends, where they would play songs by their idols, including the whole of Def Leppard's *On Through the Night* as well as songs by April Wine, AC/DC, Kiss, and British heavy metal stalwarts Judas Priest.

Pantera's approach to music was not the same as that of every other up-and-coming band. Sure, they liked to have fun, but they had a long-term vision, too. They were more focused on learning from Angus and Malcolm Young and the Van Halens than on chasing girls. If they nurtured their own music and got a major record deal, they reasoned, they'd get all the women and booze they wanted. They would look at their favorite bands and analyze the chords and rhythms behind the hooks and solos. Why are these riffs catchy? they wondered. Given their talent, drive, and charisma, it seemed almost inevitable that they were going to make it work.

* * *

In 1982, after playing live shows around Texas, the band dropped the "Metal Magic" and became known simply as Pantera (which means *panther* in Spanish). The next significant step was the departure of Donny Hart, who was far from keen on the direction the band's music was taking. Terry Glaze took over as front man, leaving Darrell as the band's sole guitarist. To begin with, Glaze had been the more skilled player, but after putting in hours of painstaking practice Darrell soon began to outpace him, so when Hart switched high schools, Glaze took the opportunity to focus on singing instead. Hart was never too far away, however, and would have a surprising reunion with the band later in the decade.

The amended lineup of Pantera—singer Terry Glaze, guitarist Darrell Abbott, drummer Vinnie Abbott, and bassist Tommy Bradford—quickly built up a reputation on the Texas club scene, where they played Van Halen and Kiss covers. The Texas underground metal scene was heavy by the standards of the time but not compared with today's bands. Darrell was such an enthusiastic Kiss fan that he'd proudly show off his Ace Frehley impressions and the Kiss stickers that shone on his guitar.

As well as playing gigs in their home state, Pantera also ventured as far as Oklahoma and Louisiana to perform, but they remained nothing more than a cult name on the live circuit. Back home in Arlington, Texas, they were fast becoming local rock stars. Despite the band's early success, however, Tommy Bradford decided he wanted to do something different with his life and left the band during his senior year of high school. Pantera needed a new bass player.

Rex Robert Brown, or Rex Rocker as he became known during the early years of the band, was born in Graham, Texas, on July 27, 1966. He went to a nearby high school and had played in other bands locally, so the remaining members of Pantera already knew him by reputation. Brown was a very talented musician, but he had recently declined the offer of a scholarship to the University of North Texas as a jazz bassist—which was just as well, because soon after that Pantera reached out to offer him a job as their new bass player.

The chemistry between the four musicians was apparent as soon as they started jamming. And with that they began to put in place the foundations of a band that would forever change the sound of American metal.

2

ROCK OUT: THE MAKING OF *METAL MAGIC*

I don't know if it came from my dad's studio or from listening to my mom's eight-track Lynyrd Skynyrd tapes back in the day . . . before I even knew what Van Halen was or Black Sabbath or Kiss.

—Dimebag Darrell to Joshua Gropp of Guitar World, 2004

PANTERA PLAYED WITH SOME OF THE BIGGEST glam-metal bands of the early '80s, including Quiet Riot, Stryper, and Dokken. If any of those bands visited Texas, Pantera would support them. They had a blast every time. Both Vinnie and Darrell were amazing players, and they had so much confidence that Terry Glaze and Rex Brown never felt like they had to do it all themselves. The Abbotts were always there to back them up.

There was an enormous sense of power in the band. When they came up with an idea, they would just improvise around it, and invariably they would pull it off. They had the arrogance of youth, and they thought they could do anything. They didn't feel like a local band: They were going to be the next big thing in metal, the next Van Halen.

Texas was so big, however, that when they first started out Pantera rarely ventured beyond state lines, except for the odd trip to Oklahoma or New Orleans. They would play anywhere that would help them build up their fan base and get the local kids to start coming to shows: at a skating rink, at the YMCA, at parties; even on the beach. The band's profile was growing fast, and they were playing so often that they soon learned what worked and didn't work. If they messed up a song, they knew they had fifty more lined up for the next show.

They were also beginning to get into the rock star life—or at least some of them were. Vinnie wasn't much of a partier, and when the band hit the road he roomed with Terry. But for Darrell and Rex, it was all-night partying. Terry Glaze has fond memories of those days:

"Ten years after we started the drinking age skipped to twenty-one, which made the crowd more college-age. . . . The drinking age was eighteen when we started, [and] that meant fifteen-, sixteen-year-old girls. It was a high school party every night . . . it was living for the moment. There were fights just like you've seen on television and movies in the Midwest. The '80s period was just girls with big hair and lots of leather. It was a great time to be in a rock 'n' roll band."

Glaze didn't socialize much with the rest of the band. After Pantera finished a run of shows he would head back to Arlington to be with his girlfriend and family. Pantera was a great escape for him; to put on a persona onstage was like a key to another, more hedonistic world, but he didn't live it twenty-four hours a day like the rest of the band. He hadn't dreamed of being a musician in school. It just so happened that he'd hooked up with some excellent players, and as soon as they started playing live they became stunningly professional as a live outfit.

Pantera were not complacent about their early success. They practiced all the time and knew they were lucky to be getting some fairly high-profile support slots. "When we started out, we went and played every little shit-hole on the face of this earth," Vinnie Paul later told Roger Scott of *NYRock*. "We played nightclubs for seven years before we ever got a record deal."

These support slots and other live appearances helped fund and promote Pantera's debut album, *Metal Magic*, which they released on their own Metal Magic Records label. Keeping things in the family, the album was produced by the Abbotts' father, Jerry (who the band nicknamed "The Eld'n"), and recorded at Pantego Sound. The fact is that *Metal Magic* would never have happened without Jerry. He was very generous in allowing the band to use the studio at evenings and weekends when other artists hadn't already booked it out. "It was just a little hole in the wall studio, but lots of records got made there," Glaze says. "It was just great to have the opportunity to learn. By the time we put out our [first] record we'd already recorded thirty or forty original songs. We were at ease with this."

Although Darrell had spent time in his dad's studio and had done the occasional piano overdub or punch-in, it was Vinnie who knew about the workings of the studio and how to make a record sound right. Vinnie was Jerry's protégé, a quiet, chunky kid who spent his time learning about sound equipment while Darrell was out partying. He was always more mature than the others, and was light-years ahead of Darrell and his buddies.

For all the support he gave his sons, however, Jerry could not fathom Darrell's style of playing or his desire to use distortion to make his sound heavier. Once Vinnie started to get into the production side of things, he helped Darrell gain more control over his guitar sound. Slowly but surely, they were getting closer to the sound Darrell wanted, even if Jerry felt sure they would damage people's ears.

At the time of the album's release, Darrell was only seventeen years old, while Vinnie was nineteen. Heavily influenced by Kiss, Ratt, and Van Halen, and filled with metal clichés, *Metal Magic* consisted of ten tracks: "Ride My Rocket," "I'll Be Alright," "Tell Me If You Want It," "Latest Lover," "Biggest Part of Me," "Metal Magic," "Widowmaker," "Nothin' On (But the Radio)," "Sad Lover," and "Rock Out." (I have chosen to refer to this album and the band's other early recordings in the past tense, as they are no longer available to buy. Old copies are occasionally available for relatively high prices on such websites as eBay and Amazon, via secondhand sellers who bought the original releases long ago.)

Perhaps one reason why the band's sound was so ordinary for the time was Jerry Abbott's unwillingness to venture into new and unexplored territory. He did not always appreciate his youngest son's appetite for off-the-wall riffs, and was often frustrated by Darrell's refusal to stick to a common agenda.

Darrell would always try to come up with the wildest riffs possible. He'd add a touch of feedback or distortion here and there, but it often met with resistance. "On our early demos, I was really frustrated with my recorded sound," he told *Guitar World*'s Brad Tolinski. "I'd tell my dad, 'Dude, I want more "cut" on my guitar—I want more treble.'" Jerry insisted his son turn down the treble knob because, he said, loud music is not to everyone's taste. Darrell, of course, wanted his music to be played loud and fast.

One day Darrell called up his friend Buddy Blaze to tell him that their record was ready. Blaze went round to the Abbotts' house to find a big box containing a few hundred copies of *Metal Magic* sitting in the living room. Darrell asked Blaze how many he wanted but Blaze said he wanted to buy a copy so that he could say he bought the first ever Pantera record. (He still owns it to this day.)

Released on June 10, 1983, *Metal Magic* was typical of the glam-metal era. The artwork, which was dripping in pinks and yellows, depicted a panther posed as a barbarian wielding a sword. It wouldn't have looked out of place on the cover of a Michael Moorcock fantasy novel. The back cover credits list the names Darrell Abbott and Vince Abbott, but they would soon become Diamond Darrell (in honor of the Kiss song "Black Diamond") and Vinnie Paul.

Although it was in the main a run-of-the-mill early-'80s metal album, *Metal Magic* did contain some moments of genuine brilliance, including "Rock Out," "Widowmaker," and the catchy "I'll Be Alright." The sharpness of Darrell's guitars certainly stood out. Much of the rest of the material was mediocre, however, while too many songs sounded like homages to other artists' work, such as the Kiss-tinged "Ride My Rocket."

In an otherwise unenthusiastic review of the album for *AllMusic*, Eduardo Rivadavia notes: "*Metal Magic*'s strongest asset from start to finish was the already discernible talent of guitar hero in waiting Diamond Darrell, even though his biggest preoccupation at the time seemed to be paying tribute to his idol, Ace Frehley."

They were still young and inexperienced, of course, and had plenty of time to learn. What they had on their side was talent—which had yet to be fully nurtured—and enthusiasm. Making the album and, subsequently, performing live helped Pantera gain much-needed experience and knowledge of how the music business works. They didn't have a big budget, a top producer, or the backing of a record label or a manager. They were totally independent.

For now, Jerry Abbott was still responsible for booking the band's shows. They would travel a long way each weekend—to Dallas or Fort Worth or Houston or San Antonio—and then start the cycle again every five weeks or so. Texas is a big place, and these cities were far enough apart that each one was a different market with different tastes and interests. But Pantera had started to form an idea of the type of band they wanted to be.

Metal Magic may have been the sound of a group of naïve rock-loving kids making some rock tunes, but they had conviction. They were playing original songs as well as covers, and with their busy live schedule had become a seasoned band almost overnight. Darrell in particular got better and better: It was like he had gone into his room to practice for six months and come out a virtuoso. He could do things that nobody else could do. There was no YouTube back then, and no one to show Darrell how to play guitar. He learned by repeatedly listening to his favorite albums and copying the riffs until he nailed them. The music came out of him; he took Donny Hart's songs and made them ten times better.

Rex Brown, meanwhile, had been in the band for a year or so by now but he hadn't immediately jelled with the others on a personal level. "They were very clean-cut in the beginning," local metal enthusiast Jerry Warden recalls. "They were kids and they had good parents. I know Jerry still very well and I knew Carolyn real well too. They were good kids and they didn't do any drugs. All of 'em were straight, Terry, Vince, and Darrell—no drugs, no marijuana. Nothing. [After] they got Rex in the band . . . one time Vince sat me down and said, 'Jerry, man, I'm thinking about kicking Rex outta the band.' And I said, 'Why, man, what's the problem?' He goes, 'Man, Rex smokes cigarettes, and the girls just don't like that. And I think that's bad for our image.'"

Ironically, Darrell would become an indulgent pot smoker and drinker in later life. For now, though, he took a hard line against drug use. Pantera roadie Walter Trachsler corroborates Warden's story. "They thought that Rex was smoking weed," he recalls. "They already knew Rex drank beer—which was a mortal sin—and when they found out Rex was smoking weed it was all over. Darrell wanted Rex out of the band so fucking bad."

They were just kids, of course, and they were going through some of the inevitable phases of adolescence. By 1983 they had all graduated from high school except Darrell, who was younger than the rest. He'd only ever held down one regular job, which was at a fast-food place called Captain D's. His friends would drive by and laugh at him because he had to wear a cardboard hat and a silly uniform. He looked like a sailor. "Dude, I can't believe you have to wear that shit," his buddies would say. But Darrell's guitar did the talking for him, and he was adamant that soon he would not be flipping burgers but working on another Pantera album.

3

HEAVY METAL RULES: PANTERA UNLEASHES *PROJECTS IN THE JUNGLE*

Being in a band is just so much more than any one person could bring to the table. It's more than just one person's vision.

—Vinnie Paul to Jeff Kerby of KNAC, 2004

BY NOW, PANTERA HAD STARTED to build a trusted team around them. Dusty Osbourne was their lighting guy, Walter Trachsler was Darrell's guitar tech, and Jerry Abbott took care of the band's live sound. To begin with, Jerry traveled everywhere with the band as road manager, driver, and sometime roadie, since most of the rest of the band and crew were underage.

REINVENTING METAL

It was in Killeen, Texas, that Darrell saw a guy named Kenny King packing up some equipment one night at a club called Woodstock, where Pantera were supporting the British band Fastway on their first U.S. tour. King picked up one 4' × 12' cabinet, put it on his shoulder, and then picked up another one and moved them both across the stage. There were some Randall cabinets too, which were heavier than Marshalls; he picked up one, slung it around, and put it up on the other shoulder. He was like a pro wrestler. Darrell asked the strong-looking seventeen-year-old if he wanted to hit the road and work for the band. King agreed, and within thirty minutes he'd packed a bag and moved from Killeen to Arlington. He recalls:

"I lived with Darrell and actually I stayed with Rex for a little bit. Rex was actually the very first person I stayed with when I first moved into Arlington, and from there I moved over to Darrell's house. . . . As a roadie you bounce around a little bit. Home was Darrell's house if I was going to call anyplace home. [Carolyn] was like my second mom . . . as far as support of the band and her kids, you couldn't find a better mother. She stood behind us one hundred percent in everything that we did. Not a bad word or anything ever came out of that woman's mouth. She was always real good to me and always gave me a place to sleep. She's always close to my heart.

"Rex was great to live with. To this very day I still consider all of 'em my brothers. They'll always be my brothers till the end—and even after that we'll still be brothers. I guess siblings don't always get along with each other, but we always seemed to do just fine. . . . I was probably the only member of the crew, Pantera-wise, that wasn't from the neighborhood or around the family. [The rest of] the road crew were just friends, people to help them just carry stuff around; just neighborhood chums. I was the only outsider, [but] me and Darrell clicked—he saw something obviously I didn't—and he offered me a job."

Heavy Metal Rules: Pantera Unleashes Projects in the Jungle

On July 27, 1984, Pantera released their sophomore effort, *Projects in the Jungle*. Released just thirteen months after their debut, the album was once again issued on the band's own Metal Magic Records and produced by Jerry Abbott. For *Projects*, Terry Glaze followed the rest of the band in adopting a stage name, Terrence Lee. (His given name is Terence Lee Glaze, so it wasn't too far from what was written on his birth certificate.) The band members enjoyed using pseudonyms and changing names; it was a way of adopting a new personality onstage and separating themselves from the real world.

Although they continued to wear their poodle-haired glam-metal influences on their sleeves, Pantera were slowly moving toward a heavier, less melodic, and more anthemic sound. *Projects in the Jungle* introduced some of the thrash-metal-type riffs that would become commonplace in the band's latter-day music, while the ninety-second-long "Blue Light Turnin'" was Diamond Darrell's own take on "Eruption," the mesmerizing guitar solo by Eddie Van Halen that is widely hailed as one of the greatest in rock history.

Despite poor lyrics and the fact that Glaze's vocal style—which had more in common with Joe Elliott's and Vince Neil's than Rob Halford's or Bruce Dickinson's—failed to match the music, there were still some gems to be found, notably "Out for Blood" and "Killers." As with *Metal Magic*, the album's greatest strength was Diamond Darrell's playing. (Metal fans would subsequently seek out Pantera's '80s albums simply for the guitars if nothing else.) Pantera were slowly going from strength to strength, and while the album suffered from definite flaws and growing pains, it also glowed with promise and innovation, albeit in moderation.

Like its predecessor, *Projects in the Jungle* has faded into the annals of metal history, and surprisingly few are aware of Pantera's true roots. It remains an important album in the band's history, however. As Martin Popoff wrote in *The Collector's Guide to Heavy Metal—Volume 2: The Eighties*: "Ignoring the indie look, which manifests itself most embarrassingly on the cheapo front cover, these are accomplished soundscapes for the era."

The band even made a music video for the song "All Over Tonight," and although it did little to raise their profile, the album itself helped increase Pantera's fan base and picked up strong reviews in the metal press. The first acceptance of glam metal in Arlington had come a year earlier when Quiet Riot released their third album, *Metal Health*, and had a hit with "Bang Your Head," which was played on the radio all the time. It may seem lightweight some thirty years later, but at the time it was metal at its heaviest.

The biggest influences on Pantera during the *Projects* era were Mötley Crüe's *Shout at the Devil*, Ratt's breakthrough album *Out of the Cellar*, and Van Halen's *1984*, as well as Judas Priest, Kiss, and Def Leppard. Pantera were a very image-conscious band and believed—rightly or wrongly—that in order to make the kind of music they wanted to make they had to dress like all the other bands. "I've got pictures of James Hetfield [of Metallica] wearing spandex," Vinnie Paul told *Electronic Musician*'s Jeff Perlah years later. "We were young kids when we started. We emulated our favorite bands."

There were definite glimpses, however, of a young, thirsty band wanting to create the kind of metal that Metallica were making out in California. These two opposing sides of the metal coin—with the likes of Ratt on one and Metallica on the other—demonstrate the collision of interests that would create tension in the band down the road. The heavier, hard-rock side of the band was Diamond Darrell's influence, with his love of Van Halen and Sabbath, while the melodic rock sound of Pantera came from singer Terry Glaze, who dug April Wine and Sammy Hagar.

Pantera looked and sounded like any other rock band of the era, but they did not share many of the same influences as the guys in Metallica. Until guitarist and singer James Hetfield met Danish-born drummer Lars Ulrich, he was into the same kinds of bands as Diamond Darrell: Van Halen, Aerosmith, Kiss, Ted Nugent, Queen, and Peter Frampton. But then Ulrich introduced Hetfield to the New Wave of British Heavy Metal, with its fast, heavy riffs and gritty, aggressive melodies. It's safe to say that without NWOBHM, bands such as Iron Maiden, Saxon, Venom, and Diamond Head, there would have been no Metallica, but for now those bands bore little influence on Pantera, who still favored the likes of Def Leppard, as Terry Glaze recalls:

"We wanted to be on shows with Van Halen and Judas Priest. All we did was practice, and we played a lot. We would play all night. We would play multiple sets. I might play seventy or eighty songs every night, so it was great training ground to learn your skills. By the time [*Projects in the Jungle*] came out we had played every little town in Texas over and over and over. We got really good. There were a lot of great musicians coming out of North Texas at that time. They were all country and rock and all kinds of stuff. There was something in the air. The reason we did the record was, if we wrote our own songs, we thought it would be a great idea to sell merchandise off the stage. Back then, bands like Metallica and Anthrax and Megadeth . . . were just kids living at home putting out records themselves, too, so we put our records out, and some of the little underground press from, say, Germany or England would review our album. Nobody knew we were living at home with our parents, but I expect those other bands were, too."

Arlington metal fan Jerry Warden would collect everything released by any of the NWOBHM bands, and would have to pay in advance for the records because the clerk at the local record store wouldn't order them if he didn't collect them once they came in stock. Warden ordered albums from Europe that most people in Arlington didn't know existed. He was good friends with Brian Slagel, a Californian metal fan who put out a fanzine called *The New Heavy Metal Revue* and had recently founded the now legendary Metal Blade Records. Slagel would tell Warden about the new Tygers of Pan Tang album, for example, or the new Diamond Head release, and of course about Iron Maiden and Saxon.

Warden is also a concert promoter, and back in August 1982 he put on shows at Heavy Meadows out in the country and even talked Pantera into performing the new Iron Maiden song "The Number of the Beast" for it. The liner notes to the first Pantera album offer special thanks to "Jerry 'Wheels' Warden" in recognition of the fact that he would drive the band from gig to gig in his pickup truck. He was also in important musical influence on the band. He had driven out to Tyler, Texas, to see Metallica on their first tour, and was definitely one of the first guys in Arlington to discover the new, heavier strands of metal to emerge in the early '80s. Eventually, word of mouth spread and the underground metal tape-trading scene began to reach out beyond Arlington and across Texas. There was an undercurrent of heavy music in Arlington, but it got heavier and heavier as more fans begun to absorb the sounds coming out of Europe.

Alongside Warden, one of the prominent figures on the '80s Texas underground metal scene was Damon Duperre. His band Boss Tweed had been one of the state's earliest heavy metal acts; they were included on the first Iron Tyrants compilation album, which was released by Azra Records, the label responsible for the first Exodus album, *Bonded by Blood*. He recalls:

"I don't know for sure if Boss Tweed influenced Pantera in any way, but they got heavier after they met and heard Boss Tweed. From about 1983 or 1984 there were a lot of bands besides Pantera and Boss Tweed playing heavy stuff, but only in underground metal clubs [of which there were very few]. Pantera and Boss Tweed also played in the more mainstream clubs, but were not always warmly welcomed."

Rick Perry of metal band Gammacide was also another local metalhead with a deep fondness for British metal. Perry went to the University of Texas in Arlington, and would frequent the nearby Fantasia Records store run by David Counter. Counter stocked British magazines like *Metal Forces* and *Kerrang!* and imported albums from the U.K. by bands such as Tygers of Pan Tang and Venom. Before the influence of the NWOBHM began to spread, American metal meant party-time hard rock, but the British bands were heavier and darker. It would be a while yet, however, before Pantera properly recognized British heavy metal beyond Priest and Sabbath.

Another Arlington metal band that owed more to Saxon and Tygers of Pan Tang than to Ratt was Walter Trachsler's group Rotting Corpse, as Trachsler recalls:

"Rotting Corpse was the first thrash-metal band in the southwestern United States. . . . When we came around it totally changed everything, because glam metal had been shoved down everyone's throats for so long that it got to the point where the people playing it really couldn't play it worth a shit, but they just got away with it. When Corpse came along it was so completely different: People were just ready for something different. At first there'd be like two or three people and we thought that was fucking cool, but it got to where we'd have five, six, seven hundred people at a show, and Pantera were playin' ten to fifteen miles away and they'd have a hundred fucking people."

Arlington, Texas, holds a special place in the annals of American underground metal as a key breeding ground for a number of bands of the era, Pantera included. Bands like Warlock, Gammacide, Rigor Mortis, Rotting Corpse, and Solitude picked up a lot of their influences from imported British metal magazines and the tape-trading scene, and because Texas is such a vast state they had no choice but to develop their own style. There was something in the water, it seemed, and in time the '80s Texas metal scene would become highly regarded by true aficionados of the genre, even if it was never as widely publicized as, say, the Bay Area scene.

Though the Arlington scene had been important to them, however, Pantera would soon begin to make connections outside of Texas—connections that would eventually give them a whole new lease on life.

4

ONWARD WE ROCK: THE RELEASE OF *I AM THE NIGHT*

When we started Pantera, there was a lot more independence....

—Vinnie Paul to Jeff Kerby of KNAC, 2004

IN 1985 PANTERA BEGAN WORK on their third album, *I Am the Night*, with Jerry Abbott once again producing, as Terry Glaze recalls:

"Jerry was very helpful. He taught us a lot of stuff. He also wrote a lot of the lyrics on a lot of those songs. Either I wrote the songs or Darrell and his dad would write the songs or I put lyrics to the songs. For the first three vinyl [album]s, that's kind of how it went. I wanted to write songs from the very beginning. That was why it was so great to be in the studio to get a chance to learn how to do it."

Pantera continued to look like a glam band, with big hairstyles and theatrical outfits, but it was obvious that they wanted to move toward a heavier, darker brand of metal, more Metallica than Quiet Riot. Their desire to create heavier music was epitomized by "Down Below," the centerpiece of *I Am the Night*. The album also contained several fantastic fist-in-the-air anthems, namely, "Onward We Rock" and "Right on the Edge," while "Daughters of the Queen" and "Come-on Eyes" (referred to on later releases as "Come [on Eyes]") offered further evidence of the band's eagerness for a heavier sound. The album closed with its sole ballad, "Forever Tonight"—something of an anticlimax after all the adrenaline that had pumped through the previous tracks. As Glaze recalls, the band's early albums served as snapshots of the time they were made:

"Whenever we had songs, we'd go in and record them. It wasn't like we were on the road for six months and said, 'Okay, let's go and do a record. . . .' It's just their father [worked at a studio], and the studio was in the same town. That's how the records came about. When we had ten songs—that's the next album. We did a lot of demoing of songs before *Metal Magic*. Those songs were the ones that we picked as our favorites for our first album, but there were leftover demos from before. There's not any *I Am the Night* outtakes. We'd already played them before we went in[to the studio] a lot of the time."

Once again, Diamond Darrell stole the show. He was slowly moving away from his early Ace Frehley–inspired sound, and without his riffs the album would have sounded even more clichéd. But there was still something missing from the band—something that did not quite fit. They needed to work on their lyrics, and Glaze's voice was obviously not going to stand up for much longer next to Darrell's earth-shattering guitar playing. In his review of the album for *AllMusic*, Eduardo Rivadavia states: "As with all of Pantera's 'forgotten' albums, it is invariably Darrell's playing that makes these growing pains more tolerable."

Released on August 16, 1985, *I Am the Night* suffered from a lack of distribution, which meant fans—particularly those from abroad—were forced to pay high mail-order prices for the album. Without the backing and financial services of a record label, the album was bound to be a commercial failure. It still sold some 25,000 copies, however, and by now the band was starting to appear in the metal press.

"They were on the cover of *Metal Forces* in 1985 for *I Am the Night*, and they got a ten-out-of-ten review," says Stuart Taylor, who would become a staff photographer for the magazine in 1988, as well as Pantera's unofficial band photographer throughout the '80s. "That was some big stuff. I still have that issue; Darrell wrote on [my copy], 'Eat This Shit . . . Diamond Darrell Lance.' People were always doubters of Pantera except for the fans."

Selling 25,000 copies of an album and picking up this sort of praise from the metal press was a great return for an entirely independent band. What Pantera needed now was a manager and a record label. Proud Texans, they were a world away from the endless stream of glam-metal bands that lined the Sunset Strip in Hollywood. Glam had evolved over the years, from the British bands of the early '70s, such as T-Rex, Queen, and Slade, to U.S. acts like Kiss, Alice Cooper, Cheap Trick, and the New York Dolls. By the mid-'80s, glam was even more outrageous; the music was heavier and the image was more feminine. Bands like Dokken, Quiet Riot, Ratt, Stryper, Mötley Crüe, and London dominated the L.A. music scene and regularly filled the city's hippest venues, such as the Whisky a Go Go, the Red Velvet, the Trip, and the Starwood. Glam was not confined solely to L.A., however: Night Ranger hailed from San Francisco, Twisted Sister came from Long Island, New Jersey had Bon Jovi, Pennsylvania gave us Cinderella and Poison, and Portland, Oregon, spawned Black 'N Blue.

Pantera did not involve themselves in the big-city glam-metal scene; they stayed local and did their own thing. What that meant, however, was that it wouldn't be easy to get noticed beyond state lines. In the beginning, they would hire friends to hand out flyers in Arlington and sell albums through the mail. Everything came from the kitchen table. There was no Internet back then, so it was difficult to buy—or even find out about—albums by obscure independent bands. Pantera would receive letters through their fan club, but sales were mostly through word of mouth. Eventually, once they had started to make their mark, they didn't need to concentrate on promotion. People would just show up whenever and wherever they were playing.

The band's reputation as one of the biggest regional bands in the South continued to grow with a headlining slot in front of 3,000 fans at the Bronco Bowl in Dallas on April 27, 1985, with Taker and Lightning also on the bill. They'd venture to Killeen to play a week of shows every month and travel to Fort Worth, Houston, and Austin. They'd play at places like the Big Wheel Skating Rink, Molly Maguire's in Dallas, Savvy's, and Heavy Meadows.

Back then Pantera would travel from gig to gig in a car with a small trailer attached, band and crew packed in like sardines. Later they upgraded to a Chevy Suburban. They had a close-knit group of friends around them, many of whom ended up working for the band, including roadies Randy Bell, Bobby Tongs (aka Daryl Arnberger,) Jimmy James, and Dusty Osbourne. To them, Diamond Darrell and Vinnie Paul were still Darrell and Vince Abbott.

"I used to run spotlight for 'em," photographer Stuart Taylor recalls. "I was homeless, so when I went on the road with them it gave me a chance to make a little bit of money to get something to eat and a place to sleep. If you drive from Dallas to San Antonio, that's five hours. I think it probably takes fourteen hours to drive across this state; it's huge . . . and you had to play the different regions. Corpus Christi is at the bottom of Texas, and that's a real good market for death metal; San Antonio's a good market for metal. . . . There were the metal places and then the more pop places. It was better way back then. . . . Pantera was more mainstream, so they could play that touring circuit, whereas the real hard bands could not. Pantera played a lot of cover material so the clubs would book them."

Not everybody stuck around, and it was often necessary for Pantera's roadies to multitask. When Darrell's long-term guitar tech Walter Trachsler moved on, he left a vacancy that needed to be filled right away. Kenny King had started off on pyrotechnics and lugging equipment in and out of venues, and was even in charge of lighting for a while. Now he would become Darrell's guitar tech, too. Ironically, King had never played guitar before, and in fact had never even picked one up, but Darrell said he'd show him how to string and tune one. King turned out to be a natural. Most guitarists, however many stagehands they employ, tend to handle their effects pedals themselves, but things were different with Darrell and King. Darrell tested him from the get-go, until one time when he couldn't get back over to his side of the stage, so King reached out and pushed the pedals for him. Darrell looked over and nodded; it was a sign of approval. Eventually, King was put in control of all of Darrell's effects, leaving Darrell free to do whatever he wanted. All he had to do was play. It was a very special bond.

Around the time of *I Am the Night*, Jerry Abbott decided he didn't want to go out on the road with the band anymore. Lighting engineer Dusty Osbourne took over on sound temporarily before Ambrose Esquibell joined the Pantera camp. The rest of the crew remained pretty consistent throughout the rest of the decade. None of them made very much money: King would take home roughly $30 a night, Esquibell $60; the band would get between $100 and $200, depending on the show. Most of the money went back into the band. Jerry had taught them that they would make the most money through merchandise, and that they had to go out there and sign autographs and mingle with their fans to sell the albums and T-shirts.

Another close friend of Darrell's, Gary Hetrick, became Vinnie's drum tech in 1985, despite having had a somewhat prickly relationship with the elder Abbott brother to begin with. He recalls:

"I remember the very first show that I went and helped him set up his drums. We opened up for the Mama's Boys. I had some blast cleaner and I was making the cymbals shine. He was like, 'Damn, my kit looks good.' After that Vinnie goes, 'Do you wanna be my drum tech?' Sometimes when we opened for people there'd already be people in the audience, and the soundman, Ambrose, he'd be wanting to do a sound check, so . . . I'd go up there and I'd be [playing] and most of the time they'd be going, 'This dude can't play the drums. This is gonna suck.' I set up the drums and ran the spotlight during the shows, and I think the biggest compliment they ever gave me was when they made the 'Hot and Heavy' video and the 'It's All Over Tonight' video. . . . I dated this chick that worked in a camera store and she let us borrow a video camera and we took it out to Savvy's in Fort Worth and this guy Joe Giron—who was a photographer from the Fort Worth *Star-Telegram*—videotaped the show. That night everybody came over to Darrell's house to watch it. . . . They'd never seen themselves videotaped. Darrell wouldn't stay up onstage; he'd get down on the dance floor and stand on people's tables while he was playing the guitar. He was doing this thirty-minute solo and Vinnie looked over at our light guy Jimmy James, and said, 'I didn't know you set up lights for Darrell's guitar out on the tables.' Jimmy goes, 'I didn't set up the lights. That's Gary on the spotlight.' They were like, 'Damn, dude.' I knew every little tab. . . ."

Pantera were beginning to make some important contacts outside the Arlington scene. Photographer Joe Giron had first come across the band back in 1981 when he was an intern at the Fort Worth daily newspaper, the *Star-Telegram*. He went out to dinner one evening with a writer at the paper, and afterward they ended up in a club. Onstage, Pantera were playing covers of Kiss and Judas Priest songs that sounded as good as the originals. Giron was mightily impressed with the Arlington band and had looked out for them ever since:

"It didn't come about until the spring of 1985 that the *Star-Telegram* decided to do a feature on the band because they were promoting a big show at the Bronco Bowl over near Dallas. It was April or May of 1985, so the paper was doing an article on a local band trying to make it on the national or international stage. When that assignment came up I grabbed it. I told the photo editor I was a fan of the band. I ended up going down and photographing the show and doing some stuff backstage. The newspaper, which was a morning and afternoon daily, ran two separate stories in the paper. Once the band saw the article—I'd given them my business card—they contacted me and said they were some of the best photos they had ever seen on the band. Things progressed from there. I would go and take some pictures at their club shows and eventually, when the band put out *I Am the Night*, I ended up doing the band photography for the album. We did some portrait stuff and they ended up using some of the live material that I had shot as well."

The band cemented another important contact around the same time through Gary Hetrick's cousin (and Darrell's future girlfriend) Rita Haney and her friend Lenise Lopez: the oft-mentioned Metallica connection. Haney and Lopez would go to metal clubs four or five times a week. They were very knowledgeable about the underground metal scene and knew all the bands. They first met Metallica when the *Ride the Lightning* tour passed through Texas in February 1985. After getting drummer Lars Ulrich's phone number from Walter Traschler (who knew Ulrich through the metal tape-trading scene), the girls met the band in Dallas and then followed them to Houston, staying an extra night with them there before Metallica traveled home to El Cerrito, California.

After the tour ended, Metallica continued to play sporadic shows around North America. When they returned to Texas in the summer, Haney suggested they play with Pantera, whom she'd first heard about through her cousin Gary. And so it was that Darrell Abbott and Rex Brown shared a stage with Metallica at Savvy's in Fort Worth, with tickets priced at three or four dollars. Because the show was completely unrehearsed and unannounced, however, only some thirty people got to see this historic performance. Not even Rick Perry of Texas metal band Gammacide knew about it, and he was going out with Haney at the time. Not that the musicians minded. They had such a blast that they decided to do it again the next night.

After one of the shows, Metallica front man/guitarist James Hetfield and drummer Lars Ulrich went over to Darrell's garage to jam. While Ulrich watched, Hetfield and Darrell riffed away all night long, swapping licks and techniques as they went. (It was from this jam that rumors began to circulate that Hetfield had borrowed some of Darrell's licks, and vice versa.) Hetfield and Ulrich were blown away by how well Darrell knew their songs, and were particularly impressed with his take on "Damage, Inc." The three men became friends and developed a high level of mutual admiration, and it was through this that Darrell—and by extension Pantera—began to appreciate and understand the heavier forms of metal.

It was also around this time that Darrell began an on-again, off-again relationship with Rita Haney. True to the metal fashions of the time, Haney had multicolored hair and always wore spandex. She was an outgoing girl who knew what she wanted, and to begin with she wasn't too sure about Darrell because of his band's reputation for glam metal. That summer, however, she and Lopez invited Darrell and Rex out to California to see

Metallica perform at the Day on the Green show in Oakland on August 31. It was in California that Darrell and Rita first hooked up, although the relationship was slow-moving to begin with—they were more like siblings than partners—while Lopez got involved with Rex around the same time. Lopez recalls the excitement of that first trip to Los Angeles:

"When we reached L.A. we were all just completely blown away. In Arlington, Texas, Pantera [were celebrities]. They had not been signed yet, so the whole plan was to shop their cassette and get them signed. We didn't do that much of that. We went to the Rainbow; I can't remember who was playing, but Blackie Lawless and Chris Holmes [of W.A.S.P.] were there. Rex was just amazed that he was in the same building with one of his idols, so he walks to the table where Blackie is eating and introduces himself. Remember that Pantera is the most popular band in the [Dallas–Fort Worth] Metroplex at this time. Rex holds out his hand to tell Blackie how badass W.A.S.P. is, and Blackie didn't even acknowledge him—bastard just kept eating. I think that Rex and Darrell really had their feelings hurt, and they were probably thinking that they might never get signed. So L.A. was a humbling experience. All I have to say is, 'Where is Blackie now?' Bet he wishes he would have shown some courtesy and shook the man's hand! I have never known Rex or Darrell to treat a fan like that."

Nonetheless, it was becoming obvious to Pantera that, if they wanted to rise above the underground metal scene in Texas, they had to somehow change and adapt to the new trends in metal. By 1986, thrash metal was the new vogue in the metal world, with bands like Metallica, Slayer, and Megadeth causing a global stir with their ultrasharp riffs and aggressive vocals. Metallica had grown bigger and bigger with a series of astonishingly powerful albums: *Kill 'Em All*, *Ride the Lightning*, and *Master of Puppets*. The last of the three was released in 1986, which proved to be a pivotal year for thrash metal following the release of Megadeth's *Peace Sells . . . But Who's Buying?* and Slayer's brutal *Reign in Blood*.

The Big Four of thrash—Metallica, Megadeth, Slayer, and Anthrax—were the total antithesis of the L.A. glam scene, and eventually all four would catch the interest of Diamond Darrell. But was it possible for Pantera to be a hybrid of Kiss, Van Halen, Black Sabbath . . . and Metallica? Back then, metal kids would listen Metallica *or* Bon Jovi—it was one or the other. It wasn't cool to like both, and you could get beaten up in high school for listening to thrash metal as well as glam. Some kids wanted to be Nikki Sixx; others wanted to be Kerry King or James Hetfield. The glam bands were posers; the thrash bands were outlaw rebels and cowboys. The two were diametrically opposed.

Pantera front man Terry Glaze did not look the part for the sound the rest of the band was headed toward. He was simply too glam. For his part, however, Glaze felt his opinion was never taken seriously enough. If ever there were a band vote, the Abbotts would never split; they'd always side with each other. Even if Glaze felt strongly about something, it didn't seem to matter:

"In the end I left for the same reason other people leave bands. I loved the two hours onstage playing music—it was the other twenty-two hours of the day that I didn't like. We never had any problems onstage . . . [it was] just miscommunication between not particularly liking one direction or the other. I was going to college and we'd be playing every weekend; I'd be down in the lobby trying to do my homework while they were partying. It was difficult. I just wanted to be heard. I never got my vote. I finally just got tired of it."

Glaze's favorite band was Cheap Trick, and he adored the Beatles and Van Halen. He liked melody. When Pantera started playing heavier music it was obvious that his days were numbered. He wasn't happy to leave the band; there was never a moment when he was onstage thinking he wanted to be somewhere else. But there had been rumblings of discontent for some time, as he recalls:

"We split everything—us four plus Jerry. We voted like a democracy and we split everything, but once their second or third album came, they didn't wanna pay their daddy anymore. Jerry was like, 'We split.' That's where the falling-out came about: over money. I can see where his point was. He bankrolled them for ten years. He invested a lot—he was there from the very beginning helping them. I never got a penny. I wish Vince would box up [and reissue] those three eleven-dollar vinyl albums, because I would buy a new house.

"Once we got more self-sufficient, Jerry didn't go on the road with us anymore. Just like all relationships, [it came down to] money and communication. By that second record they were selling a lot of merchandise. Once I got a little older I started to ask, 'Where's the money?' We're selling vinyl; we're selling T-shirts. That was not good accounting. That was my problem with the band. Not the two hours onstage."

Glaze and the others dissolved their professional relationship and went their separate ways at the end of the year. Most reports indicate that his final appearance onstage with the band was in Fort Worth, Texas, on December 31, 1985, a night on which they played a mixture of originals—including "Projects in the Jungle," "Heavy Metal Rules," and "All Over Tonight"—and covers of songs by Metallica ("Fight Fire with Fire"), Van Halen ("Eruption"), Deep Purple ("Burn"), Led Zeppelin ("Dazed and Confused"), Anthrax ("Madhouse"), and Black Sabbath ("The Mob Rules"). Glaze's final days with the band were increasingly fraught:

"I gave them notice. That was a bad idea, because they got more and more angry. I should have just packed my stuff and left. I remember the last gig: It was really weird . . . a lot of not speaking, a lot of weird tension. . . . They had already started looking for replacements. I was trying to force the issue of let's be more friendly—I felt like I tried everything I could."

Relations may have broken down, but Glaze had served Pantera well during his tenure as front man. He was a flamboyant, David Lee Roth–type figure who knew how to handle a tough crowd. There where times when the band played at venues like the Ranch, in Muenster, Texas, where he'd shout all kinds of unflattering remarks at the cowboys standing at the bar with their giant hats and belt buckles. His charm and wit won them over eventually, however, and by the end he'd have them throwing their hats in the air and tapping their toes. He was good like that.

Glaze was sad to be leaving Pantera but didn't feel like he had a choice. He went on to form a rock band, Lord Tracy, with three musicians from Tennessee, releasing just one album, *Deaf Gods of Babylon*, in 1989. His favorite Pantera album is still *Projects in the Jungle*.

* * *

Glaze's departure left an obvious void, and throughout the early months of 1986 the band went through a revolving lineup of singers as they sought out the right man to replace him. The first person they turned to was Matt L'Amour, who ended up having a brief yet tumultuous tenure with the band. Little is known about him other than that he looked like David Coverdale and could sing songs like "Children of the Sea" by the Ronnie James Dio–era Black Sabbath.

L'Amour initially joined Pantera for a run of shows in Los Angeles at the Whisky a Go Go, the Troubadour, and Gazzarri's. Not everybody was convinced regarding the band's new singer, however, as Stuart Taylor recalls:

"That Matt L'Amour guy was horrible. He couldn't sing like Terry could. I remember being in the studio with Darrell and Matt and Darrell's dad, and this guy couldn't hit those notes, so

Pantera couldn't play a lot of the material that they had. They went out to California and they ended goin' out there playing covers because they couldn't play their originals because the guy couldn't sing. I remember Darrell's dad telling him, 'Can't you tune your guitar lower enough so that guy could sing 'em?' Me and Darrell were there, and Matt says, 'Look, this is the new Pantera. Fuck all that old shit.'"

The band had fun in Los Angeles despite the limitations of their new singer. Darrell and some of the roadies took their skateboards with them and enjoyed racing through red lights on Sunset Boulevard late at night. They then traveled to Phoenix, Arizona, for a week of shows before moving on to El Paso, Texas. After just one gig in El Paso, however, they decided it wasn't working out with L'Amour; his voice wasn't right for the band, plus he had some personal issues to deal with. They were beginning to realize that Terry Glaze hadn't been so bad after all: At least he had presence and personality onstage. Even so, going almost a week in El Paso without a singer would obviously prove a struggle—until they found another singer, in the shape of Rick Mythiasin.

An El Paso native and lifelong metalhead, Mythiasin would frequent two rock clubs in town: Saso's Bar and Grill and Scorpios. He was bouncing between the two one night when he witnessed Darrell, Vinnie, and Rex arguing with Matt L'Amour in the parking lot of Saso's:

"They fired the guy, the guy was literally walking off—'I'm outta here'—and then they were like, 'You're fired.' I happened to hear this. They'd already played one night, and . . . back in the day you'd [have to] guarantee to the club owners you're going to be there the whole seven days to play. They're depending on you to draw in customers. They were like, 'Let's just pack it in and go.' I walked up to 'em and I said, 'I'll fill in for you.' They were like, 'Go away,' whatever . . . Well, I just started singing some [Bruce] Dickinson at 'em. That's what I do.

"They kinda looked up—'Really? Do you know "Run to the Hills"?' And I'm like, 'Yeah!' 'Do you know "[The] Number of the Beast?"' And I'm like, 'Yeah!' 'Do you know this song by Black Sabbath and this song by Black Sabbath?' I'm like, 'Yeah, yeah.' 'Do you know any Scorpions?' I'm like, 'Yeah.' I gave 'em a list. They started calling off Scorpions songs. 'Do you know any Anthrax, any Metallica?' I'm like, 'Yeah, yeah.' . . . [They said,] 'We're goin' back in there. We're gonna do this . . . we're not gonna be called Pantera. We're gonna be something [like] the Metal Circus. Whatever. We're just gonna play a bunch of covers. Come on, kid, let's go back in there.'"

Mythiasin could tell from the outset that Pantera were excellent musicians:

"I sang like two nights with them, and it was nothing but covers. These guys played them to a T. It was so amazing, just what they could do. Vinnie Paul was even singing—he was singing 'Blind in Texas' by W.A.S.P. while he's playing drums. They played Anthrax, 'Madhouse.' They did a Metallica song. Just phenomenal."

With their shared taste in rock from Iron Maiden to Kiss by the way of Dio, Mythiasin and Pantera appeared to hit it off. Darrell in particular felt the band had found their new singer after the first night. He even went so far as to call his dad back in Arlington and tell him they had found someone in El Paso who could sing like Accept's Udo Dirkschneider and Judas Priest's Rob Halford. Soon they were forcing Mythiasin to learn songs from *Projects in the Jungle* and *I Am the Night*. But things were moving a little too fast for Mythiasin, whose El Paso buddies were telling him that this was going to be his big break. It soon became apparent, after their second gig together, that the musicians had different views on a number of things—not just music:

"Not to knock them or discredit them in anyway, but we just weren't for each other. . . . They had a redneck mentality, Vinnie

Paul with his scarves and his big hairy boobs. Unfortunately, I kinda felt that they had issues with Mexicans, black people, gays. That kinda turned me off. Their whole attitude toward women made me weird. It was my hometown, and they were wanting me to round up all these chicks and stuff . . . .

"They just had this image thing. They were saying the job of the singer was to strut and prance away with the ladies I'd reel into the hotel room for wild orgies and drinking and drugs. It just wasn't my thing, and half the women in that audience were from my hometown. They were my friends. I dated half of those chicks before—you know what I'm saying? It just turned me off. I was so young back then. I didn't know the trappings of fame, paying your dues and being on the road. That cut my teeth back then."

One thing Mythiasin remembers vividly is how much the guys in Pantera loved their tequila:

"I took them out to Mexico and we had a vile night of drinking. Let me tell you, those boys really know how to party. I wasn't at my best the second night because we got so torn up in Mexico. It was one eye-opening experience. I was too burnt out and I knew right from the get-go."

Mythiasin wasn't the only one. Rex Brown got so drunk he had to sit on a stool because he literally could not stand straight. The band had a bar tab open and the drinks kept on coming. Given his tender age, Mythiasin had never experienced anything like it:

"They had pyros, flash bombs, all kinds of shit in this little club in Texas. I was feeling like shit and one of the road crew, he gave me a rock of speed and he whacked it into a tissue and goes, 'Here, swallow that, you'll sing like a fucking bird.' I'm like, 'Okay,' and sure enough . . . those guys were fast-living, hard-playing. I don't know to be honest with you if I would have been able to make it. I look at them today and see how Phil [Anselmo] was and how he got fucked up."

Mythiasin parted ways with Pantera at the end of the El Paso engagement. He went on to form Steel Prophet in California and today plays in the L.A. speed-metal band Agent Steel.

Back home in Arlington, Pantera turned next to a local singer, Dave Peacock. He'd played in bands of his own and attended Gunn Junior High with Darrell and Vinnie. It was obvious when they started to hang out together that they had some form of musical chemistry. Peacock already knew the Pantera material and with Darrell came up with a thirty-song set list that they could play together. They made plans to rehearse at Matley's Phase II in Dallas and a couple of days later played their first gig together. After that they went out on the road, playing in Oklahoma and Houston and at popular venues like Joe's Garage and Savvy's in Fort Worth. Peacock:

"We did a lot of covers that my band did [and] I got to sing around Dallas. The club owners wanted you to play some popular music to draw in the crowds, but if you could play some original stuff that was great too. We played some Accept, AC/DC, Judas Priest. At that time they were popular songs. A local act would play the first set, we would come out and play an all-original second set of fifteen songs, and [then] we would come out with the third set, which would be like the party set where we'd play all kinds of crazy stuff."

Peacock was paid a weekly salary of roughly $200, a little bit less than what the other members of the band were making. The rest of the band's earnings were used to pay for motels, transportation, and so on. Initially, Peacock would share a room with Vinnie when they were on the road, but after a few weeks Darrell suggested they switch rooms and have some fun. There would be some moments of introspective conversation, but for the most part they'd party until the early hours of the morning.

Vinnie and Darrell were still totally different people. Vinnie was the straitlaced member of the band; he preferred not to get drunk, electing to stay sober to make sure the band were on time for shows and that everything went ahead as planned. He could be touchy at times, whereas Darrell was much more affable. Rex Brown, too, was a party animal with a reputation for getting a lot of women. He and Darrell were always the life of the party. Roadie Gary Hetrick would always put two shots of Jose Cuervo tequila and two glasses of Coors Light on Darrell's side of the stage, and did the same for Rex; Vinnie got a pitcher of beer and a pitcher of water.

Onstage, Peacock basically followed Terry Glaze's lead: It was Pantera, but in a slightly different way. He was a likable front man. He had previously played in a band called Forced Entry, and had shared bills with bands like Warlock, so he had a lot of experience. He could sing the Glaze material well, but he didn't quite have the same level of charisma as a performer. The band had also lost some of their earlier fan base as a result of their move toward a harsh, less mainstream sound, and cracks soon started to appear in the new lineup. In the early days, Pantera had always attracted more women than men to their shows, which were often more like social events, and one point of contention was that the Abbott brothers and Brown liked to get girls up onstage to dance, whereas Peacock was keen to get the guys in the audience to rock out:

"That was my problem when I got in the band: I love the old songs but we didn't do heavier stuff, so that's where we butted heads a little bit. I got along with everybody, but when we got in the studio we'd try to record a couple of songs [and] Vinnie was like, 'This is too heavy. It sounds too much like Metallica; we want more Whitesnake, Def Leppard.' There was just a little clash there. As things went on . . . I didn't really enjoy wearing the spandex and spraying my hair."

Conversely, Peacock found that thrash metal was too cold for his tastes, but he relished the time he spent with Darrell. Although Darrell was rarely seen without his guitar, he loved to skateboard and hang out with his buddies. He'd go all the way to the top of a high-rise parking garage—at least seven stories high—and ride all the way down to the bottom. He also liked to have a laugh and play pranks—often at other bands' expense. Pantera ruled the town and had nicknames for other bands, and even if those bands didn't like the name they were stuck with it. Peacock became very aware of the respect the band commanded in the local clubs. As soon as they walked into a venue, there'd be pitchers of beer on the table waiting for them. They were big stars in a big town, even if they rubbed some people the wrong way.

Peacock also got the chance to see the band at work with Jerry Abbott at Pantego Sound, and observed that Jerry was very knowledgeable about music and new technology. Jerry looked after his boys and treated Peacock like a son, but he was a perfectionist. The music for *Power Metal*, Pantera's fourth album, had already been written. They wanted a specific sound, and Peacock's voice was not well suited to it. A lot of people thought Pantera had found their man with Peacock, but in the end it just wasn't meant to be:

"I was in the band until the weekend before Halloween [1986]. The way that ended up was we had just gotten into too much shit about the way we were recording in the studio. I didn't wanna sing songs they wanted. I didn't wanna look the way they wanted me to look. I got a handle on it. I finally just said, 'I'm not comin' with you anymore. I'm tired of y'all.' I'm sure they might have a different version of how that went down. We had a show booked in Indiana one weekend and I just did a no-show Jones and that was it for me. They called me and said, 'What's goin' on?' I said, 'Here's the deal for me. I just don't wanna do it anymore.'"

Peacock remained friends with Darrell and would meet up with him whenever the band returned to Arlington. He still has fond memories of his time in Pantera:

"I remember this one time we played in this little shitty club in Oklahoma—we had five of us back then and we were just trying to get away with everything there at those clubs. It was on a military base kind of thing. A bunch of military guys would go over there and get crazy. One night, Kenny King and the guy who did the pyro back then said, 'Hey man, on the last bomb when we hit that last track you need to get out of the way. We're just gonna blow this place.' I remember Darrell looking at me when we hit that last note and he's jumping off the stage with his guitar in the air and I just duck down in the middle of the stage and the whole place just lights up and everybody just freaked out. That was something I'll never forget. That's for damn sure."

* * *

Pantera had been through a number of singers in 1986—Matt L'Amour, Rick Mythiasin, Dave Peacock, and possibly others, too—and by the end of the year had become so desperate that they even revisited the past by rehiring Donny Hart, their very first front man. The band was very much in transition, as Hart recalls:

"At that point I don't even think they realized that they were evolving into what they became. When I joined the band I still thought that they wanted someone rather like Terry [Glaze] to sing for them, but their music was changing. They were starting to play Metallica songs and some of it required a different kind of singing. Even as I rejoined them it was not satisfactory to them. They knew that they were looking for something else."

Donny Hart's reintroduction to Pantera was not what he expected. Things had changed since the days when they were all high school kids together. They played on the club circuit for about six weeks, with Hart traveling to Oklahoma and Louisiana on weekends. He quickly discovered that audiences were crazy about Pantera, and that they were not too bothered who was fronting the band as long as Darrell, Vinnie, and Rex were still there.

He also noticed a change in how Darrell acted toward him. The guitarist had always been friendly to Hart in the past but was less so now. He was always creating something, and there was no downtime; if he wasn't writing music he'd be devising some prank or other. About halfway through his second stint in the band, Hart felt instinctively that they were holding out for somebody else, and that he was merely killing time. He also had some differences of opinion with Brown, which ultimately led to him being shown the door. His departure from Pantera was not mutual. They fired him. Or, rather, they had Jerry Abbott fire him. It was not the nicest way to end his second stint in the band, which lasted about six weeks in total, but Hart has made his peace with it.

"I still see Vince from time to time and I run into Rex from time to time. Vince doesn't really like to talk about the past too much [but] Rex is a little more forthcoming. Rex and I have more history. I've known Rex since we were both little in fourth or fifth grade, and he and I . . . we don't really talk about the bad times; we just remember the good times."

Another name in the frame to take over as Pantera front man was Jason McMaster, who went on to form the glam-metal band Dangerous Toys. At the time, McMaster was playing in a thrash-metal band called Watchtower, and recalls how he ended up declining an offer to join Pantera because he didn't think they were the right musical fit:

"At the time, I was only into thrash and doom. Funny how things switched and minds grew openly during that time. [It] did for me, for sure. I asked Dime once—I remember the date since it was my birthday, March 18, 1995—at a show in San Antonio, Texas, at Sunken Gardens [Type O Negative opening for Pantera] why he thought about me as a replacement for Terry Glaze. His response was honest, without stutter: 'You had the biggest buzz at that time.'"

Despite the trouble they were having finding a permanent singer, Pantera continued to perform live on a regular basis, and always played three sets of roughly an hour each a night. The first set was raucous party music to get the girls up and dancing. They'd play Ratt's "Lay it Down" and Dio's "Stand Up and Shout," and Gary Hetrick would have a dark red spotlight trained on Darrell the whole time. When Darrell kicked into the main riff of a song the spotlight would switch to orange and flames would go up onstage. The dance floor was often empty, however, despite the band's efforts to encourage everyone in the audience to get up and dance.

The second set was filled with Pantera originals; they were the only Texas band aside from Sweet Savage to play a full set of original material, their closet competition in the state. The third set was the heaviest of the three and would be filled with metal classics like Judas Priest's "The Hellion" and "Electric Eye."

"I think that's what kind of set us apart from everybody else when we were coming up," Rex Brown later told *antiMusic*'s Debbie Seagle. "We paid our dues, for sure."

Even so, Pantera were no longer quite the big draw they had been during the Terry Glaze era. They needed some stability. Fortunately, they were about to find the man who would bring it.

5

ROCK THE WORLD: PHIL ANSELMO, *POWER METAL*, AND THE DAWN OF A NEW ERA

Well, there are four previous Pantera albums, and the way that we look at it is [that] those were our demo tapes.
—Vinnie Paul to David Lee Wilson of KAOS2000 Magazine, 2000

AFTER GOING THROUGH SEVERAL SINGERS, and then a lull without a front man, Pantera found their saving grace in 1987 when they discovered a guy from New Orleans named Phil Anselmo. Anselmo had previously played in Samhain, featuring Will Buras from Fall from Grace and future Crowbar guitarist Matt Thomas, but it was his stint in Razor White that created the biggest buzz.

Some years later, Vinnie Paul spoke to *Metal Rules* scribe Keith McDonald about the band's introduction to their new front man:

"We were playing a club in [Shreveport, Louisiana] called the Circle and the Square, and we were going through different singers. We knew we hadn't found the right guy yet and his band would play there a week after us."

Anselmo was always hearing from his friends about this band from Texas called Pantera and how they desperately need a singer. Likewise, when Pantera played in Louisiana, people would tell them that their singer wasn't doing too well, and maybe they should check out Phil Anselmo.

Vinnie knew Phil was the right guy from the moment he heard him sing, even before they had jammed together. As soon as Phil came down to Texas they clicked right away. It was as if they were meant for each other. After several friendly meetings it was decided he should join the band and so, in early 1987, the nineteen-year-old officially became Pantera's new front man.

Phil Anselmo was born Philip Hansen Anselmo on June 30, 1968, in New Orleans, Louisiana. His parents were liberals who listened to the Beatles and King Crimson; his dad owned a restaurant in suburban Metairie called Anselmo's, which closed after Hurricane Katrina struck in August 2005. Phil attended the nearby Grace King High School. From an early age, he had a deep interest in horror films and culture; he would eventually accumulate an extensive personal library of horror films and an expert knowledge of the genre.

"I didn't like school," he told *Kerrang!* writer Mörat in 1994. "I was smart enough; I made good grades when I applied myself. My folks used to get on at me, so I'd apply a little bit and I did good, but my head wasn't there."

Phil's friend Thomas Gromaskas turned him on to Black Sabbath as a teen, and before long they were trading metal albums with each other. They'd spend hours listening to Sabbath's

Paranoid or Venom's *Black Metal*, getting stoned and talking for hours about metal. Later on, they started jamming with each other. It was just the two of them; they were the only two guys hanging around the school halls wearing Maiden or Sabbath T-shirts. They really dug the satanic imagery of Venom—the power and evil nature of the music.

Anselmo knew he wanted to be a musician from a young age. "I was raised in a house of music," he told Rafi at vampirefreaks.com. "I fell in love with it." From the age of six or seven, he knew that he wanted either "to be in music, or I was going to be a professional wrestler." He would play air guitar to Queen's *A Night at the Opera* and Kiss *Alive!*, and, like Darrell, would dress up as a member of Kiss and practice his moves in his bedroom.

One day, when Phil was putting on his full Kiss gear and applying the makeup in front of the bathroom mirror, his dad walked by and shook his head disapprovingly. Undeterred, by his mid-teens Phil knew for certain that he wanted to be in a band. His first major band was Samhain (not to be confused with Glenn Danzig's group of the same name). It was the first time he'd played music with a bunch of guys who had their own instruments and a garage to practice in, and the first time he'd heard the powerful sound of the drums being played in a room.

Phil took guitar lessons in his teens, but while his friends told him he should be a singer he wasn't quite ready for that—not yet. Samhain played covers, but Phil was already beginning to write material of his own and would often show his guitar teacher the riffs he was working on.

A quiet, shy kid who spent time working on fishing boats, Anselmo was also a huge Judas Priest fan. His next band, Razor White, would cover the Priest classics. His other favorite bands included Slayer, the British metal band Venom, and the Swiss metal monsters Hellhammer, with whom he developed a strong connection. He came to love these bands and sought out other groups with the same kind of brutality. He found emotion in this music, and it became a lifelong love. "When I first heard Hellhammer it truly disturbed me," he later enthused. "That is the key to a band: that their music stays with you and that you cannot deny its effect on you."

He was also interested in football, and played first as defensive end and then as defensive tackle, linebacker, and eventually quarterback in junior high. But music was his calling card; not sports and certainly not academia. "I used to skip school and pretend I was sick," he told *Kerrang!*'s Robyn Doreian in 1991. "I remember one particular time when I built this fake guitar out of wood and painted it blue." When he left school at age sixteen, it was to pursue a life in music.

The connection between Razor White and Pantera is an important one, and the fundamental reason for Anselmo ending up joining the latter. Steve Blaze of the Louisiana band Lillian Axe played a key role in bringing the two together. Lillian Axe were one of the first New Orleans bands to add original songs to their set lists, and would regularly cross paths with Pantera on their way in and out of Texas.

"I was judging a 'Battle of the Bands' and Phil was singing for a band called Vapid Phase and I think they won. They were only sixteen-, seventeen-year-old kids. They were doing what everybody else was doing: wearing spandex and playing metal.... They were doing Van Halen and Maiden and all the popular six-stringed metal stuff that at the time was considered a little more edgy. They were doing some pop-metal-type songs; the kind of stuff that everybody was growing up on at that time. As far as the doom stuff, I don't even think that was that popular back then."

There was a thriving rock and metal movement right across the southern states in the '80s, not just in California and Texas but in Florida and Louisiana too. In Louisiana alone there were more than twenty rock clubs; bands could play every day of the week and not hit the same club twice. It was the perfect time for Phil Anselmo to make a name for himself and build up some contacts. After Lillian Axe, Razor White would be the next upstart New Orleans melodic metal band, and would open for Lillian Axe a number of times. Phil could always be found hanging out in the dressing room, where he'd be asking Blaze or his cohorts how to play certain songs on the guitar. They were his mentors. When Blaze ran into Darrell, Vinnie, and Rex one night in Texas and heard they were looking for a new singer, he told them he knew just the guy.

Phil Anselmo had the voice, the stage presence, and the enthusiasm. He was just what Pantera needed. Although he was younger than his new bandmates, he had started out in a similar way, playing a mixture of originals with Judas Priest and Van Halen songs. He also got on well with Walter Trachsler, the former Pantera roadie whose band Rotting Corpse would often take to the stage at around 12:30 A.M. after Pantera had finished their third set. Most of the audience tended to have left by this point, but Phil hung around and befriended the band. He was perhaps the only person with as wide a knowledge of the underground metal scene as Trachsler himself.

Aside from Rob Halford of Judas Priest, Anselmo's other main inspiration, in terms of front men, was Bruce Dickinson of Iron Maiden. The importance of British metal bands Black Sabbath, Judas Priest, and Iron Maiden on the future of Pantera cannot be overstated. Ronnie James Dio was also a great influence on the young, impressionable singer, as was Paul Stanley of Kiss. For Phil, like so many other American teens of the time, listening to Kiss's *Destroyer* was an experience in itself. He also admired the German hard-rock band Scorpions as well as the British guitarist Peter Frampton, whose legendary live album *Frampton Comes Alive* left a profound impression. He was a fan of David Lee Roth, too, and even of Bono of U2, but for the most part it was Black Sabbath, Ozzy, Dio, Venom, Mercyful Fate, Metallica, Judas Priest . . . until Slayer came along, that is.

REINVENTING METAL

"Talk about infectious riffs that you were dying to know how to play," he told Steven Rosen at *Ultimate Guitar*. "Slayer reinvented thrash ... so much so that I've got at least 90 records—and I do mean vinyl—sittin' in my front room that are just pure Slayer worship."

Pantera were a hungry band—hungry to make metal and gain recognition. And they would get hungrier. Phil was in awe of Diamond Darrell's guitar skills, which, combined with Anselmo's incredible showmanship and vocal power, would create an astonishing new sound. Phil was a good vocalist, and could sing the Terry Glaze songs as well as the originals, but he had plans to make much heavier music.

He didn't go down to well with everyone in Pantera's entourage, however. One night, the band took him out in Arlington, and he got so drunk that he couldn't make it home. Roadie and drum tech Gary Hetrick was dismayed when he learned that the drunk guy sleeping it off on the couch was going to be their next singer:

"I couldn't stand [Phil Anselmo], I really couldn't. He was just a dick. The first gig they played ever was at Savvy's [in Fort Worth]. I had done a couple of years with Terry singing. Here comes Phil and the very first night and the very first song when the lights go down he starts talkin' into the mic, well, that's where I put the spotlight on Terry while he's talking to the crowd, and Phil's like, 'Get that fuckin' light out of my eyes.' I just got offended by it. Don't throw me out in front of everybody like that. I ended up quittin' cos stuff wasn't going too smoothly. It was a lot of people arguing and shit. ... I wanted to roadie so I could hang out with my friends. What kinda sucked was that I went from being a friend to subservient."

Hetrick left the fold soon afterward, not because of the way Phil was acting—although it didn't help matters—but because of the way he was treated by another member of the band. One night, after a show in Oklahoma, Hetrick was packing up the drum kit while Vinnie just sat around at the end of the stage watching him. Eventually, Hetrick walked over to Vinnie and told him that he wasn't getting paid for this; he was doing it because he wanted to help out his friends. He got three meals a day and a pack of cigarettes, and he was fed up with being treated like a servant. He got in his car, drove off, and never looked back.

Guitar tech Kenny King, on the other hand, knew from the moment Phil Anselmo stepped through the doors of Pantego Sound that he would become part of the Pantera family. The singer was young and impressionable and gifted with a voice that blew most people away. He was cocky, but it was part of his overall personality. He would also play a crucial role in helping the band cement the move away from their glam-metal roots.

For now, there still remained a glam element to their sound and image, but Phil had his sights set on bigger venues and a different kind of audience. They might have become the best-known glam band in Texas, but Pantera wanted to evolve. They needed to evolve. This was a transitional period for the band as they started to ditch the spandex in favor of ripped jeans and T-shirts. In the past, Pantera had been about as glam as a band could get, and local metal fans sometimes struggled to take them seriously when they played their heavier material. They needed somebody with Phil's street smarts and perseverance to get through this period and make people take note of how they had evolved. The difference between the Abbott brothers and Anselmo was that if they were asked to pick an all-time favorite album, Darrell and Vinnie would choose Van Halen's *Women and Children First*, while Phil would pick Slayer's *Reign in Blood*. As Gammacide's Rick Perry recalls:

"It wasn't long before they toughened up their image and started writing heavier tracks like 'The Art of Shredding' and 'Death Trap.' And unlike the rest of the guys in Pantera, who kind of turned their nose up at the thrash underground, Phil would come to the Rigor [Mortis] and Gammacide shows. I liked him. I remember he made me a compilation tape of all this obscure thrash, all these bands like Hobbs' Angel of Death and Bulldozer . . . it was like he wanted me to know he was down with the ultra heavy and ultra obscure underground. He turned me onto Exhorder before they put out a CD. He hung out with us and supported the heavier bands. . . . He wanted to make Pantera heavier, and that is exactly what he did. The force of his personality and his focus on a heavier, more brutal type of metal is the reason why Pantera eventually changed . . . ."

"I hung out with Phil after I was in the band," former Pantera front man Dave Peacock recalls, "and he would play all this heavy stuff. 'This is what I'm into, man, we're gonna turn into this shit right here.' He was able to grab the reins and make it happen. That's what turned it around for them."

It was around this time that Pantera caught the attention of Gold Mountain Records thanks to one of the label's acts, Marc Ferrari of the band Keel. A year or so earlier, Pantera had given copies of their first two albums to Ferrari after a Keel show, which he then listened to on the long bus ride between shows. It was *Projects in the Jungle* that really caught his attention. Ferrari had never heard Pantera's music before, nor had he seen them play live, but he quickly became a fan. He was always singing their praises to everybody he knew who liked rock and metal, and it was through this that Gold Mountain became interested.

Much to the frustration and perhaps envy of other metal bands in the area, Pantera were always boasting about how they were about to be signed by such and such a label, whether it be Metal Blade or Combat or whoever, but the deals always seemed to fall through. Nonetheless, they seemed to have the edge on the other Texas metal bands, having already appeared on the cover of the U.K. magazine *Metal Forces*, so when Rigor Mortis suddenly got signed to Capitol in 1987, Pantera kind of freaked out. How had a thrash band managed to get signed to a major label before they did?

Pantera knew they needed to up their game, and having Phil in the band would help them do that. The prospective deal with Gold Mountain Records came with a snag, however: The label wanted Pantera to adopt a more commercial and marketable sound. Pantera refused, and vowed to release their next studio album independently. It would prove to be one of the best decisions the band ever made.

* * *

In 1988, Pantera released their fourth album, *Power Metal*, the first to feature Phil Anselmo on vocals. It was a far heavier and more aggressive album than their fans had come to expect. Some tracks, such as "Down Below," were songs the band had previously recorded with Terry Glaze; they were so enthused about the way Anselmo sang them that they had decided to re-record the songs with him.

"[When] we started tracking *Power Metal*," he told *The Culture Shock*'s Patrick E. Douglas, "I had only been in the band barely a month. I think they were just so hungry and they had such a vicious drive about 'em that they wanted to . . . get these songs done." He was not quite ready to bring his own ideas forward, however. "A month into the fucking whole venture they've got me in front of a mic in the studio," he continued. "Of course, my lyrics were gonna be Judas Priest–like."

By his own admission, he admits that not too much thought went into the lyrics, but he knew he had something to say, and a range in his voice that echoed that of his hero, Rob Halford. He could do a better Rob Halford impression than Halford himself. In time, Phil would develop his own style, but in the *Power Metal* days his vocals sounded very much like Judas Priest's.

Produced by the band and Jerry Abbott, *Power Metal* sounded better than the three previous Pantera albums. The overall effect might still have been somewhat primitive, but the same could be said for a lot of heavy metal bands of the time. Pantera did not need a better sound, a more enhanced production. And, as ever, Diamond Darrell's guitars sounded fantastic.

Power Metal was far removed from the sometimes sickly sweet sound of the glam-metal scene that Pantera no longer played any part in. It was obvious that the emergence of thrash metal from the Bay Area and other parts of Southern California was having a fundamental impact on the new lineup of Pantera.

Darrell would tell Phil stories about how he had taught James Hetfield a few things on the guitar, and how Hetfield had advised him on how to get a certain sound through the amps. The singer really enjoyed the stories because he was a huge Metallica fan. Metallica unquestionably influenced Pantera, as Phil later explained to *Examiner*'s Elliot Levin some twenty years later:

"I gotta turn to Metallica to say they were the first ones to really bring that bite to the fucking guitars. They really upped the game. But I also have to say this: Dimebag Darrell had known James Hetfield, and Lars, and all those guys a long time, even before I'd met them."

Of course, Metallica weren't the only band with ambitions to up their game. Phil was adamant that, with the right changes, Pantera could become a nationwide concern, and he didn't care who he said it to, as Jerry Warden recalls:

"It took a badass motherfucker to come in and put his foot down to somebody like Vince Abbott and say, 'No, motherfucker, we're not going to do it like this anymore. We're going to do it like this!' Not just any man could have done that . . . that's the power that Phil had. They were a very popular regional band, and it took a very powerful personality to be able to put his foot down like that. That argument got so fucking heavy that time they made me get out of the fuckin' room. That was the only time I ever remember them doing that."

Anselmo also brought with him a far more aggressive vocal performance than anyone would have expected. The new

Pantera sounded like Ratt with a little bit of Judas Priest thrown in, "Rock the World" being a perfect example. Meanwhile, Vinnie Paul and his guitar-playing brother had been developing a powerful combination of double-kick drums and chugging guitar riffs, which over time would grow tighter, leaner, and more pronounced.

As Eduardo Rivadavia later wrote on *AllMusic*: "The music is pure '80s power metal, with Dimebag Darrell pumping out speedy riffs like he had just joined Lizzy Borden." For his part, Anselmo has always vigorously defended the album, stating emphatically to *Culture Shock*'s Douglas that *PowerMetal* was very much a heavy metal album, even if "a lot of people look at that record and say, right off the bat it's a glam record."

Released on June 24, 1988, *Power Metal* was the last Pantera album to come out on their Metal Magic label. Alongside tracks like "Rock the World," "Over and Out," and "Death Trap," the album included a lead vocal by Diamond Darrell on "P*S*T*88" and a guest appearance by Keel's Marc Ferrari on "We'll Meet Again." "I played a solo on that track," Ferrari recalls, "that's all, no rhythm. I remember it was an off-the-cuff thing: 'Hey, you want to throw something down at the end of this track?' I just winged it!"

Such was the closeness between Ferrari and Pantera that the Texan band also recorded his song "Proud to be Loud" for *Power Metal*—more than ten years before Ferrari's own version of the song was released. He had demoed the song in 1987 for Keel's eponymous fourth album, but for whatever reason it failed to make the final cut. When he played the track to Pantera, however, they loved it. Musically and lyrically, it was the perfect fit for the band at that point in time. Their version of the song later appeared in the cult movie *Donnie Darko* (in which it is credited to the Dead Green Mummies) and also in *D2: The Mighty Ducks*.

Ferrari observed firsthand how enthusiastic Vinnie was when it came to production. His own role was to offer support and arrangement ideas, and to help guide Phil's vocals. He was mesmerized by Darrell's guitar-playing abilities; watching him was like seeing Eddie Van Halen, Randy Rhoads, and George Lynch of Dokken all rolled into one.

As for Anselmo, Ferrari found the singer "pretty quiet and serious" during the sessions:

"He was very respectful to me and was great to work with. It was very clear that he was going to be a huge star along with the rest of the band. He had a great dark sense of humor, which complemented the other three guys', and he was a blast to hang out with. He had not yet developed some of the demons which dragged him down in later years."

Ferrari knew from the moment he met Pantera that they would achieve widespread success eventually, even if it would take the rest of the world a while to catch up. He loved every era of the band, from the commercial glam rock of the first two albums to the harder, metal-tinged madness of *I Am the Night* and *Power Metal*. He appreciated the fact that Pantera were uncompromising in everything they did and that they always played straight from the heart. When Keel played the Texxas Jam back in 1986, Ferrari had tried to get Pantera backstage passes but was unable to do so. He told them not to worry: They'd be playing there themselves someday soon. He still feels lucky to be part of the Pantera story.

Even at this juncture, Pantera were ahead of their peers. Countless bands on the '80s American rock and metal scene put out their own demo tapes, but Pantera released their music on vinyl and cassette, each one shrink-wrapped and professional-looking. They appealed to the hard-core metal follower. They might have been pigeonholed in the same category as Poison and Bon Jovi, but they had much more in common with Judas Priest, who had gone through a glam stage of their own on *Turbo Lover* (1986) before following it up with a much heavier album, *Ram It Down* (1988).

Meanwhile, Pantera continued to play regular shows in and around Texas, often with the same or similar set lists comprising originals like "Death Trap," "Hot and Heavy," "Hard Ride," and "Right on the Edge" alongside the Ozzy Osbourne classics "I Don't Know" and "Goodbye to Romance" and Metallica's "No Remorse." Darrell had also begun covering songs by the famed guitar wizard and teacher Joe Satriani, including "Crushing Day" and "Echo," both from Satriani's classic 1987 album *Surfing with the Alien*.

It was also around this time that Pantera started to get other bands to open for them. By 1988, they were among the highest-paid bands in Texas, and were taking home some $1,500 a night. With a support band in tow, they would still receive a high fee but no longer had to play the three sets of old. They also signed an endorsement deal with Randall Amplifiers, which meant they needed a bigger vehicle to carry all the equipment in. In the old days Vinnie Paul had driven the band around in a Pontiac with a little one-axle trailer for the gear; now they were able to upgrade to a Ryder truck.

To many, Pantera were still a run-of-the-mill glam-metal band—or so it seemed at the time. They brought nothing new or especially challenging to the fold, but what they did was play professionally and expertly. They played good-time party metal, but they did it so well that they raised the bar for all the other local bands. Their stage shows—with lighting, sound, and Darrell's magnificent guitar tones—were the envy of other every other band in Texas. They'd put on a massive concert in a tiny club but it was their show, and it was always impressive.

There were hundreds of these kinds of bands in the '80s, but what the commercial failure of the first four Pantera albums did was allow the band to nurture their talents and develop new ideas out of the limelight. In fact, without those albums the latter-day version of Pantera would never have existed. Those albums contained the odd flash of thrash-metal brilliance but they relied too heavily on clichés and unconvincing melodic rock choruses and melodies.

Even so, the release of *Power Metal* and the growing success of bands like Metallica had caused Pantera to give serious consideration to their spandex-clad image. Thrash metal may have started to show signs of fatigue but the Big Four—Metallica, Megadeth, Slayer, and Anthrax—were doing remarkably well, having each released at least one masterpiece of the genre. As with any trend, there reaches a saturation point, and glam metal was hit hard by the success of Guns N' Roses, who merged punk with hard rock to create a totally raw yet catchy American sound. Pantera were all about metal, however, and although *Power Metal* retained a candy-coated, poodle-haired sheen, there were big hints at the groove-metal riffs that would become the band's signature sound in latter years.

It was around this time that Pantera met Slayer, one of the fiercest metal bands in the country. Still stuck on the seemingly never-ending Texas club circuit, Pantera were booked for a show in Dallas on a Friday, with Slayer due to play on the Saturday evening as part of their recently commenced *South of Heaven* tour. Being an avid fan, Phil had already bought his ticket for the show. As it happened, all members of Slayer bar drummer Dave Lombardo went to see Pantera perform on the Friday night, much to Phil's delight.

"Kerry King ended up getting on stage with us and played 'Reign in Blood,'" he recalled in an interview with Rafi from vampirefreaks.com. "After that me and him got to talking and hit it off really well." The pair quickly bonded over a shared love of Judas Priest and exchanged numbers. A few weeks later, Phil's phone rang. He couldn't understand who was on the other end of the line at first, and then he realized: It was Kerry King! They would end up seeing each other several times over the next few months. "The first time he just came to hang out," Phil recalled.

"The second time he called me and said, 'Look, this time I don't want to just come down for no reason.'"

King told Anselmo that he wanted to jam, and when Slayer next visited Texas, Kerry joined Pantera onstage. They blitzed through some classic material, including songs from *Power Metal* as well as Slayer's "South of Heaven" and "Reign in Blood," even some old Priest songs too. When King hooked up with Darrell he taught the Pantera guitarist a few new tricks: things that were going on in the burgeoning underground American metal scene at the time, but which were a world away from what Darrell was influenced by. King played out of key and at an incredible speed. It was totally different from the way Darrell and his heroes played the guitar, so it gave him a whole new perspective on how to make a metal riff.

Kerry King became a hugely influential figure to Pantera over the next few years. He would call Phil and joke that he wanted to join Pantera, and he'd watch them at local gigs. He and the band quickly developed a twin-guitar sound that recalled their mutual heroes, Judas Priest, and as Diamond Darrell learned the Slayer songs he noticed how dense and intricate the riffs were. But while many other bands of the time merely imitated Slayer, Pantera were developing a sound of their own.

Something else Phil brought to Pantera through 1988 and into the following year was a sense of fan community. The tape-trading culture was in its prime during the '80s as metal fans traded tapes of their favorite bands in an effort to spread the word and find out more about the underground metal scene. Word of mouth about certain bands began to spread around the country and then across the Atlantic as fans in the U.S. and Europe built up contacts and correspondence with each other through fanzines and magazines such as the U.K.'s *Metal Forces* and *Kerrang!*

Phil was an avid tape trader. He listened mostly to thrash metal, but he was into the hardcore bands too and admired the grueling work ethic of punk. On the club circuit, booking policies were dictated by what was popular at the time, and so the majority of small rock clubs wanted their acts to look like Poison or Cinderella and play sugar-coated glam metal. Phil, however, had never bought a Poison record in his life. When he slipped a Slayer song into the band's set list, he was doing the opposite of what the band had done previously with Terry Glaze. He was a flexible singer—that's what the band liked about him. He could hit the high notes but also growl and scream. He was determined to drag Pantera out of the glam-rock rut, and he would use his influence and interests to do so, as he explained to *MMN*'s Kenny Herzog:

"The next thing you knew, instead of just a bunch of poofy-haired metal guys and chicks, there were hardcore kids coming in, there were thrash kids. The places were packed, so what could the clubs say, 'We're not gonna let you play because you don't look glam anymore'?"

Nobody was going to mess with him. Pantera dominated the Texas metal club scene and nobody told them what to play. Phil had the street-smart attitude to take the band to the next level. Interacting with the audience was his main concern, and back in the days before Pantera became a worldwide band they'd go into a club and tell the audience that this was their stage too. The fans would go crazy.

Most of the Arlington metal bands got along well with each other, but some felt Pantera were posers, particularly after they began to make their stylistic shift away from party metal at the end of the decade. To his credit, Phil went out of his way to connect with some of the other metal bands in the Arlington area—bands like Rigor Mortis, Gammacide, and Rotting Corpse, with whom the other members of Pantera had never really made an effort in the past. That was just the way he was. Even so, some of these bands still felt Pantera used their position on the Arlington scene against them, as Rick Perry of Gammacide recalls:

"I remember Walt [Trachsler] from Rotting Corpse and I going to a new Arlington club called Metal Works [run] by a guy named James Craven who also had a music store where Darrell gave guitar lessons. Anyway, we booked a gig for Gammacide and Rotting Corpse. A short time later the club owner called back and said our gig was canceled. We found out later that they guys from Pantera told James that he shouldn't book us because our fans would trash the place."

The snub prompted a low-level feud between the bands. "We would talk shit about them in local magazines," Perry continues, "and they would retaliate by putting little hidden comments on their flyers that Rick Perry was a drug addict...."

In later years, Darrell would become an enthusiastic supporter of Perry's industrial metal band Puncture. Prior to that, however, Perry remembers him as a friendly guy who nonetheless wasn't always too keen to help out his fellow Texan musician:

"Darrell knew I was as a big a Priest fan as he was, and one time Pantera played at Joe's Garage, he invited me up to jam 'Green Manalishi' and 'Metal Gods.' They had all these Randall stacks on stage, and their roadie plugged me into one on Rex's side of the stage but it had no distortion—a totally clean sound. And so, during 'Green Manalishi,' me and Darrell are trading leads; he has this godlike tone, tons of sustain and echo, and I'm going 'ticka-ticka-ticka.' So they looked like they were being cool, inviting the guy from Gammacide to get up and jam with them, but they kind of gave me a crappy sound on purpose, to make a fool of me."

Soon, however, Pantera would have much wider concerns than petty squabbles on the Arlington metal scene. As 1989 dawned, a new chapter of the band's history would begin in earnest.

In the '80s, most metal bands dressed in glam attire. Pantera simply thought that that was what they were supposed to do. It took time for them to understand that big hair, makeup, and flashy clothes do not play music. Musicians do.

"That [glam look] was our first incarnation of the band back in '83, when we were all fourteen-year-old kids," Vinnie Paul later told Keith McDonald of *Metal Rules*. "All we knew was emulating our heroes."

Pantera—and their fans—have since disowned those first four albums, even the Anselmo-charged *Power Metal* with its goofy album cover. They are not listed on the band's website, and fans rarely talk about them. They have been lost to the annals of metal history like the treasures of Atlantis. Even so, Pantera had learned a lot about rock and metal during that time, not just through playing their own gigs, which they did sometimes seven nights a week, but also through supporting a plethora of bigger names—from Stryper and Ratt to Quiet Riot and Uriah Heep—as they passed through Texas. It was the perfect training ground for what was to follow.

PART TWO

SOUTHERN COWBOYS FROM HELL

6

AT THE CEMETERY GATES: FINDING A LABEL

The fact that you got signed to a major label, it was huge, you know? It was like this kick-start to your career, but then you realize that you're starting all over again, it's just at a different level. . . .

—Phil Anselmo to Chris Akin of Addicted to Vinyl, 2010

B Y 1989, ALTHOUGH THEY CONTINUED to play sporadic live shows, Pantera had drifted from view. It is not uncommon for bands to struggle to find a deal in their early days, and this was the case with Pantera during the late '80s. They'd shopped their demos around to all of the major labels in Los Angeles but were still yet to find a deal. It was a particularly frustrating period for guitarist Diamond Darrell, who watched on as one of his former bandmates hit the big time. After leaving Pantera, Terry

Glaze had formed Lord Tracy and released *Deaf Gods of Babylon* on the MCA subsidiary UNI Records. He had subsequently been on tour with Darrell's idol, former Kiss guitarist Ace Frehley, while Darrell sat at home wondering how it had all panned out like this. Maybe Glaze had made the right decision to leave.

Earlier in the year, Darrell had auditioned for the vacant guitarist slot in Megadeth. He passed the audition, but he had one stipulation before accepting the role: He wanted to bring his brother Vinnie along with him. Megadeth already had a fine drummer in Nick Menza, so front man Dave Mustaine said no and recruited guitarist Marty Friedman instead. It was a blessing in disguise, however, as the Abbott brothers would return to Texas and focus their time and energy on Pantera with renewed enthusiasm. A much-needed bout of good luck was just around the corner, too, when Atco Records A&R man Mark Ross came to see the band play at the Basement in Dallas in September.

Some accounts would have it that an opportunistic Ross decided to check out some bands at a tiny club in Texas after being left stranded there by Hurricane Hugo. Ross, so the story goes, had never even heard of Pantera, let alone have seen them live before, but was so impressed with the band that he left the gig halfway through to call his boss, Derek Shulman, and demand that Shulman sign the band. But although this story has been circulated for many years, and has a nice ring to it, it is simply not true.

A shrewd and knowledgeable businessman, Shulman had been responsible for the success of Bon Jovi and a number of other melodic rock bands of the '80s. He had been aware of Pantera since their glam-metal days, back when he worked for Polygram Records, and had even seen them perform in Dallas with Terry Glaze. Some time later, he was given a videotape of the band playing material from what would become *Cowboys from Hell* by Polygram lawyer Jules Kurz, and was suitably intrigued. The video, he felt, offered something completely new:

"Mark Ross, who worked for me, was down in Texas on another mission, actually, and there was a show that he was supposed to go to near Dallas. I said, 'Listen, I know that Pantera is playing in Arlington or somewhere close by.... I want you to go check them out because I haven't seen them play with this new music for a couple of years.' Anyway, he went down to the show in Texas. He called me. He said, 'Whoever this band you told me go see, they're unbelievable. You should come down and see them again.'"

A week later, Shulman went to see the band play in Texas. There were fewer than fifty people in the audience but he knew after just three or four songs that he was going to sign the band. "I went from being from someone who was interested in signing the band to becoming a huge fan," he says. "They were unbelievable."

Shulman had come close to signing the band before, but had always felt there was something missing. Now they had added the missing ingredient: Phil Anselmo. Shulman was mesmerized. There are many key elements to getting a record deal—timing, luck, and drive among them—but as far as Shulman was concerned, Pantera had it all. Anselmo was an incredible front man—a true rock star before he was even a rock star; Diamond Darrell a supreme guitarist; Vinnie Paul an amazing drummer; and Rex Brown a suitably robust bass player. Negotiations were concluded swiftly, and by the tail end of the year the deal was done.

Atco Records was founded in 1955 as a division of the Atlantic label, its name a contraction of Atlantic Corporation. Among the label's first hits was Bobby Darin's "Mack the Knife," while during the '60s it released records by Sonny & Cher, Buffalo Springfield, and the Who. By the '80s, however, it had become a much smaller concern run by a team of dedicated metal fans, and when Shulman took over he was given free rein to do as he pleased.

Beside Shulman, one of the key figures was marketing manager Steve Kleinberg, who had moved over from Polygram at Shulman's request, having previously worked with Def Leppard, Bon Jovi, Cinderella, and L.A. Guns. Kleinberg's first two projects at Atco were Pantera's *Cowboys from Hell* and AC/DC's commercial comeback, *The Razor's Edge*. He felt like the luckiest guy in the world. He'd already witnessed the power and intensity of the Pantera live experience at the Basement in Dallas and had been impressed at the way the band played on while fights broke out between the burly, beer-swilling cowboys in the audience.

What Pantera needed now was a firm and experienced manager to guide them to success. At Shulman's urging, the band hooked up with Walter O'Brien of Concrete Management, part of the New York–based Concrete Marketing firm, whom Shulman made known since his days in the British prog rock band Gentle Giant. O'Brien had come to Shulman with the cult band Metal Church, who had just left Elektra Records and were looking for a new deal. Shulman wasn't interested, even though he liked the band, but he told O'Brien about another act he'd just signed to Atco—one he felt would soon become one of the most important metal bands of all time. O'Brien recalls:

"I flew with Mark Ross to Dallas to see them. I was unsure because I knew the band from their early indie days and was never that impressed. But the second they got onstage and started tearing it up and jumping all around, I was blown away. I instantly begged them to let me manage them, and they did.

"Everything you see from Pantera is just what they're like. It was hysterically funny, full of energy. Vinnie was all business back then; the other guys were interested, of course, and Dime just wanted to make sure I got drunk. But it was clear these guys had the energy and charisma to go all the way."

The first time O'Brien went out to dinner with the band, Darrell asked the waitress to light him up "with one of them double-side-key deals." The waitress looked at Darrell like he was green until Vinnie or Rex told her it meant he wanted extra hot sauce. O'Brien and the band soon became good friends and would go bowling together regularly. Darrell would jump down on the ball-return machine and ride the balls like a rodeo bull until the staff threw them all out.

Back at Atco, Shulman knew that the kind of music Pantera were going to make would not be welcomed with open arms by MTV or mainstream radio, and that the only way the band would break through was on the road. Playing live in places they'd never played before would become an important part of marketing the band. Even if only fifty people turned up, those fifty people would tell fifty more about the band, and word of mouth would spread around the country's metal scene about this new band, Pantera, even though they weren't really "new" per se.

Pantera in turn knew that they were not getting any younger, and that now was their time to make their mark on the world. Phil in particular was determined not to let life pass him by, and was very aware that what the band was about to create would come to define them. "I want to be there, I want to know exactly where I'm gonna go, what I'm gonna do with my money, how I'm gonna treat people," he told *Kerrang!*'s Mike Gitter in 1993. "I want to be very conscious of it."

Another sign that a new era was about to begin was that most of the band's old road crew had moved on. Walter Trachsler, Jerry Abbott, and Gary Hetrick were already out of the picture, and now Kenny King was about to leave too:

"It ended October 31, 1989, [at] a club called Bear Creek. We were loading out and carrying some equipment up the ramp and . . . I slipped and I twisted my left ankle pretty bad."

The accident left King unable to drive the band's truck, which in turn led to a confrontation with sound engineer Ambrose Esquibell, who King insisted should take over driving duties.

"He was getting rather pissed. I said, 'I'm not gonna fight you. . . . We're not gonna do this.' . . . It was me being hotheaded, losing my temper. That night, when that happened, Vince and Rex were watching the whole thing . . . me and Ambrose having this confrontation. I said, 'Screw it. Give me my money—I quit.' That was stupid. I let my pride overgrow what I should have done and went and talked to Darrell. . . . To this day it kills me, because this has never been resolved between me and Darrell."

King and Darrell would remain friends and see each other from time to time, but they never discussed King's last night with the band.

"After I quit we're still brothers, we were still good to each other, [but] this is something me and him never got to sit down and talk about. I said I was through. I never went back and talked to Darrell. I never went back to talk to anybody. That was the end of my guitar-teching."

King's replacement, Grady Champion, was already familiar to the band. He had played guitar in Cat Daiquiri, one of the first bands to support Pantera; when the two bands played together, King would take care of Champion's equipment, too. It was a fairly smooth transition. After King quit he made a list of all of Darrell's effects and where they came in during the set list, which he then handed over to Champion, since Darrell was never going to go back to pushing his own pedals.

As soon as they got signed, Pantera upgraded to a sixty-foot RV for touring, but before long they had run the thing into the ground and went back to using a bus instead. They were not the kind of band to move upscale to a multimillion-dollar vehicle. They had an identity and a way of life that suited them. The trappings of the rock 'n' roll lifestyle might go to a lot of musicians' heads, but that was never the case with Pantera. They were grounded and honest, true to themselves and their fans. They had also grown up, and now was the time for them to go out on their own with a new sound and a fresh image to match.

They had ambitions to play to thousands of people around the world and did not want to be confined to the small sweaty clubs of Texas.

Even so, there was still some conflict within the band as to how they should proceed, with not everyone convinced by Phil's enthusiasm for the breakneck speed, frantic riffing, and sheer energy of bands like Metallica and Slayer, as former Pantera guitar tech Walter Trachsler recalls:

"From the very beginning, [Phil] was like, 'I'll be in this band but I'm gonna take it in a different direction.' Then they were like, 'You're in the band but you ain't changin' what the fuck we're doin'.' . . . They were never buddy-buddy . . . probably the person that most took to Phil was Rex. Rex has always been a person that takes to everybody. . . . He doesn't try to push himself or his shit off on everybody else. Rex and Phil just as people were more along the same lines. Vince was the type to sit back; he's gonna do his own thing but he's gonna wait and see which direction things go. Darrell was the type of person that's gonna force his own thing; that's all there was to it. He wasn't doing anything else. That's his M.O. Rex was the type of person that would adapt to situations, and so would Phil."

Pantera's first four albums had provided them with a means to hone their craft by trial and error, and without those albums, what was to come next would have sounded vastly different. What was clear, however, was that if Pantera were to find success beyond Texas and the South, they needed to evolve. Now it was time to demonstrate that evolution on record.

7

PSYCHOS FROM THE SOUTH: THE RELEASE OF COWBOYS FROM HELL

At this point we knew this was the direction we wanted to take the band. It was time to put a little chance on the table too. . . .

—Rex Brown to Rich Catino of Metal Asylum, 2010

PANTERA HAD ALREADY BEGUN WRITING and recording tracks for what was to be their major-label debut at their own Pantego Sound in Texas, where they had made all of their previous albums. In fact, they had already cooked up demos of the *Cowboys from Hell* material even before A&R guy Mark Ross came to see them live and changed everything for the band. The sessions were a way of shedding their glam-metal skin and embracing their southern roots. They took elements of country and hillbilly music but added them to heavy metal to create a new image.

REINVENTING METAL

On their past albums, the guys in Pantera were just a bunch of teenagers trying to find their musical voice; now, with Phil Anselmo on board, they had found it. He brought out the heaviness in them: all of it.

The general consensus is that the first track the band wrote for the album was the title track, often abbreviated to "CFH," which has since become the band's trademark anthem. Back in 1989, Darrell arrived late to a house party in Fort Worth, Texas, having spent time working on a riff, which he then played to Phil in his car. Phil said they had to use the riff immediately and "Cowboys from Hell" was born right there and then. According to Walter Trachsler, however, the song had a rather more convoluted past:

"It was a Metallica song. One hundred percent. James Hetfield came up with that. It had nothing to do with Texas, nothing to do with cowboys. It was one of those times they came to the [Abbotts'] house to hang out. . . . There's a picture on my Facebook of James Hetfield sittin' on a couch playing one of Darrell's guitars. When this picture was taken, James was playin' me that fuckin' song. We're hanging out in the front room with James playing guitar and I said, 'Hey dude, you're gonna come up with any new Metallica stuff?' He said, 'Yes, as a matter of fact [I'm finishing this off] wanna hear it?' I said, 'Yeah.' Well, back then, all we tried to do was play fast stuff. Everything was a million miles an hour. He starts playin' and it was a fuckin' slow song. He played all the way through and it was a slow song. I was like, 'Dude, what the fuck? What's that called?' He said, 'Cowboys from Hell.' They never put it out, so Rotting Corpse—six maybe, seven years later—we went and did a song that was as much as I could remember that song called 'Cowboys from Hell' and everything we recorded we recorded at Pantego Sound with Vince, so he heard everything we did. He goes, 'Hey man . . . what was that song called?' That was the only one that he ever said anything about . . . dude, [that song] came from San Francisco."

Pantera demoed a total of eleven songs. Only one failed to make it onto the final album: "The Will to Survive," an interesting song with Phil singing in an upper range—the closest he got to a Rob Halford–style falsetto. It just didn't fit with the rest of the album (nor indeed with *Power Metal*, for which it was also demoed back in 1987).

"The Will to Survive" would later be included on the twentieth-anniversary edition of *Cowboys from Hell*, where it served as another strong example of Diamond Darrell's distinctive blend of heaviness and the blues, as Rex Brown subsequently explained to *Metal Asylum*'s Rich Catino:

"He really used the blues as a tool. ['The Will to Survive'] got some real tasty bluesy licks. And he was also playing around [with] 'the box,' which is just around twelve notes that are real tasty, and then he could also rip your head off."

There had always been an underlying blues aspect to Pantera's music—unsurprisingly, given that the Abbotts grew up around Texan blues players—and they would never fully disassociate themselves from the genre. "The box" was Darrell's term for a group of notes—a kind of scale—that he would play around with during studio sessions while he was trying to get the right sound. It was how he came up with the original riff to "Cowboys from Hell."

After completing the demos for the album, Pantera returned to Pantego Sound at the turn of the year with a new producer, Terry Date, who had been recommended to the band by Atco Records boss Derek Shulman. Both he and manager Walter O'Brien felt Date was the perfect man for the job, as O'Brien recalls:

"They had done a great set of demos of most of the songs on their own, in their dad's studio, Pantego Sound. They were going to hire Max Norman [best known for his work with Ozzy Osbourne and Megadeth], but his manager kept dragging it out while waiting for a better job to materialize. We wanted to get going, so I convinced the band to bring Terry Date in for the weekend, see if they got along, and then he'd stay and produce [the album] if they felt good about him. They did, they clicked, and when Max's manager finally called the next week to say Max was available—meaning his 'better' job fell through—we told him no thanks."

The Michigan-born Date brought with him an incredible amount of experience, having previously worked with Overkill, Dream Theater, and Metal Church, among others. He also had some bold ideas, such as advising Anselmo to drink port before he sang to warm his throat. It had apparently worked for Chris Cornell of Soundgarden, and it would work for Anselmo, too.

Having played these songs at local gigs, Pantera knew that their fans really liked the new material, but in their hearts and minds they were already working toward their next album. Fortunately, in Terry Date they had a producer who would push them every step of the way, as Rex Brown explained when asked by Rich Catino of *Metal Asylum* about the difference between the original demos and the final album: "Terry really pushed us for excellence. There are some interesting intros Darrell did on those demos, but [we ended up with] a balls-out record. I definitely like the finished versions."

The biggest difference between the demos and the final studio versions was in the arrangement of the songs, and it was here that the band took a massive step forward. One such example is "Cemetery Gates," which runs to more than six minutes and shows the breadth of the band's talent and vision. Rex came up with the original idea while jamming on his orange Kramer acoustic bass during some downtime for the band. Darrell liked what he heard and started playing along, and Rex then added a piano part. They then took the bare bones of the song to the rest of the band and Date before overdubbing additional guitars and drums. It has since become a classic Pantera track.

Now, with a revered producer on their side and the backing of a major label, Pantera could finally become the sort of original metal band they had long felt they were destined to be. After completing the recording sessions at Pantego Sound the band and Date headed to the Carriage House in Stamford, Connecticut, to mix the album, before handing it over to Howie Weinberg at Masterdisk in New York for mastering.

Cowboys from Hell opens with the title track, which is driven by one of the most groove-laden riffs in all of metal, and rarely lets up from there. "Primal Concrete Sledge" demonstrates the chugga-chugga guitar style that Pantera would become famous for, while the superlative "Psycho Holiday" is topped off by a great vocal performance. "Heresy" is a thrash-metal monster driven by pounding drums; the aforementioned "Cemetery Gates" is one of Pantera's most accomplished compositions, featuring some intricate guitar and mesmerizing shifts in tempo. "Domination" is another track powered by chugging riffs, while the central guitar solo proves just how incredible Diamond Darrell's guitar playing had become. "Shattered" captures Phil Anselmo's best Rob Halford impression, an exemplary vocal performance that marks him out as one of the best singers in metal. "Clash with Reality" features more progressive guitar work and some angry, angry vocals, "Medicine Man" is one of the band's catchiest tracks, and the frenetic "Message in Blood" is another of the album's strongest moments—in all senses. "The Sleep" offers some respite in the form of a mid-tempo stomp with mournful vocals, while "The Art of Shredding" brings the album to a close with a manic journey into hardcore metal.

As with the band's previous albums, one of the standout elements throughout *Cowboys from Hell* is Diamond Darrell's guitar playing. He had really come into his own during the making of the album, and the advice he had once received from his old man, Jerry, about playing by the book and not doing things too differently, was no longer applicable. In some respects—albeit unintentionally—Jerry had held his son back; now it was time for Darrell to ignore the recording manual and do things his own way; to bring in some distortion, add some feedback, and play those frantic, breakneck riffs. His playing was rhythmic and melodic, yet he used unconventional notes and pitch harmonics that would soon be blowing the minds of the band's fans.

Although Darrell had by now developed a style all his own, his playing still bore the influence of some of his guitar heroes, notably Randy Rhoads and Black Sabbath's Tony Iommi, who inspired Darrell to detune his guitars to C-sharp—and sometimes even lower—for a deeper, more menacing sound. The chord passages on "Cemetery Gates," meanwhile, were said to have been inspired by Ty Tabor, the guitarist in hard-rock band King's X.

There was a brutal and progressive edge to the way Darrell played his guitar and how Terry Date made the band sound. The heavy grooves, complicated chord structures, and innovative guitar work were different from what was happening in the American metal scene at the time. Sure, Metallica had experimented somewhat with *Master of Puppets*, and they'd gone even further with . . . *And Justice for All*, but they were starting to pull back now, and had opted for a more commercial sound on *Metallica* (also known as *The Black Album*.) Pantera wanted to make their mark on the American metal scene, and that meant cooking up a completely different sound.

While Darrell's guitar playing was at the heart of the band's new sound, Phil, too, was becoming a force to be reckoned with. He had been somewhat intimidated while working on *Power Metal*, well aware that the rest of the band had been playing and recording together for years. Now, on *Cowboys from Hell*, the others were beginning to get a sense of his full potential, both as a singer and as a songwriter.

The overall intensity of the album is almost overwhelming. Aside from Phil's falsetto vocals, which recall a much deeper Rob Halford of Judas Priest, the band had all but abandoned their musical roots. *Cowboys from Hell* has thrash-metal riffs in abundance and a far more extreme and aggressive sound than many would have expected from the band that had made *I Am the Night*. The riffs are more technical and intricate, the drums heavier and faster, and the band's collective force more complex and abrasive. Some would dub this sound "power groove" or "groove metal," even as others were adamant Pantera were a thrash-metal band. Genre debates aside, the band had shown that they had a lot to say, and that what they had to say was worth listening to.

* * *

Released on July 24, 1990, *Cowboys from Hell* was a giant leap forward for the band both in terms both of the sound of the band and of their commercial success. It was the band's first chart hit, even if it would not reach its U.S. peak of Number 27 until 1992. It may have been a slow burner in terms of chart success—the album also reached Number 46 in the Swedish charts in 1995—but it did nonetheless provide the band with some much-needed mainstream attention. Until now, ZZ Top had been the heaviest band from Texas to make it big. Most well-known hard-rock and metal bands came from New York or California or Seattle; Pantera were about to change that.

The album's eye-catching cover art shows the band in an old saloon, obviously in reference to the title. Darrell in particular was keen to be involved in all creative matters, including photos, packaging, and videos, and would often travel to the Atco offices to meet with designers and video directors. On *Cowboys from Hell*, he is posed in the center of the shot, playing guitar. Vinnie is shown counting money, Rex is leaning on the bar, and Phil is jumping into the air to Rex's left. It's a terrific shot displaying the earlier humor of the band. They took their music seriously, but they also had a sense of camaraderie, too.

"It's definitely tongue in cheek," Phil told *Examiner*'s Elliot Levin. "I'm not sure who came up with that idea, I remember sitting down and us talking about it, and the only thing I can really remember about it is when we actually did that shoot I actually stood up on a bar stool...."

Initial reviews of the album were very positive, with most critics hailing Pantera as a new force to be reckoned with in the metal world. Those who were already familiar with the band from their previous albums, meanwhile, could hardly believe the shift in sound and image. That said, there was a clear appetite for the album among fans and critics alike, particularly those who had been left cold by the grunge explosion. Pantera were quickly hailed by many as the next big thing in metal.

Cowboys from Hell spawned three singles: the title track, which hit Number 31 on the U.S. *Billboard* Mainstream Rock Tracks chart; "Cemetery Gates," which peaked at Number 18 on the same chart; and "Psycho Holiday," which failed to chart. A slightly shorter version of "Cemetery Gates" was used on the soundtrack to the 1995 movie *Tales from the Crypt Presents Demon Knight*.

Promo videos were made for each of the singles, and would soon appear in heavy rotation on MTV. Like a lot of bands, Pantera did not especially relish the video-making experience. They hated sitting around all day, waiting for the cameramen to set up. They were most at home onstage. Fittingly, then, the videos for "Cowboys from Hell" and "Psycho Holiday" were shot at one of the band's favorite venues, the Basement in Dallas, and simply show them playing live.

"I'm not saying I'm the most pure dude in the world," Darrell told H. P. Newquist of *Guitar Magazine* in 1995, "but I really don't care about what I look like or what I do in the videos." Nonetheless, the *Cowboys* promos proved popular enough with fans that they were released on VHS, alongside additional band footage and live performances, as *Cowboys from Hell: The Videos* on April 2, 1991.

Cowboys from Hell remains a highly influential and important metal album and has stood the test of time remarkably well. In a review for *BBC Music*, Greg Moffitt notes: "Where most imitators merely pile riff upon riff, Pantera wrote songs, and *Cowboys*... doesn't just hinge on an all-out aural assault." In a recent poll of the all-time greatest heavy metal albums for *IGN*, *Cowboys* featured in nineteenth place, while it was ranked number eleven on *Guitar World*'s 2006 list of the "100 Greatest Guitar Albums of All Time." It was also named the nineteenth most influential metal album of all time by the popular website metal-rules.com.

Such is the enduring popularity of the album that some of its most famous tracks, such as "Domination" and "Cemetery Gates," have been covered by a wide range of other bands either onstage or on record, including Apocalyptica, Glória, Angelus Apatrida, Bullet for My Valentine, Evile, Dream Theater, Michael Angelo Batio, and Between the Buried and Me.

Even so, *Cowboys from Hell* was only a taster of things to come. As Anselmo explained in a later interview with *Examiner*'s Elliot Levin: "*Cowboys* was a good launch-pad when it came out, but [it was] not the complete genuine article."

* * *

With a new album in the can—and a much heavier one at that—Pantera also revised their look. It was also no longer about denim and leather (as Saxon once sang), but something more casual, more American. Dimebag, for example, now wore knee-length shorts and a T-shirt onstage, while Anselmo had shaved his head and exposed his collection of tattoos, which gave the band a hardcore punk–like image. He had grown tired of the long-haired metal scene of the '80s and wanted to start a new trend to change metal for the better. "I was fucking damn dead sick and tired of [the] prototypical long-haired . . . lead singer, 'How's everybody feeling out there tonight,' you know?" he later told Levin. The change came as a surprise to many, as Derek Shulman recalls:

"Phil was certainly nothing more than I'd seen before. I did get a bit of a shock when I turned up after *Cowboys* became quite a big record for them and they were getting into *Vulgar* and he shaved his head. I was a little upset by that, but apparently he was ahead of the time as well. Phil and the band were always ahead of whatever movement they were in and they were the leaders. Sometimes it was hard to understand it, but they really were."

Some observers, however, would claim that Phil was merely mimicking hardcore punk singer Henry Rollins, formerly of Black Flag, but the Pantera front man always disputed such accusations. Rollins is muscular and toned, while Anselmo looks more like a brawny bar-brawler. "My band don't sound nothin' like Rollins," he told *Kerrang!*'s Jason Arnopp in 1994, "and my performance ain't nothin' like him."

Some among the more devoted, tape-trading metal community would also accuse Pantera of mimicking the groove metal sound of Exhorder, who hailed from Phil's hometown of New Orleans. Exhorder's debut studio album, *Slaughter in the Vatican*, came out a few months after *Cowboys from Hell*, but they had been around since 1985, and their demo tapes had been in circulation since 1986. Phil loved those demos, particularly *Get Rude*, and told singer Kyle Thomas as much. He had proved instrumental in spreading the word about the band, and was even asked to move back home and replace Thomas in Exhorder after the New Orleans group temporarily split up in 1988. It was a tempting proposition, particularly since, back then, Pantera were not yet making the music Phil wanted them to make.

Thomas and Anselmo were very similar singers, and when Kyle heard that Phil was seriously considering this new opportunity he decided to rejoin Exhorder himself. Phil made it clear that he was an Exhorder fan first, so there were no hard feelings. He would later introduce Thomas to the rest of Pantera, but, as had so often been the case in the past, not everyone in the band was so welcoming, as Thomas recalls:

"I knew everyone but the drummer. Phil introduced me to him in 1988 or so, and he [Vinnie] was so rude—walked off in the middle of me talking to him, in midsentence, ten seconds after I started talking. It wasn't like he was busy—it was their first show in New Orleans, there may have been twenty people there, and he just walked away toward the bar. I never looked back on that one. I don't need [him] either. If he ever cares to explain that one to me and I misunderstood him, feel free, but it seemed pretty cut-and-dried. Rex and Darrell were always very nice to me."

By 1991 Pantera had the backing of a big label and a much less controversial album title, and thus achieved far more success than Exhorder, who sadly never went beyond cult status. By Thomas's own admission, Exhorder didn't work hard enough; their drummer was still in college, and often their main impulse was simply to get drunk. They only did a few tours, and the major opportunities never came along. But the stylistic traits of *Cowboys from Hell* and *Slaughter in the Vatican* have been compared and contrasted over the years since—far too excessively in some cases. Did Exhorder rip off Pantera, or was it the other way around? Are the similarities between both bands *that* obvious, or was it just publicity hype? Certainly, the drum parts on Pantera's "Primal Concrete Sledge" owe a debt to Chris Nail's drums on "Slaughter in the Vatican." But was this really any different than Led Zeppelin deriving influences from old American blues players?

Around the time of Exhorder's second album, *The Law* (1992), guitarist Jay Ceravolo made some negative remarks about Pantera's glam past in an interview with *Metal Maniacs*—remarks he had said were off the record, but which were published nonetheless. The interview added fuel to the supposed feud between the two bands, but Kyle Thomas is quick to downplay it:

"I got on the phone with Phil not long after an interview with Exhorder came out. That article really poured gas on that fire, and we really weren't happy with each other one bit. Phil was angry and hurt and felt that we were just jealous. Maybe we were. I never wanted them to not have what they earned—I just wanted to live out my dream as well. I have, to an extent: being in the magazines, touring the world with multiple bands, video on MTV, etc. Money talks, though, and I sure wish that I could have earned more of it living that dream.

"Some parties have really gone overboard about [the conflict between the bands]. I went to see [Pantera] once as Phil's guest, and in the middle of the concert, someone in the upper level unraveled a giant banner that read 'EXHORDER' . . . I wanted to crawl under a rock. Afterward Rex asked me about it, basically baffled by it. He was like, 'What the hell?' All I could say was, 'It wasn't me, man.' Darrell used to come out to see us play in Texas, and one time he came out pretty angry after the same article that pissed off Phil was released. He was pretty ticked, and filmed himself speeding toward us as we were about to leave the club . . . he'd slam the brakes, reverse, and do it again. He did it like twenty times. Then he drove off. It's kind of funny in retrospect. I'd laugh my ass off if I saw it today. Nothing ever came to a fistfight or anything, but there was tension."

Psychos from the South: The Release of Cowboys *from* Hell

Although the so-called feud between Pantera and Exhorder was largely the product of press hype, it is still discussed today. It became Thomas's cross to bear—his proverbial albatross—to the extent that he rarely speaks about it, and in fact has walked out of interviews in the past when it is brought up. The truth, however, is that he bears no ill will toward Pantera whatsoever. He has defended them in the past—and continues to do so—while Anselmo has always praised Exhorder. The supposed feud between them has been maintained over the years by the fans, even though there has always been room in the metal community for both bands.

Exhorder split up a year after the release of *The Law* but reformed in 2008. While Pantera grew more and more popular, Exhorder stayed obscure, but they deserve far more acclaim than they have yet received for their undiluted brand of razor-sharp, technically accomplished American metal.

* * *

Leaving overzealous fan debates aside, Pantera spent much of 1990 touring in support of *Cowboys from Hell*. Their first major cross-country jaunt was with thrash bands Exodus and Suicidal Tendencies; after that, they toured with Mind over Four and Prong. Among the venues they played that year was the Ritz in New York City. Phil believed New York was the wildest place the band played—and also the toughest. It was also a great place for Pantera to check out artists and bands that were inspired by Pantera, among them California heavy metal outfit DevilDriver, formed in 2002; Dez Fafara; Slayer; Biohazard; Sepultura; Prong; Sick of It All; Agnostic Front; and Anthrax.

By 1990, most of Pantera's original road crew had moved on. The "Road Dog 1990 Crew," as it was known, consisted of road manager Guy Sykes, guitar tech Grady Champion, lighting tech

Sonny Satterfield, sound tech Ambrose Esquibell, and a drum tech who went by the name Scarsdale. Before each show, Phil would do an hour-long workout with push-ups, crunches, skipping, sit-ups—a full-body workout. He found that he needed to psych himself up for a show, mentally and physically.

"That was a tough tour, man," he told *Examiner*'s Elliot Levin. "Playing in front of a mainly Suicidal [Tendencies] audience—and no offense to Exodus, but Suicidal was *the* band on that fucking tour—that was a challenge."

Outside of Texas, and perhaps a couple of other southern states, Pantera were practically unknown. They had a strong regional following, but metal fans elsewhere had not taken to them at all. They stuck mostly to the same set list throughout 1990—"Domination," "Psycho Holiday," "The Art of Shredding," "Cowboys from Hell," "Message in Blood," "Primal Concrete Sledge," "Cemetery Gates," and "Heresy"—but it seemed as though the only thing people ever thought or cared about was what Pantera sounded like before Anselmo joined in 1987. To begin with, the audience response to the new incarnation was lukewarm at best. But the band played on, feeding off the crowd's apathy like ravaged animals and driving themselves to become tauter, more polished musicians. Before long, they had achieved a remarkable, machinelike tightness. The interaction between Darrell and the rhythm section was second to none.

Unlike some bands, Pantera were not unattainable or inaccessible. Phil would even invite fans to come up onstage and sing with him. The band had a great interaction with those who liked them, but getting the cynics on their side was a lengthy, time-consuming, and draining process. They would have to earn the trust of not only of a small regional audience but a whole world of metal fans—and that would be a tough job, particularly when their front man looked and acted like a hardcore dude.

Prior to signing a contract with Atco, Pantera didn't realize how much work they'd have to put in as a major-label band. Darrell had read all the stories about Kiss guitarist Ace Frehley and drummer Peter Criss rockin' 'n' rollin' all night and partying every day, but in truth, those hell-raising hedonistic ways only lasted so long, and what had kept Kiss alive and well all these years was the workhorse mentality of Paul Stanley and Gene Simmons. For Pantera, signing a record deal meant nonstop touring and recording.

There were still plenty of perks of the job, however, such as the time they ended up jamming onstage with another of their heroes. One day, Phil and Darrell were in a hotel room in Canada, before a show, when the phone rang. On the other end of the line was an accented voice Phil did not recognize: It was Rob Halford of Judas Priest. He told Phil he was coming to see Pantera perform that night, and asked if he knew any Judas Priest songs. Phil thought he was dreaming: He knew everything about Judas Priest, and here he was, chatting to Rob Halford on the phone. After the conversation, Phil looked around to Darrell with a funny expression on his face and told them that Halford was coming down to jam with them onstage. They were in a dream world for the rest of the day.

That evening, Halford joined Pantera onstage for powerful versions of the Priest classics "Grinder" and "Metal Gods." Such was the obvious onstage chemistry between the self-proclaimed Metal God and the Texan group that Pantera were invited to open for Judas Priest on their *Painkiller* tour of Europe, which would give them their first exposure on the continent on a bill that would also feature the Canadian thrash metal band Annihilator.

The tour began on January 31, 1991, in Copenhagen and ran through to March 31 in Dublin. As the opening act, Pantera played a short set; in Madrid on March 10, for example, they

REINVENTING METAL

performed "Domination," "Psycho Holiday," "Cowboys from Hell," "Cemetery Gates," and "Primal Concrete Sledge."

Annihilator had never even heard of Pantera before the tour started, but received a suitably comical introduction to them when they both arrived in Europe and the Texan group revealed that they were missing a drummer. Vinnie, it transpired, had missed the plane because he'd been sitting in a restroom reading the newspaper. The Canadian band couldn't believe what they were hearing, and it prompted guitarist and founder Jeff Waters to come up with a new nickname for Pantera's drummer: "Vinnie the Pooh."

Pantera were almost unknown in Europe, except to some members of the metal press and serious metal enthusiasts. The crowd response to them on this tour was often far from positive, and at some shows, Pantera were booed by the famously traditionalist European metal audiences. Some wondered why Judas Priest had taken Pantera on the road with them at all. As a genuine metal fan, Rob Halford knew that Pantera were going to be the next big thing in metal, and yet the audiences didn't get it, and neither did the metal press. Even the guys in Annihilator were unconvinced to begin with, as Jeff Waters recalls:

"Rob Halford got it. He got it way before the tour started. He saw it probably because of his experience and his longevity and [because he] was so in touch with metal. He saw another legend coming up. But we didn't get it. We—as Annihilator—hung in the bus and thought they were slightly rednecky Americans, and we were more happy, polite, and friendly Canadians; silly and immature Canadians. We didn't clash like it was a bad mix [but] it was an odd mix. We definitely [weren't on] the same page."

Watching from the side of the stage, however, Waters and his bandmates soon realized that there were in the company of some incredible musicians:

"That tour gave me a huge lesson, and gave everybody huge lesson, which was: You don't shit on the metal crowd! You're spitting and telling them to fuck off. We did appreciate the shuffle moves and the great musicianship and the great guitar playing; and the singer was energetic and a really crazy front man.... That taught me a very early lesson as a kid—twenty-four-years old at the time—taught me if your neighbor next door is practicing guitar, and you think maybe the guy's not very good ... don't ever fucking underestimate being different or being new or being creative or being weird or being not in the mold, because Pantera taught everybody a lesson. I ended up being slightly influenced by some of their songs and records in my playing and stuff like that. It's funny how that all completely turned around."

As the tour progressed, Halford and Anselmo formed a close friendship based on mutual respect and admiration. Phil spent so much time in Halford's dressing room, in fact, that erroneous rumors of his alleged homosexuality began to circulate. Halford had not yet come out of the closet, although he would several years later, but as far as Phil was concerned, as Vinnie Paul later put it: "That is the most untrue rumor I've ever heard in my life. ... Phil Anselmo has had his fair share of pussy on this earth, trust me."

In fact, the reason for Phil's frequent visits to Halford's dressing room was simple: He was teaching his idol how to warm up his voice before a show. Yes, that's right: He was showing Halford, a metal legend, how to sing in his aggressive, rugged style night after night without killing his vocal cords. Halford would later mimic Phil and Pantera in his underrated solo project Fight, which he formed after leaving Judas Priest in May 1992, while he and Pantera would also team up that year for "Light Comes Out of Black," which appeared the soundtrack to the original *Buffy the Vampire Slayer* movie. The Fight material is grittier than Priest's, and the Pantera influence is obvious. Halford also shaved his head and exposed his collection of tattoos by wearing shorts and T-shirts—just like Phil. As the '90s began, metal had entered a new era, even if European audiences were slow to appreciate it. American bands had taken British and German metal and put their own spin on it. Overseas fans might not have been quick to latch onto Pantera, but they got there in the end.

Pantera and Annihilator partied hard on tour. There were drugs and drinks at the ready, and while of the musicians drank to avoid the drugs (or vice versa), others did both. The two bands became good friends, although there were some issues along the way. Pantera were always playing pranks on people, and sometimes these went too far, at least for the guys in Annihilator, who weren't too thrilled when the Texan group left bottles of their urine—with the caps loosened—in the bus driver's bunk. Waters was also puzzled by the amount of time Pantera would spend filming themselves doing silly stunts like making themselves throw up after eating too much ham, although it all paid off in the end when the band included some of the footage on their highly successful *Vulgar Video* collection.

Waters and Brown would sometimes rub each other the wrong way: partly, according to Rex, because Waters was always bumming cigarettes off him. "Buy your own fucking smokes, Waters!" he'd yell. On the other hand Jeff, like others, found Vinnie more withdrawn than his bandmates. He was somewhat distant and focused more on the business side of things. While the others were off partying, Vinnie would be poring over the books with manager Walter O'Brien and tour manager Guy Sykes.

Waters spent more time with Darrell, who, it turned out, had been born the same year as Waters, and had a similar attitude—a mix of charisma and ego—as the Annihilator front man recalls:

"We kind of avoided each other for the first few weeks. Then we got together and we were like, 'What, you like the same guy as I do? The same guitar player?' We'd go through the ropes and stuff; we'd go through the blues and Tony Iommi. . . . [We] realized that there was not one single influence that was different between the two of us. We had the same musical background. It was pretty fucking mind-blowing . . . ."

Most nights, after finishing their own sets and taking a shower, Jeff and Darrell would kick back with some beers and watch Judas Priest—always from K. K. Downing's side of the stage. They almost never missed a Priest show.

"[We] weren't best friends; it wasn't like that . . . none of us ever had that relationship with Pantera, and they didn't have that with us. We were young and had a little bit [of] attitude and ego because we had two massive-selling albums at the time. We were partying all the time and drinking, and that usually happens to people who are young and party every night and get told they're really good. You're on tour with Judas Priest and it's hard to hold your young ego in check . . . ."

Both guys also got on well with the Priest road crew, particularly guitar tech Andy Battye, who had previously worked for Metallica's James Hetfield. Battye knew that neither Annihilator nor Pantera could afford a hotel room, so whenever they had days off he would let them hang out in his hotel room rather than on the tour bus. He could see that they were all good guys and musicians, and they'd sit back, drink beer, and chat about metal.

Generally speaking, the bands would sleep on the bus until midday or so, when they arrived at the next city on the tour. Most of the places merged into one—except for when they rolled into war-ravaged Yugoslavia for a show at Dom Sportova in Zagreb on February 26, 1991, as Waters recalls:

"I remember it was early afternoon, like two o'clock, rolling into this place, waking up with our regular diet [of] a Coca-Cola and a cigarette. A healthy lifestyle! We look out the window and I remember we were pulling into this arena, and we saw a whole bunch of commando-looking guys with guns and these big black dogs. We're talking like two hundred—it looked like an army was there. We got off the bus thinking: This looks like a violent country. We didn't know. I didn't know if Pantera had a clue what was going on politically or what was going on in that part of the world. I sure didn't.

"We got into the arena, security took us in, and the manager of Priest—Jayne Andrews, the same manager they have now—came in and said, 'Listen guys . . . you have to get the fuck out of here tonight. Right after your show, get off the stage, go, drive, run away.' We're all like, 'Why?' 'Because there's going to be a war!' We thought, Ah, cool! A war! Right on, we're metal—just a bunch of idiots, right? 'There's no girls, there's no partying—you're going to get on that bus . . . get on the bus and leave.'"

There may have been a war going on, but Darrell still had time for a prank. After each show the two support acts would share a buffet tray containing an assortment of meat, fruit, and vegetables, which they'd eat either in their dressing rooms or back on the bus. That evening, everybody was in such a rush to leave that they didn't notice what Darrell and Jeff were up to: namely, urinating all over the food tray. Unbeknownst to them, however, one of the catering ladies had caught them in the act. After making the food look reasonably presentable she took the trays up to the bus and warned everybody else onboard not to eat anything. Darrell and Jeff got their comeuppance in the end as the two bands and their crews sat and watched them eat the piss-soaked food.

Waters left Europe having learned a lot from Pantera during the tour, especially about the business side of things. He would often hear Vinnie and Darrell or maybe Phil having meetings at the back of the bus about the band's business affairs. At the time he wondered why they weren't out partying, but it soon dawned on him that Pantera had a vision—an agenda. They were plotting their future world domination. After the tour Pantera went on to achieve incredible fame and wealth while Waters lost his girlfriend, his house, and almost his record deal, too. After a spell in rehab he was gradually able to get his life and band back together, thanks partly, he says, to what he had observed of how Pantera operated.

After playing the last of their European dates with Judas Priest, Pantera began their own three-month Cowboys & Idiots tour at the Palace in Hollywood on April 8, 1991. After warming the crowd up with *Cowboys from Hell: The Demos* they would blast their way through a set featuring "Domination," "Psycho Holiday," "The Art of Shredding," "Cowboys from Hell," "Message in Blood," "Primal Concrete Sledge," "Clash with Reality," "Heresy," and "Cemetery Gates."

They spent most of the rest of the year on the road. On August 17 they were invited to perform at the Monsters of Rock festival in Donington Park, U. K., as part of a bill that included AC/DC, Metallica, Mötley Crüe, Queensrÿche, and the Black Crowes. They also played Monsters of Rock shows in Germany, Italy, and the Soviet Union, the last of which was to an audience of more than 1.5 million people.

They were not about to let success change them, however. Back home in Arlington, the Abbotts and Brown would still hang out with their childhood buddies, while Anselmo still loved nothing more than a good horror movie. "Look, I lived in a car for half a year, I lived in a tin shed for the other half," he told *Kerrang!*'s Mike Gitter in 1993. "I know what it's like to be hungry. I know what it's like to not have, and now I've got a little."

It helped that they were surrounded by a team of loyal and dedicated people: Atco's Derek Shulman and Steve Kleinberg, manager Walter O'Brien, U.K. A&R man Derek Oliver, booking agent John Dittmar, tour manager Guy Sykes, photographer Joe Giron, and of course their road crew, notably guitar tech Grady Champion. These guys each had a significant part to play in the rising success of the band, and they all had good relationships with them. By the end of the year, Pantera had played more than three hundred dates in support of *Cowboys from Hell*, but even now there was no time to rest. It was time to get back to the studio to make their next album.

Top: The first lineup of Pantera, 1981: Donny Hart, Vinnie Abbott (aka Vinnie Paul), Terry Glaze, Darrell Abbott, and Tommy Bradford. (Courtesy of Terry Glaze)

Right: A rare shot of a very young Darrell Abbott with Terry Glaze singing in the background, circa 1981. (Courtesy of Terry Glaze)

Top: Pantera in 1982, possibly on Halloween, at the Longhorn Ballroom in Dallas, Texas. Left to right: Rex Brown, Vinnie Paul, Terry Glaze, and Darrell Abbott. (Stuart Taylor/Frank White Photo Agency)

Left: Darrell Abbott doing his thing at Graham Central Station in Texas, 1984. (Stuart Taylor/Frank White Photo Agency)

Metallica's James Hetfield with Darrell Abbott at Darrell's mom's house in Texas, 1985. (Stuart Taylor/Frank White Photo Agency)

Donny Hart briefly returned to Pantera for a second and final stint with the band in 1986. Left to right: Rex Brown, Donny Hart, Darrell Abbott, and Vinnie Paul at the Ranch in Muenster, Texas. (Stuart Taylor/Frank White Photo Agency)

Onetime Pantera singer Dave Peacock and Darrell Abbott onstage, 1986. (Stuart Taylor/Frank White Photo Agency)

Wowing the crowd in Muenster, Texas, 1985. Left to right: Rex Brown, Terry Glaze, and Darrell Abbott. (Stuart Taylor/Frank White Photo Agency)

The band entertain their buddies at Vinnie and Darrell's mom's house, 1986. (Stuart Taylor/Frank White Photo Agency)

Darrell Abbott, Rex Brown, onetime Pantera singer Matt L'Amour, and Vinnie Paul, 1986. This was taken outside of Pantego Sound, where the band recorded all of their early records. (Stuart Taylor/Frank White Photo Agency)

Top: Pantera's most iconic lineup, circa 1987, looking like they belong on the Sunset Strip. Left to right. Rex Brown, Phil Anselmo, Vinnie Paul, and Darrell Abbott. (Stuart Taylor/Frank White Photo Agency)

Left: Phil Anselmo onstage, 1987. (Stuart Taylor/Frank White Photo Agency)

Anthrax's Scott Ian with Darrell Abbott in the late 1980s. (Stuart Taylor/Frank White Photo Agency)

Slayer's Kerry King with Pantera in Dallas, 1989. (Stuart Taylor/Frank White Photo Agency)

A badass-looking Pantera following a major makeover: Darrell Abbott, Vinnie Paul, Phil Anselmo, and Rex Brown in Dallas, April 1990. (Stuart Taylor/Frank White Photo Agency)

The Abbott brothers onstage in February 1995 during the *Vulgar Display of Power* tour. (Stuart Taylor/Frank White Photo Agency)

Phil Anselmo, March 1990. (Frank White)

Left: Rex Brown onstage during *The Great Southern Trendkill* tour. (Frank White)

Bottom: The band pose for the camera in the studio, November 1991. (Stuart Taylor/Frank White Photo Agency)

Right: Anselmo looking mean onstage during Ozzfest, June 15, 1997. (Frank White)

Bottom: Vinnie Paul standing up for the crowd, looking very "metal." (Frank White)

Darrell Abbott, October 1994. Check out the Ace Frehley tattoo. (Stuart Taylor/Frank White Photo Agency)

8

DEMONS BE DRIVEN: THE RELEASE OF *VULGAR DISPLAY OF POWER*

The versatility and tightness between Vince and Rex, Rex and Dime, was like nothing I've seen before or since. When it came time to execute the vocals, we all got along.
—Phil Anselmo to Metal Odyssey of Hard Rock Hideout, 2010

BY 1992, METAL WAS FAST BEING superseded by grunge. Seattle bands like Nirvana, Soundgarden, Pearl Jam, and Alice in Chains were breaking into the mainstream with a new form of alternative rock that merged hardcore, punk, and even traditional metal with deep, introspective lyrics. The success of albums like Nirvana's *Nevermind* and Pearl Jam's *Ten* meant that record companies lost interest in commercial hard rock, and many bands that had been successful in the '80s entered the new decade without a record contract. While some, like Metallica, were able to survive the grunge explosion, others weren't so lucky—particularly the kinds of glam-inspired bands satirized in Soundgarden's "Big Dumb Sex."

Fortunately, Pantera had never been interested in being trendsetters, and they did not let the changing times affect them. In that regard Atco Records was 100 percent behind them. Even when (ultimately futile) attempts were made to market the band or steer them toward a different sound or image, they were deflected away by the people around them. "You could call us stupid-lookin' glam-ass motherfuckers from '80s or whatever," Phil Anselmo told *Kerrang!*'s Jason Arnopp in 1994. "Okay, we weren't cool then. Heavy metal absolutely ain't cool at all, anymore, so we're definitely not cool now."

In the earlier days of the Anselmo era, Pantera were certainly easy to work with, partly because they were just grateful to have a record deal in the first place. They were affable and hardworking, even if Phil a little too aggressive at times. What was more important, however, was the dynamic between the four men as musicians, as Derek Shulman recalls:

"In a band you need this kind of chemistry. There's different kinds of chemistry. There's Phil, who was the mercurial singer who could sometimes be very unpredictable. There's Dimebag, who was always very affable but such a brilliant front guitarist. You had Phil and Darrell in the front: A hard rock star band has to have that. So we had Phil, who's very aggressive but a great front man, and Dimebag, who [when] he did his thing was a great sideman . . . then of course Vinnie; his drumming was incredible, and Rex was a very solid character, [a] very peacemaking kind of character, who you would be dying to see right there every time."

With their next album, Pantera continued to venture into heavier, more extreme, and more brutal areas of metal. Their aim was to make a landmark album on their own terms, and the result, *Vulgar Display of Power*, would become their commercial

Demons Be Driven: The Release of *Vulgar Display of Power*

breakthrough. Recorded right on the back of almost two years of solid touring, it captured the band at their best.

"When we did the record, I know for a fact we were amped," Phil Anselmo told *Metal Hammer*'s Dave Everley some twenty years later. "We were on our A-game. We were at our strongest, mentally and physically." As Vinnie Paul recalled around the same time: "I thought that [album] really set the tone for what the band was all about from that point on."

Like its predecessor, *Vulgar Display of Power* was recorded and mixed by the band and producer Terry Date at Pantego Sound in Pantego, Texas, and mastered at Masterdisk in New York City by Howie Weinberg. The album's title is derived from a line spoken by Father Damien Karras in the horror classic *The Exorcist*.

The band had laid down some rough ideas for songs while on tour. The main thrust of "Walk," for example, came about during a preshow warm-up when Phil barked at the band that they needed to get some songs ready for their new album, and Darrell let rip with the riff in response. They didn't write the rest of the song there and then, but they knew the riff was a keeper.

Lyrically, meanwhile, Phil was entering his most profound and introspective territory to date. The words to his new songs embodied feelings of despair, hostility, anger, violence, and frustration. Like any wordsmith, he took influence from past experiences and general human urges, channeling his emotions into words rather than actions, although from the way he was onstage it was obvious that he had a lot of fire in his belly. The words came straight from the heart, as he explained to *Noisecreep*'s Amy Sciarretto: "I meant every motherfucking word. . . . There are snippets of those lyrics that are words to live by, when things get cruel."

He had certainly led a colorful life, and he knew that he and his bandmates had to be resilient. They had to show people what they could do, what they were capable of. Nobody felt this more than Phil himself. In the past he had felt restrained by his role as the new guy, but on *Vulgar Display of Power* he was given the lyrical freedom he craved. "I was doing my own thing, totally," he explained to *Kerrang!*'s Jason Arnopp. "They'd go in the studio and do their tracks during the day, and I'd go in at night. We'd record at different times, although we'd write the shit together."

Recording at different times helped the musicians gain a wider perspective on the songs as a whole as well as their own individual parts. What was also important to the band, however, was capturing as truly as possible the energy and aggression of their live performances. Like Eddie Van Halen, Diamond Darrell was keen to capture a live, raw feel in his playing, which meant placing as few rhythm guitar parts behind the lead breaks as possible. Audience reaction was constantly on his mind: If he thought a riff wouldn't go down well when he played it onstage, he wouldn't include it in the studio version either.

As well as finding a new freedom in the lyric-writing process, Phil was also starting to write guitar riffs, which he would then show to Darrell. One of these riffs formed the basis of the screaming metal monster "Mouth for War." "The thing about Dimebag is he would grab the guitar, I'd show him somethin', but by the time he grabbed it, he just had this grip on the guitar that was fuckin' inhuman," he told Steven Rosen at *Ultimate Guitar*. "I can't explain it—just not human. I sounded very mortal. Believe me, the riff [for] 'Mouth for War' as you know it sounded very, very mortal compared to what it is now . . . ."

Vulgar Display of Power is an album of thick, brutal songs, intelligent lyrics, and magnificent musicianship—and is one of the all-time great metal albums. The opening track, "Mouth for War," is the perfect encapsulation of Pantera: the anger, the frustration, the intricate guitar work, the hardcore vocals, the pounding drums and deep bass line. Track two, "A New Level," is an astonishing attack on the human senses and a clear sign—if it wasn't already obvious—that the band were moving into even heavier territory than on *Cowboys from Hell*. "Walk" is a defiant metal anthem for the masses, while "Fucking Hostile" takes us into hardcore metal territory, with Vinnie Paul's double kick drums working overtime.

"This Love" begins with some deceptively mellow guitar chords and soulful vocals before the lights go down and the metal begins, the abrupt changes in tempo lending the track an almost unnerving volatility. "Rise," on which Phil tackles the subject of racism, inspired by an encounter with two black kids back home in New Orleans, is like a long-lost Slayer track. It's seriously fast, even by Pantera's standards. "No Good (Attack the Radical)" has the feel of a living, breathing animal with razor-sharp claws, while "Live in a Hole" is a showcase for the remarkable chemistry between the band members. "Regular People (Conceit)" is a chance for Vinnie Paul to shine and strikes the perfect balance between groove and hardcore, while "By Demons be Driven" is Phil Anselmo at his most profound. The final track, "Hollow," is a surprisingly mournful, touching song that shows a different side to the band, although it does nonetheless descend into metal madness midway through.

Shortly before the album's release, Pantera reconnected with former front man Terry Glaze at a show Glaze was playing in Dallas with his current band, Blowphish, a more melodic outfit he'd formed following the demise of Lord Tracy. He recalls:

"[Darrell] showed up and after my gig he had a limo out in the parking lot in Dallas. He said, 'Come out, I wanna play you the new record . . . .' [We] got in the limo and he had a cassette tape, and he put on 'Mouth for War' and he was air-guitaring to it. And he goes, 'What do you think?' I said, 'I think it's incredible.' I said, 'I love Van Halen.' We kind of hit it off, and then . . . after *Vulgar Display* came out—I lived in Los Angles by this time—they were playing at the County and I went up to see the show and we just kind of all [had] big hugs and they were cool. They were doing really good. I actually got on the bus [and] rode with them up to San Francisco. I went to Reno with Darrell and gambled with him for a night. And then they put me on a plane and sent me back to L.A...."

Released on February 10, 1992, *Vulgar Display of Power* was an immediate hit with metal fans and critics alike, many of whom loved the sharp twist in musical direction. The first of the band's albums to be given a Parental Advisory sticker, it became an instant metal classic, and remains the most stellar, dynamic, and visceral of Pantera's albums. Everyone in the band was proud of the album, and its legacy cannot be overstated.

It was obvious that the band had well and truly left their glam-metal influences behind them, while even Anselmo had dropped his falsetto vocals in favor of a more aggressive and abrasive style of delivery and now sounded more like Henry Rollins than Priest's Rob Halford or Eric Adams of Manowar. The album was not without its critics, however, with some attacking Pantera for what they perceived to be weak lyrics and others claiming that the band was too focused on creating heavier music over everything else.

Vulgar Display of Power hit Number 44 on the *Billboard* 200 and Number 64 on the U.K. album chart, and reached Number 69 in Germany. Sales would remain robust over the next few years, during which time several singles were drawn from the album. The first, "Mouth of War," peaked at Number 24 on the *Billboard* Mainstream Rock Tracks chart and Number 73 on the U.K. singles chart, and was accompanied by a video directed by Paul Rachman, who had previously shot videos for all of the singles from *Cowboys from Hell*. "This Love" hit Number 5 on the *Billboard* Mainstream Rock Tracks and Number 6 on the Hot 100. "Hollow" reached Number 17 on the *Billboard* Mainstream Rock chart, while "Walk" (1993) hit Number 2 on the same chart and Number 23 on the Hot 100, peaking at Number 35 in the U.K. The band also treated their fans to a promo EP titled *Hostile Mixes* featuring three remixes by Justin K. Broadrick of Godflesh and a fourth by J. G. Thirlwell of Foetus.

With *Vulgar Display of Power*, Pantera had emphatically found their sound. Reviews of the album were strong, with a wide array of journalists raving about its innovative riffs and melodies. For *Entertainment Weekly*, it was "one of the most satisfying heavy metal records since Metallica's early '80s cult days . . . eleven caustic songs of unabashed brute force . . . a fully realized album that goes way beyond metal's usual crunch-and-burn." It also came fourth in *Guitar World*'s listing of the top guitar albums of the year.

The critical consensus remains positive, with the album featuring in the highly regarded book *1001 Albums You Must Hear Before You Die*. It was also named one of the "50 Heaviest Albums of All-Time" by the U.K.'s Q magazine in 2001, while *IGN* named it the eleventh most influential metal album.

Pantera spent most of 1992 touring in support of the new album, gradually building their fan base as they went. By now they had really taken off as a live band, and fans were going crazy for them. It appeared that Atco's marketing plan—which was effectively to not market the band in a conventional sense at all, but just to send them out on the road to build a fan base—had been a stroke of understated genius.

"I think especially me, and pessimistic youngster I was . . . I think I knew our strengths, which were definitely our live performance," Phil Anselmo told *Examiner*'s Elliot Levin twenty years later. The band would play around with the set list to keep things interesting, but it would often run as follows: "Heresy," "Mouth for War," "Domination" / "Hollow," "Fucking Hostile," "This Love," "Primal Concrete Sledge," "Cemetery Gates," and "Cowboys from Hell." At some shows they would also pay tribute to their heroes by playing Motörhead's "Ace of Spades" and a pair of Judas Priest tracks, "Grinder" and "Metal Gods."

After spending the early months of the year in the U.S., Pantera spent June and July in Canada, where they were joined on selected dates by White Zombie, Sacred Reich, Skid Row, and Soundgarden. At the end of July they visited Japan for the first time before playing a couple of shows in Brazil.

By now Pantera were playing much bigger venues, and although Phil continued to charge around and jump on and off stacks of amps, the days when he could invite fans up onto the stage to head-bang and go crazy were long gone. It was largely a question of insurance. Following an incident earlier in the year in Oklahoma, where a member of the venue's security staff had been hurt during a scuffle, the band had employed their own security guard, Big Val, to act as a liaison between band and venue. Phil was suspicious of the incident, given that nothing like it had ever happened at any of the hundreds of gigs the band had played previously. "These days," he explained to *Kerrang!* scribe Mörat, "we're getting sued for a quarter of a million bucks because some fuckin' security guard got hurt in Oklahoma when the kids went ape-shit."

On September 12, 1992, Pantera once again joined the Monsters of Rock festival in the wealthy city of Reggio Emilia in northern Italy. The show was headlined by Iron Maiden, with Black Sabbath, Megadeth, Testament, Warrant, and Pino Scotto also performing; Pantera were third from bottom of the bill. They played five additional dates on the Monsters of Rock European tour in September before supporting Megadeth on their *Countdown to Extinction* tour around the continent.

Pantera did what they always did: They put on a great show. They'd come a long way from the tour with Judas Priest a year earlier, when they'd often been booed offstage. Word had spread, and they now had a growing legion of fans. Occasionally they'd have an off night—there'd be times when Anselmo was in a bad mood and didn't have his usual rapport with the crowd—but in general Pantera went down a storm. They also had fun with Megadeth on the tour—perhaps more so than they might have expected.

"I don't know how Phil feels about this tour right now," Megadeth front man Dave Mustaine told *Kerrang!*'s Robyn Doreian in 1992, "[but it's] probably a little better than when he went into it, because people talk so much shit about us."

There was some talk of Megadeth feeling threatened by having such a strong support band. "I think some of the guys from my band saw them [Megadeth] recently, and they're just a little fucking paranoid, in my opinion," Phil told Mörat of *Kerrang!* magazine. "I said something to the crowd one night about us going on the Megadeth tour. I said, 'This is a song that we send out to that whole memory—this is called "Domination"!' . . . I didn't put two and two together, y'know, but they did, so they're all thinking I'm slagging them. But they should know better than that."

After completing the Megadeth tour, Pantera headed back to the U.S. to round out the year with yet more shows. It was around this time that two members of the band decided to change their stage names. Rex Rocker reverted to the name Rex Brown, while Diamond Darrell had become Dimebag Darrell, as Walter Trachsler recalls:

"Everybody called him Diamond Darrell. Everybody, at school, anywhere he went . . . I said, 'I ain't fucking calling you that.' I called him Dime and I changed it to Dimey. This was to fuck with him—to take the hot air out of him . . . I've never kissed Darrell's ass in my entire fucking life. One day we're in Darrell's room and some friends were over and Darrell was just talking shit about Rex—Rex this, Rex that . . . Rex was so bad smoking weed and all this shit. And out of the blue, I said, 'All right, Dimebag.' And everybody's looking at me, like, 'What the fuck? What the fuck did you say?' . . . And then the motherfucker chased me down the street. He was so mad at me for fucking with the thing in the first place . . . 'When people are here, you call me Diamond . . . don't fucking call me anything else.' Fuck that dude, I'm not doin' that shit . . .

"But then when we'd play at the clubs—we're little kids but we're playing to adults—I would call him Dimebag and [people] thought that was fucking cool, so everyone started fuckin' calling him Dimebag. He hated it but it turned into that. And that's where the fucking name came from, one hundred fucking percent."

For Rex and Darrell, changing names offered a chance to shed ties with the past. *Vulgar Display of Power* was the last album to list them as Diamond and Rocker. Their glam-metal roots were well and truly behind them.

Another more subtle change came in the way Phil Anselmo sang onstage, as it became apparent to fans that he could no longer hit the high, Rob Halford–style notes he used to. It was fine when the band was only playing two or three nights a week, but now that he was expected to do it six or seven nights a week it was killing his voice.

Vocal troubles aside, however, Phil had lost none of his enthusiasm for touring. "We knew that the more we played, the more visible we were and the more we killed," he told Chris Akin of *Addicted to Vinyl*. "Every single time that we played, no matter who we played with—people would come back."

As 1993 began, Pantera went straight back on the road. They toured Europe in January and February, with a gig at the famous Marquee club in London among the highlights; then it was back to the U.S. for more sporadic dates into the summer. They ended the year with a run of shows in South America in December at the Coliseo Rubén Rodríguez in Bayamón, Puerto Rico—where Phil reportedly walked offstage because he was unable to jump down and perform among the fans—and the release of *Vulgar Video*. The band's second official video collection, it features guest appearances by Kerry King from Slayer and Rob Halford from Judas Priest as well as performances of "Walk," "Domination," "Primal Concrete Sledge," "This Love," "Mouth for War," and a cover of the Kiss classic "Cold Gin" with Skid Row.

By the end of the year, Pantera had built up such a strong and powerful fan base that they could now make any kind of metal album and their fans would love it. Those fans had latched onto a new kind of metal: one that was as hard-edged and furious as anything from the Bay Area, yet still undeniably melodic. Had they wanted to, they could have done what Metallica had done and made a more commercial album, like the California band's self-titled 1991 release, but Pantera were always more extreme—more guttural—than that. Their next album would prove that they did not want to be pigeonholed. Metallica might have become the biggest metal band in the world, but Pantera were now the most interesting.

9

STRENGTH BEYOND STRENGTH: THE RELEASE OF *FAR BEYOND DRIVEN*

It's an imperative quality to have that well-roundedness to go in any genre of music. Everyone was rounded out in Pantera in their own way.
—Phil Anselmo to Metal Odyssey of Hard Rock Hideout, *2010*

WHEN IT CAME TO MAKING DECISIONS about Pantera, the Abbott brothers were like one person. They trusted each other implicitly, and were never dogged by the kind of rivalry that would so often affect other siblings in bands. Instead, the Abbotts fed off each other's strengths. As time passed, Vinnie began to loosen up a bit, while conversely Dimebag became more interested in the business side of things now that the band was selling millions of albums. Despite the success of their first two major-label albums, both men knew exactly what kind of band they wanted Pantera to be—and, more importantly, exactly the kind of band they didn't want it to be. They would not compromise their sound for the lure of the great Yankee dollar. Phil Anselmo felt the same way. "I'd say a prime example of selling out, and I'm nervous about saying this, would be a band like Celtic Frost," he told *Kerrang!*'s Robyn Doreian in 1992. "They were all doom and gloom, then the next record they were glam . . . ."

Pantera had done a lot of touring over the past few years, and had become a much tighter outfit as a result. They took that with them into the studio when they came to make their third Atco album, *Far Beyond Driven*. The album was recorded at Abtrax Recording, where Jerry Abbott now worked in Nashville, Tennessee, with producer and engineer Terry Date. It was the first time they had made a record outside Texas, although they returned to their home state to master the album at Dallas Sound Lab.

Many of the songs on the new album stemmed from the band's time on the road. Dimebag liked to churn out a riff during a concert, and if it got a strong reaction from the crowd he knew it was worth keeping. The song "25 Years" came together one evening when the band just started jamming onstage; after Darrell started playing the lead riff, Phil had an idea as to where the song should go next, as Darrell explained to *Guitar World*'s Brad Tolinski:

"He said, 'Dudes, go into a straight chug right there.' This is in front of hundreds of people! We just put the crowd on hold for a few minutes while we put the song together." The crowd didn't seem to mind, however—in fact, they seemed to enjoy getting the opportunity to see how the band worked.

The band had begun to experiment more in the studio, notably on "Becoming," which was named for a passage in the bestselling Thomas Harris novel *Red Dragon*, and which featured Dimebag playing through his DigiTech Whammy pedal. Elsewhere, they invited Marty Friedman of Megadeth to play guitar on "I'm Broken," later said to be Slayer guitarist Kerry King's

Strength Beyond Strength: The Release of *Far Beyond Driven*

favorite Pantera track. They also recorded what would become a classic cover of Black Sabbath's "Planet Caravan," while "Good Friends and a Bottle of Pills" made reference to the Ted Nugent song "Good Friends and a Bottle of Wine," from his album *Weekend Warriors*.

For the latter song, Dimebag avoided the standard guitar solo and just let his guitar feed back, while the intro features the sound of Vinnie's snare drum echoing through Darrell's guitar pickup. "That song was just something that happened to me one night," Phil told *Kerrang!*'s Jason Arnopp in 1994. "I kinda wanted to write a song like that, and the music sounded the way it does, so I decided to just do a narrative over the top." It was Pantera's idea of having fun. They wanted to try something different, and indeed a bit of experimentation is not a bad thing, particularly when you know you're going to be on the road for long periods of time, often in unfamiliar territories. (It's easy to become tired of playing the same old material—how many times has Motörhead played "Ace of Spaces?")

When it came to writing lyrics for the album, Anselmo, ever the lone wolf, became even more contemplative and introspective than before, as evidenced on tracks like "25 Years" and "Becoming." These songs were largely about his life before Pantera. His childhood had not been easy; it was one of anger, bitterness, neglect, and family betrayal. Thinking about it made him angry, but he channeled his negative emotions into songs.

What the rest of the band loved about Phil was how his lyrics came straight from the heart. He did not mind sharing his personal feelings with the world, and knew that by writing about such personal experiences he could inspire a whole generation of disenfranchised youths. As Vinnie Paul explained to *NYRock*'s Roger Scott:

"One time, in Alabama, we had some church group carry around crosses and stuff out in front of the show, but none of those PMRC [Parents Music Resource Center] and other of this crazy stuff has come after Pantera. Maybe when they read the lyrics, they see a lot of reality."

As the years passed, Phil felt more flexible within the band, and more able to write with more freedom. They didn't always get along well with each other—especially when Dimebag tried to write lyrics, which drove Phil crazy—but on the whole the others respected what he had to say. "My life is complex," he told Jason Arnopp at *Kerrang!*, "but I don't think my joys would interest anybody—they're the same as what AC/DC were talking about years ago: fucking chicks and getting loaded, taking drugs . . . .

"Another thing about my lyrics on this fuckin' record," he continued, "is that the songs don't just encompass one thing." On "Strength Beyond Strength," for example, he touches on the subject of legalizing marijuana, which he felt enhanced his perception of things, and was no different in a lot of ways from drinking alcohol.

One of the most controversial and thus well-known songs in the Pantera arsenal is "5 Minutes Alone." The story goes that this song was written after a show in San Diego where the band had become so frustrated by a heckler that Anselmo allegedly told the rest of the crowd to beat him up. The heckler's father sued the band, and a war of words ensued between the two parties. Ironically, the resulting song would become one of the band's most cherished recordings. Dimebag came up with the main riff in his garage one day while fooling around with his eight-track; rather than play with different notes, he let the same one ring out until it screeched.

The eventual album, *Far Beyond Driven*, opens with the overly aggressive "Strength Beyond Strength." There are some uneven breaks, and the bass struggles to stand out, but the drums and guitars—as ever—are excellent. "Becoming" is a standout, with its catchy, chugging riff, while "5 Minutes Alone" has more of a hardcore mentality but has a chunky riff to keep the metal

Strength Beyond Strength: The Release of Far Beyond Driven

fans happy. "I'm Broken" is more old-school than its siblings; the guitar work is like some mental Black Sabbath–Judas Priest hybrid.

"Good Friends and a Bottle of Pills" offers one of several opportunities for Rex Brown to shine with a deep bass groove, but the overall effect is tarnished by vocal effects and an almost desperate need to shock with the lyrics. "Hard Lines, Sunken Cheeks" and "Slaughtered" are both notable for their groove-laden riffs, while "25 Years" slows things down to a more mid-paced setting, even if the seemingly constant breaks become somewhat tiring. "Shedding Skin" is a powerful track both musically and lyrically, while "Use My Third Arm" has a rugged lead guitar riff but is spoiled by Anselmo shouting too much, and "Throes of Rejection" has nifty bass line and a deep, thumping melody. The album closes with the band's fantastic cover of Black Sabbath's wistful "Planet Caravan."

Overall, *Far Beyond Driven* is a good Pantera album but not a truly great one. Although it is flawed in places, it does contain moments of sheer brilliance and innovation. The main problem is the way it tries to outdo *Vulgar Display of Power*, as if the band were desperate to be heavier and louder than before, but with less balance and cohesion. On top of that, Anselmo tries too hard to shout and scream rather than sing, which he had done so well on the band's two previous Atco albums.

Released on March 22, 1994, *Far Beyond Driven* was the first Pantera album to reach Number 1 album in the United States and even hit the top spot in the Australian album charts. It also reached Number 2 in Sweden, Number 3 in the U.K., Number 7 in Germany, Number 8 in Austria, Number 14 in New Zealand and Norway, Number 21 in Switzerland, and Number 47 in the Netherlands.

Never afraid of controversy, the band had originally wanted to use an image of a drill entering an anus on the album cover; in the end it was replaced by a striking blue-hued illustration of a skull being drilled, but the record still came with the now obligatory Parental Advisory notice.

As well as the regular edition, the album was also released in a special collector's slipcase format and in a box set called *Driven Downunder Tour '94: Souvenir Collection* in Australasia, both of which are now considered to be rare collector's items. The latter edition contained an original live set, the *Alive and Hostile E.P.* and the *Walk* EP, a collection of remixes and live tracks from *Vulgar Display of Power* and *Cowboys from Hell* that had originally been released in Japan in 1993.

The album also spawned four singles. The first, "I'm Broken," was a significant success abroad, hitting Number 19 in the U.K., Number 32 in Sweden, and Number 49 in Australia. It also earned the band their first Grammy Award nomination, for "Best Metal Performance." "Planet Caravan" reached Number 21 on the *Billboard* Hot Mainstream Rock Tracks chart and Number 26 in the U.K.; "Becoming" (1994) hit Number 18 on the *Billboard* Hot 100; and "5 Minutes Alone"—the B-side of which featured a cover of Poison Idea's "The Badge" that had originally been recorded for, but then axed from, the soundtrack to *The Crow*—peaked at Number 13 on the Hot Mainstream Rock chart.

Pantera felt that the success of the album was a major achievement, and that they were blessed to have such a devoted fan base, even if they were frustrated at being labeled an overnight success, which was emphatically not the case. Either way, the fact that such a bold and extreme metal album had hit Number 1 showed that they were doing something right. "It just fuckin' floored everybody in the music industry," Vinnie Paul told *Soundwave Touring* writer Cameron Edney. "They were saying who the hell is this band Pantera. . . . We knocked out Bonnie Raitt, we knocked out Ace of Base, we knocked out all these bands they thought would have a number one record . . . ."

Strength Beyond Strength: The Release of *Far Beyond Driven*

By now, Pantera were a force to be reckoned with in the world of metal. Atco had put a lot of effort into marketing the band from the get-go, and this time around even arranged for MTV to follow them through twelve U.S. cities on a breakneck five-day tour to promote their latest work. All the hard work seemed worthwhile, as Pantera became one of the biggest metal bands in the world. By the end of March, *Far Beyond Driven* had sold 185,000 copies in the U.S. alone, and it would remain on the *Billboard* 200 for twenty-nine weeks.

Faced with this renewed success, Pantera seemed more eager than ever to continue performing. "It's the same as it used to be, but just on a different level," Dimebag told *Kerrang!* writer Mörat in 1994. "It ain't all easy. I still go out and blow my fucking mind every night, get drunk, crank my stereo up and don't give a shit, and I still look forward to playing."

Certainly, Dimebag had a vision of where Pantera was going, and he was determined to stay true to that vision, even as the mainstream media continued to ignore or misunderstand the band. Critics greeted *Far Beyond Driven* not with open arms but rather with dubious raised eyebrows. Reviews were mixed, with many concluding that the album was worthy enough but not in the same ballpark as *Cowboys from Hell* and *Vulgar Display of Power*. *Rolling Stone* described it as "a kind of aesthetics of thud," noting that "the real art smolders in the noise itself." In the U.K., *Melody Maker* decided: "Like great techno, it's utterly flawless music, free of any error, minimal and animal enough to make a screaming bloody mess of the head."

Subsequent reviews of the album have been similarly mixed. In an astute review for the *Classic Rock Music Blog*, Mark Polzin wrote: "Most critics agree that *Driven* is the last great Pantera album, yet some wouldn't even go so far as to include mention of this record in the same sentence as *Cowboys* or *Vulgar Display*. I fall in with the former camp, not the latter."

Ultimately, *Far Beyond Driven* may not be viewed with the same reverence bestowed upon *Cowboys from Hell* and *Vulgar Display of Power*, but it's not far off the mark set by those albums, and is emphatically the most extreme metal record ever to hit Number 1 on the *Billboard* 200.

From the outside, it seemed as though all was well in the Pantera camp as *Far Beyond Driven* made its way to the top of the charts. The MTV cameras captured a group of musicians who were always happy to sign album sleeves and chat with fans about the band and metal in general. Inside, however, cracks were beginning to show. Label boss Derek Shulman was about to depart for Roadrunner Records, breaking apart the close-knit team—completed by manager Walter O'Brien and producer Terry Date—that had worked together since the turn of the decade, while further tensions within the band would soon start to have a pronounced impact on their creative drive. And then there was the Phil Anselmo problem.

10

FIVE MINUTES ALONE: COMMUNICATION BREAKDOWN AND BAND TENSION

Pantera—the core of Pantera, me, Vinnie, and Rex—have been together forever. Phil joined us almost seven years ago, and since then we've been just going at it.
—Dimebag Darrell to H. P. Newquist of Guitar Magazine, 1995

PANTERA SPENT MUCH OF 1994 on the road in support of *Far Beyond Driven*. The tour began in March and covered a large swath of the U.S., with Crowbar as the support act. Since hitting Number 1, Pantera had gone from playing clubs and small venues to amphitheaters with capacities of roughly 16,000. They had come a long way from their early glam-metal club days, but, as Phil bawled to *Kerrang!* writer Jason Arnopp, "We get absolutely no motherfuckin' respect!"

Respect or not, however, touring was the band's life—it was what they were all about. They loved their fans and their fans loved them back. The shows were always a spectacle from a fan's point of view—there was something powerful and profound about them that few other bands could compete with.

The band traveled to Japan in May before heading to the U.K. for the annual Monsters of Rock festival in Donington Park on June 4. "It will definitely be a metal bill," they told *Kerrang!*'s Mayhem column. "I think we're gonna have a different set for the show—we're already talking about pulling out all the stops. Maybe people could send in a dream set list for Aerosmith at Donington. That'd be interesting!"

Aerosmith were the headline act that year, while the rest of the bill featured Extreme, Sepultura, Therapy?, and Pride and Glory. It was an odd experience for Pantera. Being such a heavy band, they were not used to playing alongside some of these more melodic acts. They also had to play without a sound check, while the damp weather came in stark contrast to the warm Texan sun. It might not have been their greatest performance, but not everybody in the audience was there to see Pantera, and the band would have to get used to playing to more eclectic crowds.

The band may also still have been feeling the effects of the previous night at Rock City, a famed rock venue in Nottingham, in the English Midlands, where Vinnie and Darrell had found themselves getting into heated arguments with two journalists from *Kerrang!* magazine, Paul Rees and Mörat. Mörat recalls:

"Most of the *Kerrang!* staff had gone up [to Donington] a day early to be on site for the festival, but Rock City was only a cab ride away, so we all ended up there, getting drunk. A lot of the bands of the lineup for the next day were there, including Pantera, and everyone was wasted . . . Basically, Paul had made a joke in *Kerrang!* about Vinnie looking like the fat bloke from [the comic book series] *Asterix* . . . and, understandably, Vinnie didn't like it, so he came up to Paul and threatened him.

Kerrang! could be overly personal, and it was one of the times they got caught out. Much as I like Paul, he probably needed to know not to go there. It wasn't really much of an altercation: Paul weighs about ninety pounds soaking wet, and he was terrified when Vinnie had a go at him, but that's all it was, some finger-pointing and a few stern words."

Pantera had suffered years of jokes about their glam-metal past; this was a step too far. While Rex tended to let these things slide, Vinnie could be a bit of a bully, and continued to throw his weight around. "I can take jokes just fine," he told another *Kerrang!* writer, Jason Arnopp, "[but this] was the worst interview I've ever read, and if I see him again, I probably will hurt the motherfucker! No tellin' what he might have done to my career."

Paul Rees, former editor of *Q* magazine, now has a more sober perspective on the incident. "It was a cheap shot and I regretted making it. One of our editorial staff at the time had a deaf brother and he could lip-read. He told me that he could see Vinnie and two burly crew members discussing 'hurting someone.' Vinnie approached me, threw his arm round me, and informed me I was an asshole. I did require a change of underwear, and I left the club like a jet-propelled hare, since Mörat's judgment of the battle was right."

There was a separate altercation later the same night between Mörat and Dimebag. Mörat—who had always got on best with Phil, with whom he shared a similar taste in obscure metal—had interviewed the band in New York not long before. In the piece he had described how Dimebag was about to take a private jet to see bubblegum rockers Warrant, and it may have been this that tipped Darrell over the edge. He recalls:

"I can't remember what part of that he took exception to, but he came up and started poking me in the chest with his finger, so I grabbed his finger and offered him outside, at which point he called his personal security guy over. . . . Phil Anselmo came over, and we'd always got on pretty well, so he led me away to the bar. Me and Phil stayed up drinking all night, which in hindsight probably wasn't a good idea, because he was still obviously drunk on stage, but they dedicated 'Fucking Hostile' to me, and it became kind of a running joke. I worked with Pantera a few times after that, and if I took my jacket off Dimebag would make out that he was running away . . . and then we'd get drunk. I think maybe they liked the fact that I'd stood by what I'd written."

In June the tour moved back to the U.S. for two months of shows with support first from Biohazard and Sepultura and then from Sepultura and Prong. Midway through the tour, however, Sepultura front man Max Cavalera broke his leg, so the band had to sit out a number of dates. Pantera wanted Slayer to step in as a replacement, but Slayer were on a headlining tour of their own in support of their forthcoming album *Divine Intervention*. It was around this time that rumors began to circulate about poor ticket sales. Pantera had no trouble playing to large audiences in Texas, but some cities, such as Los Angeles, were less welcoming, and the band ended up playing to thousands of empty seats.

Further controversy ensued when Phil Anselmo was accused of hitting a security guard during a gig at Darien Lake in Buffalo, New York. He was subsequently charged with assault and spent several hours in custody before being released on $5,000 bail. Anselmo initially claimed that the whole thing had been an accident—that the mic had been pulled out of his hands while fans attempted to climb onto the stage, and that in the ensuing melee he had inadvertently struck the guard—but when the case finally went to court in May 1995 he pled guilty to attempted assault and issued an apology. He was sentenced to one hundred hours of community service. By this point, the band were always dealing with several lawsuits filed by fans who had been hurt while stage diving, and tensions were beginning to mount.

In August, a fan was killed after stage diving at a Motörhead gig in Germany, prompting widespread debate about whether stage diving should be banned. Pantera were keen for their fans to be able to do what they wanted, but were also aware that some people in the audience were just out to cause trouble. "Obviously we prefer non-seated places to play," Vinnie told *Metal Hammer*'s Ian Winwood, "but we've been sued about half a dozen times in the States when someone gets up on our stage, jumps off, breaks their ankle, and then decides they're going to sue the band."

In September and October, Pantera toured Europe with support from Downset before heading to Australia for several dates in November. They then resumed touring commitments in North America in early 1995, and would spend the rest of the year playing sporadic bursts of shows everywhere from Scandinavia to South America. "Brazil, Mexico, and Puerto Rico were insane!" Anselmo told Metal Odyssey of *Hard Rock Hideout* in 2010. "The most rabid first show was in Puerto Rico, man, it was dangerous. There were gang members everywhere outside, it was chaotic."

The most infamous moment of the tour, however, came on March 4, 1995, at the Verdun Auditorium in Montreal, when Phil stopped performing and made a speech in which he criticized African-American rappers and their culture, claiming that "rap music advocates the killing of white people." A number of people in the audience—including local journalist Mitch Joel, who wrote to the band's management and the music press about the incident—felt that the speech had racist connotations. A few nights later, Pantera played a gig in Long Island, New York, during which Phil apologized for his outburst in Montreal and stated that Pantera was not a racist band; the following morning, he issued a full public apology, insisting that he had been drunk in Montreal and that his onstage remarks had been misconstrued. He went on to explain how his upbringing in the cultural hotbed of New Orleans had shaped his views as an adult.

It was neither the first time nor the last, however, that Phil Anselmo would be accused of being racist. A year earlier, MTV had claimed that he was wearing a T-shirt with a "white pride" symbol on it; in fact, it was the logo of the obscure thrash band Carnivore (fronted by Type O Negative's Pete Steele, now deceased), known for their right-wing views. Nonetheless, the issue of racism would continue to linger for some time. Footage of him ranting to audiences at other shows can be viewed on YouTube, prompting some damning comments about his reported white pride beliefs.

At the time, many wondered whether Phil was starting to crack under the strain of fronting Pantera at the height of their fame. By December 31, 1995, when the band played a New Year's Eve show at the Tarrant County Convention Center in Forth Worth, Texas, the band had played almost four hundred shows over two years in support of *Far Beyond Driven*.

During that time, Phil had begun to distance himself from the rest of the band. While the others spent their downtime in bars or strip clubs, or amusing themselves by smashing up coffeepots and vases, the band's front man preferred to spend his money on horror movies and boxing magazines. "I'm just not into smashing up shit," he told Mörat of *Kerrang!* in 1994. "The rest of the band are, though. They love doing that shit and they always have done. I don't think they ever really thought about it . . . ." (Such was his love of boxing, meanwhile, that he had a trainer with him on tour, and he would later write for the website *BoxingInsider*.)

Phil had built up a reputation—mostly due to his tattooed and bulky hardcore image and onstage performances—that was possibly at odds with the real person. "My whole goal in life is to make friends and help out," he told Jason Arnopp at *Kerrang!*. "A lot of people see that in me. A lot of fuckin' people would murder for me, and I would do the same for them." He cherished his friendships. "I'm a sensitive fuckin' person. I know how much I give and give. It's tough reading how people think bad things about you. And they're doin' it because they don't know me."

The others had always defended the fact that Anselmo rode around in his own tour bus, insisting that they needed space from each other because of their hectic schedules. Much of it also had to do with the fact that the Abbotts didn't smoke, whereas Anselmo and Brown did, so there was a smoking bus and a nonsmoking bus. Photographer Joe Giron says that he "never had any issues" with Phil:

"He was always the same person. He had gone through a few rough patches with things but he was never mean toward me or anybody else. He was a pretty welcoming individual. He wanted to have his privacy, and most musicians do. Dime and Vinnie were a little more outgoing and would share more of themselves with the band and that type of deal. Phil, at least in front of me, was never mean. . . . Rex was just a little more quiet; not as assertive as the other guys. . . . I don't think he was as headstrong a personality as Dime or Phil or Vinnie, but he certainly made contributions to the band; otherwise it wouldn't have been Pantera without Rex and without the tightness he had with both Vinnie and Dimebag. Rex and I got along in terms of playing golf. Him and Vinnie would go and play golf on days off from the tour instead of sitting in the hotel room all the time . . . just hanging out hoping your hangover would go away. That nice fresh air out there on a warm sunny day was usually a good way to get rid of that. They were Texas born and bred. They wished that everywhere was Texas."

Being in a band is like being married: There has to be a level of compromise and an ability to respect each other's space. What was also true, however, was that Phil enjoyed his own company, and that this would create a lack of communication in the long run—particularly since the other three had grown up together, and remained as close as ever.

As the tour progressed, Phil began to suffer severe back pain as a result of his energetic live performances and the rigors of touring life. After a series of MRI scans he learned that his crazy onstage behavior—jumping on and off drum risers and running back and forth across the stage—had caused him to rupture the lumbar disc in his back. He had also damaged a second disc and gradually worn away the cartilage between them, causing him chronic pain.

Such was the severity of the problem that he was asked if he wanted to be fitted for a wheelchair. He was told that the problem could be rectified by extensive surgery and a long period of recuperation, but at this stage that was simply not an option, with yet more live dates on the horizon, including a slot at Ozzfest. And so he soldiered on, but it would cost him in the long run. The pain grew worse in the winter, especially when the band toured Europe in harsh weather. Inevitably, he needed to medicate.

"I got put on the heaviest painkiller known to mankind," he told *Revolver*'s Brandon Geist. "It's called methadone. Most people relate methadone to heroin, but I saved every bottle, every document—everything was for my back."

Eventually, he sought out a stronger substitute for the legitimate prescription painkillers and muscle relaxants he had been prescribed, and those substances soon started affecting his performances, making him sound slurred and drunk onstage. Some nights he'd seem completely out of control, like a madman possessed by some demonic force. Except that it wasn't a demonic force—it was heroin, as he explained to Geist:

"When I was in my middle twenties, I could walk through walls. There wasn't a man big enough to kick my [ass]. I'd rock with anyone, and I don't remember losing a fight. And then I tried a drug called heroin, because deep inside of myself I thought— I knew—there was no way that any drug could conquer me. No way. But the second time I did it in my entire life, it killed me."

He was angry—at the media, at magazines, at whoever crossed his path. He wanted to piss everybody off. In hindsight, however, he knew that this anger was aimless, and that it came as a result of all the alcohol, drugs, and pure adrenaline coursing through his system.

"I was hurt and hurting," he told vampirefreaks.com's Rafi. "I . . . don't think I knew how angry it was making me. I had a lot of anger inside me because I think I felt a little flipped off. . . . I was in my prime and I feel like I was cut in half."

PART THREE

THE GREAT SOUTHERN TRENDKILLERS

11

UNDERGROUND IN AMERICA: THE RELEASE OF *THE GREAT SOUTHERN TRENDKILL*

We've been evolving as Pantera the band—we're not just another one of those groups where one or two guys are in the spotlight. We're a fuckin' band in the truest sense of the word.
—Dimebag Darrell to Nick Bowcott of Guitar World, *1996*

PANTERA STARTED WORK ON THE FOLLOW-UP to *Far Beyond Driven* in late September and October 1995 and carried on working on the album until Christmas, with a release slated for the spring of 1996. They had already written a couple of tracks on tour, and decided to play a few low-key dates to try out the new material in front of an audience and see what kind of reaction it got.

Pantera never had a regimen when it came to writing songs. They'd hang around, have a few drinks, and jam, and the songs would start coming together from there. They'd tape everything and decide if they liked it later on, having played back what they'd recorded. Most of the album was recorded back home in Texas at Chasin Jason Studios, a converted garage in Dimebag's backyard, with Terry Date and Vinnie Paul sharing production duties. It was later mixed at Larrabee Sound Studios in Los Angeles and mastered at Sterling Sound in New York.

As the sessions continued, however, the band's internal troubles grew ever more pronounced. Having already taken time away from the band earlier in the year to record *NOLA* with his side project, Down, Anselmo now decided to record his vocals for Pantera's latest album at Nine Inch Nails front man Trent Reznor's Nothing Studios in New Orleans. Walter O'Brien recalls:

"It was a constant conflict. He lived right through the woods from Pantego Sound for the first couple albums, but once he moved back to New Orleans it was like pulling teeth. By *Great Southern Trendkill* he made Dime fly back and forth with the master tapes so he could add vocals and make mix and music suggestions. . . . That was the real start of the end. Phil wanted to stay in New Orleans; the band were working in Dime's studio in Texas. Communications fell apart; cooperation was nonexistent. And the tone of that album is just depressing and confrontational. To this day I can't listen to that album at all because of what went down during its recording and touring."

The band had almost always written the music first before Anselmo added his vocals. He carried a book of lyrics with him and would note anything down that he might want to use in a song. Working apart from the rest of the band, Anselmo double-tracked his vocals on some of the tracks—something he had not previously done before—to create a deeper and more menacing effect. He also brought in Seth Putnam of the absurdly named

Boston grindcore band Anal Cunt to add his high-pitched screams to "13 Steps to Nowhere," "The Great Southern Trendkill," "War Nerve," and "Suicide Note Pt. II."

Despite the growing tension between the band members, Pantera knew they had to be at the top of their game, particularly when the mixed critical response to *Far Beyond Driven* was followed by widespread praise for albums by Sepultura, Machine Head, and Fear Factory. Pantera were angry as hell, and it showed, especially in the intricate guitar riffs. Dimebag remained loyal to his Randall amps and his blue 1981 Dean ML with the Kiss stickers, but he would also regularly pick up new equipment in pawnshops in Texas and elsewhere. He also continued to hone his sound, detuning his guitars to give the album an even deeper sound. His riffs on *The Great Southern Trendkill* are amongst the fastest he had ever written, while his solos grew more focused yet more intricate, and at times more melodic. Some metal fans had bemoaned the lack of guitar solos on *Far Beyond Driven*, but *The Great Southern Trendkill* showcases some of his most remarkable lead playing. He wanted to retain a live vibe in his playing, however, and avoided adding a solo just for the sake of it. The solo had to complement and enhance the rest of the song: It was about the song, not the skill, and how the band sounded as a unit. If a particular song didn't warrant a solo, he wouldn't play one.

Like a lot of guitarists, Dimebag had a backlog of riffs that he had come up with over the years, and to which he would return when it came to writing a new album. "Some of the riffs on [*The Great Southern Trendkill*] date back to our *Cowboys from Hell* and *Vulgar Display of Power* periods," he told *Guitar World*'s Nick Bowcott. "Hell, a couple of ideas even go back to before we got signed." "Floods," for example, was based around a riff he had written back in 1988.

Often overlooked by both critics and fans, *The Great Southern Trendkill* was an important addition to the Pantera canon.

It came out at a time when rap-metal was making big strides in the mainstream music world, but, as ever, Pantera remained true to their traditional heavy metal roots and refused to follow the trends of the day. "All of the previous albums have their own identity, none of them sound like the last one, and we'll continue with that," Vinnie Paul told *Metal Edge*'s Gerri Miller. "I can tell the people out there not to expect a commercial radio record from Pantera, since that's not what we're all about."

The album also shows the extent to which Phil Anselmo had become dependent on drugs. His lyrics frequently reference drug abuse, notably on "10's" and "Living Through Me (Hell's Wrath)," while he discusses suicide on the two-part "Suicide Note" (the first half of which was nominated for a Grammy Award in 1997). He berates the media on "War Nerve" and writes about the end of the world on "Floods," while the title track and "Sandblasted Skin" tackle the fickle nature of popular culture.

The Great Southern Trendkill opens with the title track, which sounds unlike anything the band had ever recorded before. It lacks the grooves and chugging riffs that helped make Pantera popular, but it does contain some interesting darts around the fretboard. "War Nerve" is a full-throttle dose of hardcore metal, although the musicians sound like they are trying a little too hard, while "Drag the Waters" combines some expansive guitar work with ultra-tight rhythm playing. The more restrained "10's" is a somber song with a guitar riff reminiscent of the style of Alice in Chains' Jerry Cantrell, while "13 Steps to Nowhere" features some excellent drumming and Anselmo at his most aggressive. "Suicide Note Pt. I" is mournful and ambient, while "Pt. II" is far more extreme and visceral. "Living Through Me (Hell's Wrath)" has a beastly thrash riff at its heart, "Floods" is deep and full of yearning, and "The Underground in America" returns the band to their most extreme levels of anger and frustration. The closing track, "(Reprise) Sandblasted Skin," is a supercharged song tackled at breakneck speed with a sturdy lead riff.

Underground in America: The Release of The Great Southern Trendkill

While *The Great Southern Trendkill* may not be as immediately approachable as the band's previous three major-label albums, it introduced new layers and textures that show the band in a whole different light. The blues influence on the band was still prevalent—with ZZ Top's Billy Gibbons, known for his use of pinch harmonies and pentatonic scales, still a big inspiration to Dimebag—but they had also taken a few more experimental turns this time around. As well as the aforementioned vocal overdubs, they added cowbell to "Drag the Waters" and keyboards and twelve-string acoustic guitar to "Suicide Note Pt. I." The keyboard parts were played by Big Ross, aka Ross Karpelman, who was also a member of Anselmo's band Down.

Although *The Great Southern Trendkill* was different from previous Pantera albums, there was no chance of the band selling out. They had made an album for metal fans to love and for metal haters to despise. "[It] was basically a big bird-finger to the music industry," Vinnie Paul told *Metal Rules*' Keith McDonald. "The most anti-commercial record ever."

The album was released on May 7, 1996, by EastWest Records, which had recently merged with Atco, although the same core of people continued to work with the band, and hit Number 4 on the *Billboard* 200. Given how unpopular metal seemed to have become in the mid-'90s, Pantera were doing extremely well to maintain so high a level of commercial success. "We know that some of the bands out there have opened up some doors and helped get more radio time for metal bands, but we're doin' fine," Rex Brown, who had no time for the fickleness of the music industry, told *Vox*. "People say metal's dead, but we keep selling records and tickets, so those people are full of shit, man."

Three singles were released from the album: "Drag the Waters," "Suicide Note Pt. I," and "Floods." None reached the main *Billboard* chart, but "Drag the Waters" hit Number 10 on the Mainstream Rock Tracks chart, and Number 27 in the U.K.; Dimebag directed the accompanying music video.

Reviews of the album were mostly very positive. "*The Great Southern Trendkill* is dark, thunderous, and technically brilliant," Robyn Doreian wrote in *Metal Hammer*, "but at the same time somehow disturbing." The U.K.'s *Melody Maker* concluded: "It makes my brain hurt, my eyes water, and my genitalia retract like a startled turtle. I cannot think of higher recommendation, considering the kind of album it is." For *Spin* magazine, the album was a work of "mature speed metal and perfect summer fun: twisted power ballads, rap-style toasting, almost radio-worthy melodies, plus all the right jackhammer drum jolts, wrestler bellows, and guitar lurch . . ." *Guitar World* would subsequently include "Floods" in fifteenth place on its list of the greatest guitar solos of all time.

Despite the critical praise bestowed upon the album, however, Pantera fans still tend to prefer *Cowboys from Hell* and *Vulgar Display of Power* to the band's subsequent releases. *The Great Southern Trendkill* has become the forgotten album among Pantera's major-label releases, and is rarely spoken of to this day. It appears not to have stood the test of time.

On September 23, 1996, Pantera released *The Singles 1991–1996*, a six-CD box set, in Australia, where it peaked Number 40 on the charts. Almost a decade had passed since the band had made *Power Metal*, their long-forgotten first album with Phil Anselmo. It's fair to say that without him, Pantera would never have become the band they did. But he had also taken them to the edge, and things were about to get worse.

12

HELL'S WRATH: BAND LIFE AIN'T EASY

There are a lot of tapes and loops and samples and record-scratching and shit like that [on other people's records, but] for us, we have always been a very straightforward, honest, and traditional band.
—Vinnie Paul to David Lee Wilson of KAOS2000 Magazine, 2000

MUSIC GOES AROUND IN CIRCLES, and trends that fall out of fashion often become fashionable again somewhere down the line. As musical movements become over-sanitized—as did grunge, for example—fans get fed up and move onto something else. When this happens, a lot of bands burn out; only a select few manage to outlive the changing times. Bands like Slayer and AC/DC remain consistent, and they have earned their place at the top of the pile through longevity and hard work. Pantera belong in the same category.

"I'm not a fan of alternative music," Vinnie Paul told *Metal Edge*'s Gerri Miller. "But you know, heavy metal is never gonna die, it's always been around. It's had its ups and downs and right now it's real slow, there's not a lot of new exciting bands out there."

"Funk-metal became big at one time, and hip-hop-metal . . . [and] grunge, even, the Nirvanas and whatnot," Phil Anselmo explained to *MMN*'s Kenny Herzog. "There was ample amount of chances for any band to turn their back on their original genre, and that's something that was a no-no in the Pantera camp."

Pantera had created a niche audience all their own—an audience that had grown over the years but that remained fiercely loyal. Pantera refused to play by the rules or follow trends. They set them. It helped that they were never reliant on TV or radio. There were no rules, and no one told them what to do or how to sound. Instead, they had built themselves up through constant touring and hard work, and would continue to do so. (They had also become something of a salvation for Atco Records during a lean period for the label.)

In June 1996, following the release of *The Great Southern Trendkill*, Pantera kicked off another high-profile tour of the U.S. with White Zombie, with support on selected dates from Eyehategod, Deftones, and Minority. Pantera had become a seriously heavy band—certainly on the live front—and that's the way they liked it. Some fans and critics made them feel guilty for being popular, but it was hardly their fault that people loved them for making great music and being one of the meanest bands on the live circuit. They had an awesome time at every show, playing a set made up of tracks from their latest album mixed with past favorites like "Walk," "5 Minutes Alone," "Planet Caravan," and "Primal Concrete Sledge."

However, the tour would be dominated by an incident that occurred when the band played a homecoming gig at the Coca-Cola Starplex in Dallas on July 13. An hour after the show, Phil Anselmo overdosed on heroin. Thankfully, security guard Big Val found him immediately and summoned the paramedics who were already at the scene and were able to give Phil a shot of adrenaline after his heart stopped beating. He was then rushed to a nearby hospital. By now, it was obvious that the drug had taken control of him, and that something needed to be done about his addiction. Not only could it wreck the band's future—it could also kill him.

An Atco employee, who has asked not to be named, was with Phil on the tour bus the day before his overdose. They sat together and spoke about Phil's problems and addictions. After the overdose, the employee called Big Val to ask: "What the hell happened?" He felt like it was his fault because he had not intervened the night before. If Val hadn't found him, Phil probably wouldn't be here today. The Atco employee told Val: "I need you to do me a favor. I need you to get Phil, when he can, [to] call me. I need to talk to him." When Phil called a couple of nights later, however, the employee's wife answered the phone, so he was unable to confront the singer about how upset he was about what had happened, and how angry he was about the situation.

Until now, none of the people around Phil had seen him do heroin. "It was always back of his own bus or in his room," manager Walter O'Brien recalls. He had managed to keep his addiction from his bandmates, and had even reportedly hidden two previous overdoses from them. O'Brien remembers that night in Dallas vividly:

"We knew he was withdrawing a lot and being miserable [and] that he was smoking a lot of pot. But it turned out he had been using heroin with his New Orleans friends behind all our backs. The first time we knew was when he overdosed in Dallas backstage. It was devastating. . . . We all ran into his dressing room and saw the medics pull his body onto the stretcher. He had turned blue already and everybody was crying and screaming. It was the worst day of all of our lives, I'd say."

Phil's spell in hospital forced him to think about his actions. He vowed to quit heroin, while the band's management ordered him to issue a press release and apologize to his fans and bandmates. The public confession, sent out in his own handwriting, went a long way to convincing the band's audience that everything would be fine—but in truth that was far from the case.

"The hospital revived him, but instead of him learning an important lesson, he started feeling more invincible," O'Brien continues. "That was really the beginning of the end of everything."

Anselmo wasn't proud of his addiction—in fact, he was kind of embarrassed by it—but it had overtaken him. Wherever he was in the world, he needed his drugs.

In the meantime, Pantera resumed touring. They were like a blitzkrieg onstage—a tidal wave. On July 26 they played a show at Vancouver's Pacific Coliseum with White Zombie and Minority, subsequently reviewed by Kevin Templeton for *Drop-D Magazine*:

"All in all, I really thought it was great to see the contrast between White Zombie's flashy stage performance and Pantera's stripped-down, wall-of-amps style. All things considered, I would have to give Pantera the slight edge on this evening, due to the sheer strength of their material and their overall impact on the dancing hordes."

In September, Pantera crossed the Pacific for a run of shows in Japan, Australia, and New Zealand. As a rule, the band preferred to play in small, sweaty clubs, but by now they had grown accustomed to playing in larger amphitheaters. What bugged them about these bigger venues was that they were seated: As far as the band was concerned, sitting down at a Pantera show defeated the whole purpose of the thing. Where possible, they would opt for a general admission policy, but that wasn't always an option. Sometimes they'd end up having to pay for thousands of dollars worth of chair damage, but it was always worth it. The band took great pride in convincing the more uptight members of the audience to get up and join the mosh pit, as Anselmo explained to *Kerrang!*'s Mörat in 1992:

"If you're an uptight little pussy and you just wanna sit there and fold your arms and go, 'Man, I don't like this,' you should just stay home and watch MTV and have a fucking ball!"

There were no such problems with the fans down under, as Vinnie Paul recalled in an interview with Cameron Edney of Soundwave Touring:

"I remember heading out the back of the arena in Sydney and there was this big twelve-foot fence—it may have been higher actually—and the fans would not leave. They were climbing on this fence chanting, 'Pantera!' If there wasn't barbed wire at the top they would have been over; it was like everybody left the 10,000-seat arena and went and stood up at that fence. I was scared, man. . . . I thought the fence was going to cave in, the fans were chanting Pantera as loud as they could go, they were fucking awesome!"

Pantera had a hard-core following right across the world; long gone were the days when they were only known to metal fans in Texas and perhaps readers of the cult U.K. magazine *Metal Forces*. "The kids fuckin' get it man, and that's what it's all about," Rex Brown told *Vox* magazine. "It's obviously really important, and we wouldn't fuckin' be where we are without them."

The sound of the crowd before the start of a show was usually enough to psych up the band members before they took the stage, although Vinnie Paul would also stretch his muscles and listen to some old-school metal to get himself in the right frame of mind. Sometimes he'd have a couple of shots of vodka, too. Dimebag, on the other hand, gave *Guitar World*'s Brad Tolinski a list of essential products for life on the road:

"Beer, Taco Bell, joints, whiskey, a Walkman, and a little acid for long bus trips."

Pantera were known as a band that worked hard and partied harder. They would sometimes rack up more than two hundred live shows per year, but they made sure to enjoy themselves on the road, too. Vinnie Paul had opened up a strip joint called the Clubhouse in Dallas and enjoyed checking out similar clubs across the globe. "The ones in Japan are really good," he told Spence D at *IGN*. "They only have a couple of 'em, and they're very expensive. It's like eighty dollars just to get in the door. And they bring all the girls in from Australia and New Zealand, so that's a plus. The ones that they have in Europe are really dodgy."

After returning from Australasia, Pantera began a winter tour of the U.S. with support from Biohazard and Neurosis. Tension continued to grow between Phil and his bandmates, and it was obvious that the front man was still struggling with his various demons. He wasn't comfortable with the way fans hung around outside the venues, waiting for the band to come and go. He didn't enjoy signing autographs and talking to fans about the band, and had generally lost faith in the whole "rock star" image. He didn't care what people thought of him, and if anything he'd rather be at home, drinking and listening to metal.

In hindsight, the released of Down's debut album, *NOLA*, in 1995 was a clear sign that all was not right between Phil Anselmo and Pantera. He might have been the front man of one of the biggest metal bands of the decade, but Down was his baby and he found working on his side project much more enjoyable than being in Pantera. Metal journalist Mörat spent a lot of time with the band in the '90s and so had a good perspective on the relationship between the musicians at the time. He says:

"Because there were two brothers in the band I think it made Phil and Rex kind of outsiders, no matter what, and it made sense that they hung out more together. Phil was still a bit of a loner, though, or if not a loner then keen for company that wasn't necessarily tied up with Pantera. . . . He's a thinker, which is probably what led to the drugs—he was trying to block something out. Considering all the times we hung out, the last time I saw him I went back to say hi and he just looked at me blank like he didn't recognize me or I wasn't there, he was so strung out. I think some of his demons come from allowing that to happen . . . ."

In the meantime, the Abbotts did their best not to let the various cracks that were appearing in the band detract from day-to-day life. Photographer Neil Zlozower first shot Pantera in the early '90s at a headlining show at the Hollywood Palladium and worked with them again on several occasions later in the decade. He found them all very professional and easy to work with, even if Phil often seemed to be off in his own world:

"Vinnie and Dimebag were always a pleasure to work with. I did this one session with Dimebag where he came to my studio and it was right around 1996. He came in. He was great. We did a lot of shots of him on a white background. He was there for a few hours. I got a few drinks with him. . . . Vinnie and Dime both liked drink. But then he put [on] this Uncle Sam beard and he painted it white and had his sunglasses on. . . . It was a pretty unique take! I got a good night that night. Vinnie I've shot a few times for magazines and he's always a pleasure to work with. Always wants to come in and do his shoot as fast as possible because he doesn't like coming to Los Angeles. He always wants to come in, do his shoot, and then he's off to the Rainbow. He always wants to go to the Rainbow."

Pantera's last show of 1996 was on December 21 at the Rosemont Horizon in Chicago. It had been a whirlwind year, and although *The Great Southern Trendkill* had not been received quite so well as *Far Beyond Driven* or *Vulgar Display of Power*, Pantera had proven that they were not a one-dimensional band. They could be as innovative or experimental, in a technical sense, as any other metal band in the country. Metallica had infuriated their fans by moving away from their thrash-metal origins, leaving only Slayer to compete with Pantera in terms of sheer relentlessness. Certainly, in the live arena, Pantera were unbeatable—no one could touch them. The only problem was the band's erratic front man, but unfortunately that problem was not one that they would be able to solve any time soon.

13

SOUTHERN SHREDDERS: OZZFEST, *OFFICIAL LIVE,* AND SOME MUCH-NEEDED DOWNTIME

It's always special meeting my heroes. Sammy Hagar is one of my best friends; I love him.

—Vinnie Paul to Ramsey Ramirez of Magx Online, 2010

PANTERA RARELY HAD FORMAL REHEARSALS. They'd maybe do two or three days of preproduction before a tour, or if Phil wasn't in town Rex, Vinnie, and Dime might get together to learn some new songs. By now, having played together so many times, each of them knew, instinctively, what the other was going to do onstage. They were an incredibly tight unit.

After a brief Christmas break the band returned to the road in early 1997 for a headlining tour of the U.S. with support from Clutch and Neurosis. Then, in March, they traveled to Mexico,

Chile, and Argentina as the opening act on the Lost Cities leg of Kiss's *Alive/*Worldwide tour. It was a dream come true for Dimebag Darrell, who had worshipped the band since his teenage years, while his brother was similarly excited. "They're one of the reasons why we started doing what we do," Vinnie told *NYRock*'s Roger Scott. "We've known Paul [Stanley] and Gene [Simmons] for quite some time, and Gene's come out and jammed with us, several times, it was just amazing—they treated us so good."

Rex Brown was similarly excited, telling *antiMusic*'s Debbie Seagle: "Doing photo shoots with Gene Simmons and him playing on your bass rig . . . it's mind-boggling, so you just go with the flow and let it happen." It was an important tour for Kiss, too. It was the first time the four original members of the band had played together since 1979, and it proved to be a massive success.

The nature of Pantera's music meant they would go down a storm at rock and metal festivals the world over. They knew what their fans wanted and they stuck with it, never trying to be anything but a metal band. "We're not afraid to carry around a heavy-metal moniker," Dimebag Darrell explained to *Electronic Musician*'s Jeff Perlah. "It's who we are and what we do. A lot of bands have shied away from that—they've said, 'Don't call us metal,' and tried to change their styles. We don't bend, man."

Pantera would soon be playing on the main stage of America's highest-grossing (and rapidly expanding) touring metal festival: Ozzfest. The tour began on May 24, 1997, in Washington, D.C., and finished on June 29 in San Bernardino, California. While it was only in its second year, Ozzfest had become the most popular touring attraction in the U.S., with almost every metal band in the country eager to join the crazy train that took its name from its founder, metal legend Ozzy Osbourne. The festival did a lot not only to revive Osbourne's career but also to promote other metal bands, especially after grunge had all but

Southern Shredders: Ozzfest, Official Live, and Some Much-Needed Downtime

destroyed metal as a mainstream concern in the early '90s. For a few years, metal bands had had to soldier on underground; now they were back in the limelight.

Pantera would play a shorter set than usual on the tour, one generally comprising "Cowboys from Hell," "A New Level," "Walk," "Becoming/Throes of Rejection," "5 Minutes Alone," "Sandblasted Skin," "Domination"/"Hollow," "This Love," and "Fucking Hostile." They were delighted to be on a bill that included bands that had been around for a long time as well as lesser-known new acts. "There's so many bands that are on the bill," Brown told Seagle, "and it's pretty refreshing just to go and see the new bands that are up and coming."

This year's bill included Ozzy Osbourne himself, Marilyn Manson, Type O Negative, Fear Factory, Machine Head, Powerman 500, Coal Chamber, Slo Burn, Drain STH, Downset, Neurosis, and Vision of Disorder. It was an interesting mix of bands, offering something for metal fans old and new. The presence of Manson—the current bogeyman of American metal—caused the most controversy, and resulted in several protests outside venues, but it also helped quash the idea that metal was done for. The tour was a sold-out success.

For Pantera, part of the privilege of taking part in the tour was the presence at the top of the bill of their idols Black Sabbath. Ozzy Osbourne, Tony Iommi, Geezer Butler, and Bill Ward continued to have a profound influence on Pantera, and to feature on the same bill as them was a highly significant milestone for the Texan group. It was a childhood dream come true, in fact. Touring with Black Sabbath meant that they had now shared stages with three of their biggest influences: Kiss, Sabbath, and Judas Priest.

Meanwhile, the Atco employees who joined Pantera on the tour soon learned that drinking alcohol was not an option but a requirement. Even with band and crew physically spent after a long day and night, Dimebag would pour everyone a glass of some booze or other. He got one of the label's employees so drunk that he passed out in a puddle of his own vomit in the parking lot of the PNC Bank Arts Center in New Jersey. The police found him and rushed him to the hospital. When he got back to his office the next day there was a bottle of Crown Royal on his desk, compliments of the band.

On July 29, a month after the Ozzfest tour, Pantera released their only live album, *Official Live: 101 Proof*, comprising songs recorded during the band's U.S. tours of 1996–97. The album was produced by the Abbott brothers and mixed at Chasin Jason Studios, with Sterling Winfield assisting with the engineering. It hit Number 15 on the *Billboard* 200 and was a Top 20 hit in Australia, Finland, and New Zealand, despite stalling at Number 57 in the U.K.

Live releases tend to be stopgaps between studio albums, but *Official Live* followed in the footsteps of such seminal live recordings as AC/DC's *If You Want Blood . . . You've Got It*, Kiss's *Alive!* and *Alive II*, and Motörhead's *No Sleep 'til Hammersmith*. The album cover shows a whiskey bottle with the title "101 Proof" indicating the alcoholic content and a "No. 5" in reference to the fact that this was Pantera's fifth "official" release (ignoring their early self-released albums).

Official Live opens with a wild version of "New Level" before the band blast through thirteen more songs, including classics such as "5 Minutes Alone," "Cowboys from Hell," and "Cemetery Gates," and newer cuts like "War Nerve" and "Fucking Hostile" (here listed simply as "Hostile"). There's also a neat medley of "Domination" and "Hollow" (billed as "Dom/Hollow"), while the climaxes of "Becoming" and "I'm Broken" are merged with elements of "Throes of Rejection" and "By Demons Be Driven," respectively.

Taken as a whole, the fourteen live tracks offer a perfect encapsulation of Pantera's onstage prowess as arguably the best live metal band of the '90s. The album closes with two brand-new tracks recorded by the band during a break from touring as a way to ease back into the studio. "Where You Come From" sees the band back in groove-metal mode, and is all the better for it, while "I Can't Hide" is hard-core metal madness with an indelible melody.

Reviews of the album were generally positive, and *Official Live* is still well thought of even if it has not quite gone down in the annals of the all-time metal greats. In *The Collector's Guide to Heavy Metal—Volume 3: The Nineties*, Martin Popoff writes:

"This band live was insane. Incredibly, the sound they got on record turned out to be reproducible onstage; Dime put on a great show of stomping metal might mischief, and Phil could be counted on to say stupid shit to get a rise, chuckle, or to impart a little metal obscurity to those in the circle of such."

The only thing missing from the album is a sense of Pantera's visual sensibility. They were a very interesting band to watch, but inevitably a live recording gives little indication of how they behaved onstage.

Official Live: 101 Proof was released at a time of celebration and consolidation for Pantera. Several weeks earlier, *Cowboys from Hell* had gone platinum for the first time after achieving sales of one million copies in the U.S. *Vulgar Display of Power* and *Far Beyond Driven* would each reach the same landmark later in the year. It was further proof—if proof were needed—that Pantera had become one of the biggest metal bands in the world.

True to form, Pantera played a handful of live dates to promote the album's release before embarking on a full U.S. tour in September. The tour began at the Starwood Amphitheatre in Antioch, Tennessee, in September and ended at the Coast Coliseum in Biloxi, Mississippi, in December, with support first from Machine Head and Coal Chamber and later from Anthrax. The band played a remarkably taut set featuring most of the songs included on *101 Proof* as well as other live favorites such as "Mouth for War" and "Hard Lines, Sunken Cheeks."

On November 11, 1997, Pantera released their third official VHS collection, *3 Watch It Go*, which brought together tour footage with promo videos for "Planet Caravan," "I'm Broken," "5 Minutes Alone," and "Drag the Waters."

Unsurprisingly, they began 1998 with yet more touring around the U.S., sharing stages this time with Anthrax, Sebastian Bach, and Coal Chamber. Despite the sheer number of shows they played, Pantera were always a very spontaneous band; they had a core list of songs they would play, but things could quickly change if they had fun jamming around an idea backstage. They thrived on that kind of mentality.

The band made a return trip to South America in May before heading to Europe in June for a series of festival dates. Among the highlights were the Italian Gods of Metal festival in Milan on June 6 and the U.K. Ozzfest at the Milton Keynes Bowl on June 20, on a bill that also featured Black Sabbath, Ozzy Osbourne, Foo Fighters, Soulfly, Slayer, Fear Factory, Therapy?, Coal Chamber, Life of Agony, Human Waste Project, Hed PE, Entombed, and Pitchshifter.

Later in the summer, the band received a Grammy nomination for the *Official Live* version of "Cemetery Gates" in the category of "Best Metal Performance" (they eventually lost out to Tool's "Enema"). It was long-overdue recognition for one of the band's finest songs. By now, however, the media had begun to focus on the friction within the band. It was time for the members of Pantera to take a break from one another.

* * *

Before Pantera were ready to think about a new album, they each worked on side projects as respite from the stresses of life in the band, and it is worth mentioning them here.

Phil Anselmo was a busy man for sure. "I'm a fuckin' musician, man," he told D. X. Ferris of *Alternative Press* in 2002, "and to limit myself to just one style of music would be limiting the whole spectrum of what it is to be a musician. I can write any which way I please."

He had already released *NOLA*, his debut album with Down, in 1995, and some blamed the album for the communication breakdown between Anselmo and the Abbotts. When he was asked by Nick Bowcott at *Guitar World* if he was bothered by Phil's side projects, however, Dimebag Darrell didn't seem overly concerned: "No, not at all. Phil's a musical guy and he likes to stay busy. That's what he does, he jams all the time—just like me."

For his work outside Pantera, Anselmo adopted the nickname Anton Crowley, which he derived from the Church of Satan founder Anton LaVey and the English occultist Aleister Crowley ("the Wickedest Man in the World"). He played guitars on the 1999 Necrophagia album *Holocausto de la Morte* and had a brief spell in the black metal supergroup Eibon, which also featured Satyricon's Satyr Wongraven, Darkthrone's Fenriz, Mayhem's Maniac, and Necrophagia's Killjoy.

He then began another side project, Viking Crown, issuing an EP, *Unorthodox Steps of Ritual*, in 1999. That first release was basically a one-man show, while the follow-ups, *Innocence from Hell* (2000) and *Banished Rhythmic Hate* (2001), feature Stephanie Opal Weinstein (aka Opal Enthroned) on keyboards and Necrophagia front man Killjoy on vocals. Anselmo and Opal married at his home in Louisiana on October 31, 2001, and would work together on various musical projects during the three years they were married; a disagreement with Killjoy, however, led Phil to withdraw from a planned collaboration as Enoch.

Phil Anselmo was not a fantasist, and nor did he enjoy being idle. "If you have the good common sense to know that music is good in a lot of different directions, you've got to find that direction yourself," he told D. X. Ferris. "I don't half-ass much. I'm a doer."

Meanwhile, the Abbott brothers and Rex Brown formed Rebel Meets Rebel with outlaw country musician David Allan Coe. Coe had originally met the Abbotts at Billy Bob's in Fort Worth, where the three musicians discussed the similarities between country and metal—notably the rebellious nature of the music. "At the time we gave him some Pantera CDs and DVDs and he said he'd briefly heard of us, but not much," Vinnie told *KNAC*'s Jeff Kerby. "He ended up calling Dimebag the next day and he said, 'I watched that video, and you guys are just like me. It just blows me away that you play my song before your concert.'"

Coe liked the Abbotts so much that he suggested they write some songs together. They recorded together sporadically between 1999 and 2003, but their self-titled debut album as Rebel Meets Rebel was not released until 2006.

Dimebag was a restless musician. Even when he wasn't on the road or in the studio he'd be at home jamming with his four-track or playing guitar with friends. He'd always have his guitar with him. He was forever coming up with new riffs—by now he'd written thousands of them—but the idea of making a solo album never really crossed his mind. His focus remained with Pantera. He and his brother did, however, form another side project called Gasoline. The project stemmed from the fact that Pantera had always performed a New Year's Eve show until the late '90s, when their bandmates reportedly decided they didn't want to do it anymore. The Abbotts loved those celebratory shows, however, so much so that they decided to form their own little band to play songs by Pat Travers and Ted Nugent and general have fun as they saw in the new year. They even came up with some original songs with titles like "Get Drunk Now" and "This Ain't a Beer Belly, It's a Gas Tank for My Love Machine." They continued to play together as Gasoline for the next few years, even in one instance playing in support of Drowning Pool.

To keep their fans happy, Pantera put out *3 Vulgar Videos from Hell* on October 5, 1999. The DVD collection brought together the previous VHS releases *Cowboys from Hell: The Videos*, *Vulgar Video*, and *3 Watch It Go*. As well as music videos and live performances (including several songs shot at the 1991 Monsters in Moscow show), the set includes ultra-rare band footage shot between 1989 and 1997 and features a wide variety of guest appearances from some of rock and metal's most well-known artists, including Rob Halford, Kerry King, Skid Row, White Zombie, Sepultura, Alice in Chains, Sacred Reich, Exodus, and Suicidal Tendencies. Manager Walter O'Brien recalls:

"All Dime ever wanted to do was show everyone a great time. We used to argue most about the home videos. He just took forever adding more and more video footage even after we would go over the two-hour limit. The label would argue we could only go so long—people weren't buying videos anymore at that time. But Dime wanted [what] he wanted, and that was it for him. I was always stuck in the middle. I often tell people, if Dime got everything he wanted in the videos it would have had to be X-rated. If you think the videos are wild now, you should see the stuff left on the cutting room floor. Actually, no—nobody should see that stuff. But he knew his audience, and the videos sold like crazy. He would go right to the edge to make people laugh and have a good time. He was a true rock 'n' roll character of the highest order."

Thanks to these videos, Pantera had an image of rock 'n' roll excess comparable only to those of Van Halen and Mötley. The kinds of things shown in the videos—Darrell dying his beard pink, Vinnie smashing up a television set, Rex sprawled over a toilet—were not necessarily representative of the band's day-to-day life, but a lot of people got the wrong idea and assumed that Pantera spent every day wrecking hotel rooms. The fact is that they'd spend the whole day waiting to go onstage for a two-hour show, so they needed something else to do. Filming themselves acting out pranks and stunts was a way to avoid boredom and have fun.

With Dimebag, someone always had to bear the brunt end of a bad joke. He was always devising some stunt or other, whether his bandmates were interested or not. (Phil certainly wasn't, and while Rex would go along with most things, Vinnie would often just sit and watch.) It was indicative of a mean streak in Darrell's personality, as Walter Trachsler recalls:

"When we were children if he was borrowing your toy—like, 'Hey, let me play with that'—when he got it, he was just gonna fuckin' break it. He loved to break people's bicycles. If you let him ride your bike, he was gonna break it. . . . He would ride it and break the forks off of it. Then he would just fuckin' throw it and walk away. And all his buddies would follow him. Darrell was a mean motherfucker, dude."

14

GODDAMN ELECTRIC: PANTERA HIT THE STUDIO FOR *REINVENTING THE STEEL*

We thought the timing was perfect for a new album.
—Vinnie Paul to Therese McKeon of Shoutweb, 2000

ON NEW YEAR'S EVE, 1998, Pantera joined a reunited Black Sabbath for a special show at Bank One Ballpark in Phoenix on a bill that also featured Soulfly, Slayer, and Megadeth. They had originally planned to have returned to the studio to start work on a new album by now, but then they received a call asking them to join Sabbath on a full U.S. tour that would take them through January and February, this time with Deftones, Incubus, and System of a Down among the support acts.

There was no way Pantera could refuse another chance to tour with their heavy metal heroes. Ozzy and Sharon Osbourne had been very supportive of the band, and had given them tremendous exposure by inviting them to play at the various Ozzfest shows of the past few years, as booking agent John Dittmar recalls:

"Sharon Osbourne and [her assistant] Jennifer Perry were instrumental in helping Pantera at several points.... They always treated the band great and played a big role in the continued development of Pantera."

It was evident too that Black Sabbath had a lot of respect for Pantera, and that the Texan band's special brew of metal had gone down well with Sabbath fans, who not only craved fast and heavy music but also enjoyed the band's distinctive monolithic riffs and toe-tapping melodies.

More than anything, however, Pantera could just not believe they were on the road with Black Sabbath. "It's incredible," Rex Brown told *antiMusic*'s Debbie Seagle. "Sometimes it's just—you can't even speak anything out of your mouth ... [but] we're peers with them now, which is great, you know?"

After completing the Black Sabbath tour, Pantera joined Metallica and Monster Magnet for a special show at Mexico City's Foro Sol on April 30. The only downside to all of these live engagements was that the band still hadn't made it back into the studio, as Vinnie Paul explained to *Shoutweb*'s Therese McKeon:

"It's funny because people come to our shows and they come backstage and say, 'Great show. What a great concert ... so, when's the new record coming out?' And I say to them, 'When we're finished touring then we'll make the new record!"

Meanwhile, some of the band had begun to enjoy the fruits of their labors. Phil Anselmo had bought himself a large new house in Louisiana, which he dubbed Nodferatu's Lair. He had decided to move back to the town where he was raised because he was fed up with the attention from local kids and metalheads in Texas, where his home was more like a tourist attraction.

The band's few recent recordings had all been one-offs. They recorded a cover of Ted Nugent's "Cat Scratch Fever," which Nugent himself was not too keen on, for the *Detroit Rock City* soundtrack, and a version of "Electric Funeral" for the Black Sabbath tribute album *Nativity in Black II*. "We still do covers!" Vinnie Paul told David Lee Wilson of *KAOS2000 Magazine*. "We never want to forget the club days and or where we came from and what inspired us to do what we do. We still pay homage to them all."

The band also wrote a new song, "Puck Off," to commemorate the Dallas Stars' run up to the 1999 Stanley Cup Finals. The song was included on the compilation album *Dallas Stars: Greatest Hits*, and was indicative of a friendship that had sprung up between the Texan band and their local NHL team. That summer, Vinnie hosted a Stanley Cup victory party at his home, during the course of which Canadian-born center Guy Carbonneau reportedly dropped the cup itself from the roof of Vinnie's house into a poolside deck. (Fortunately, an NHL-approved silversmith was able to repair the cup.)

On September 12, the Abbott brothers suffered a massive personal blow when their mom, Carolyn, passed away. It was a difficult time for them but they sought solace in their work, and at the tail end of the year Pantera finally started work on a new studio album, their first since *The Great Southern Trendkill*.

The album itself would not end up taking very long—it was finding time to get started that had been the problem, as Vinnie Paul explained to Spence D at *IGN*: "You know, we also put the live album out, which included two new studio tracks. A lot of people kind of forget about that. As soon as we did that, that came out in '98, we were gonna do one short tour and then hop right in the studio—and then Black Sabbath called us."

The starting point for their new album was a song called "Yesterday Don't Mean Shit," which the band wrote at a hotel room in Toronto during the second leg of the Black Sabbath tour. It set the feel and texture for the rest of the album, and made clear that, as ever, the band was only interested in looking forward, not backward.

"We did our growing up on independent records," Vinnie Paul explained to *KAOS2000 Magazine*'s David Lee Wilson. "Elektra Records [the new parent company for Atco/EastWest] has offered us large sums of money to own the rights to those records and to rerelease them, but the way that we look at it is everything that we have accomplished has been since *Cowboys from Hell* came out in 1990, and that is really what we are all about and that is how people know us."

Reinventing the Steel was recorded at the band's own Chasin Jason Studios in Dallas and produced by Dimebag Darrell, Vinnie Paul, and Sterling Winfield, who had previously worked with the band on *Official Live: 101 Proof.* (It was later mastered at Masterdisk by Howie Weinberg.) Despite the strong relationship the band had developed over the years with producer Terry Date, Pantera had wanted to self-produce an album for some time. "I co-produced all the albums before and really understood how we worked in the studio," Vinnie explained to *Metal Rules* writer Keith McDonald. "It just worked out. It was a lot of fun and was just the right time."

The band still had a lot of respect for Date, who was working with Deftones at the time, and continued to keep him involved in the process. "I definitely stayed in touch with him the whole time through the project," Vinnie told *Yahoo! Music*'s Janiss Garza. "[I] sent him some tapes here and there. And he was just, like, 'Thumbs up, man! It sounds like you've got it.'"

Pantera wanted to make a metal album that was fresh and vital, and they knew that to do so they would have to take their time. "It was probably the smoothest record we ever made," Vinnie told McDonald. "We didn't have any deadlines put on us by the record company."

The Abbotts knew they had the experience and knowledge to handle the production of the album, but what was now lacking, in Dale, was an important conduit between the band and their singer, the ever-distant Phil Anselmo, who was still struggling with his personal demons. Phil didn't much like traveling to Texas to record, either, and was reportedly not overly keen on the band's new material. He and the Abbott brothers were living in different worlds; Rex just did his best to get along with both parties.

For *Reinventing the Steel*, Pantera believed in quality rather than quantity. They'd rather have ten solid tracks than fifteen average ones. The title of the album was a play on the idea that the band wanted to reinvent their sound while sticking determinedly to a heavy-metal framework. Metal had been through some big transitions since Pantera's genre-defining *Cowboys from Hell*, and they felt that it had lost a lot of its "steel" in the process, particularly in terms of the way nu-metal groups used loops, scratching, and samples.

"There's bands out there that say they're hard rock or metal but they have a lot of hip-hop or rap mixed in," Vinnie explained to *Shoutweb*'s Therese McKeon. "Well, they do what they do. What they do is different than what Pantera is about. There's a lot of music out there today using computer programs and synthesizers."

Pantera strove to create an organic metal sound uncontaminated by passing musical trends. "I get asked, 'What is a typical Pantera fan?'" Vinnie continued. "There is no typical Pantera fan." One of the best things about Pantera's fan base was the surprising range of age groups. They went from kids to fifty-year-olds, and they all sang along to Pantera's songs at live shows. The new album would need to appeal to them all.

"We wanted to put out a straight-fuckin'-on, cut-the-fuckin'-fat-off, fuck-the-trendy-shit, hard-ass-fuckin' Pantera album," Rex told *Vox*. "*Trendkill* was more eccentric; *Steel* is fuckin' balls-out metal, man."

By now Dimebag was unquestionably one of the most important and influential guitarists in modern American metal. "One of the most important things for a player to learn is to use their ears," he told Lisa Sharken at Seymour Duncan. "Go after what you like, and once you've dominated learning everybody else's licks, take whatever elements you've retained and then use them to forge your own style."

Dimebag was always keen to ensure that his riffs worked as well onstage as they did on record. On *The Great Southern Trendkill*, however, he had explored new guitar sounds and some heavily layered techniques that didn't always translate so well on tour. This time around he returned to a harsh, raw guitar sound that he hoped would go down just as well when the band went back out on the road.

Lyrically, the band had grown ever more introspective over the years, with Anselmo never afraid to express his feelings in song. "There's a lot of songs in the past where Philip Anselmo is kicking and screaming like a little kid, hoping someone will notice fucking how not happy I am right now," he explained to *Examiner*'s Elliot Levin. "And it's well documented, but it's the truth."

The big change on *Reinventing the Steel* was that many of the songs are about the band itself. "We'll Grind That Axe for a Long Time" talks about how they stayed true to their sound and image while their peers—and even some of their idols—had sold out, while "I'll Cast a Shadow" deals with their profound influence on the metal genre. The latter song took a while to come together. Usually, the band would finish a song in just a few hours, but they ended up leaving "I'll Cast a Shadow" aside and returning to it after the rest of the album was completed.

The album's distinctive artwork is centered around a photograph taken at a bonfire the band attended. They were all having a good time with some friends when someone dared Phil's assistant, Dustin, to run through the fire naked—which he did.

Fortunately, they had a camera with them and were able to film Dustin running through the bonfire with no clothes on (footage of which was also used in the video for "Revolution Is My Name"). It was a marked change from Pantera's previous album artwork, but the result was another iconic cover image.

Reinventing the Steel begins with "Hell Bound," a hard-core metal song with an accessible melody. "Goddamn Electric" is a fantastic tribute to Pantera's heroes Black Sabbath, featuring a guest solo by Slayer's Kerry King that was recorded backstage at an Ozzfest show in Dallas on a portable tape machine. The head-banging "Yesterday Don't Mean Shit" is one of the album's standout tracks, "You've Got to Belong to It" is driven by some powerful double-kick drums and excellent axe work, and "Revolution Is My Name" has a memorable melody and is notable for Anselmo doing more singing rather than shouting. "Death Rattle" is a fists-in-the-air anthem—and very punk-sounding, too. "We'll Grind That Axe for a Long Time" is built around a hard-as-nails lead riff, while "Up Lift" is a more groove-laden track with a lot of growling by Anselmo. "It Makes Them Disappear" is another Black Sabbath-style beast with an ambient melody and chugging riffs while "I'll Cast a Shadow" is a moody, dark, and powerful track that closes the album in fine style.

Reinventing the Steel would prove to be Pantera's last album, and is a fitting return to form after the more experimental material on *The Great Southern Trendkill*. While some of the songs are slightly underwritten, the music is fantastic, with some strong riffs and indelible melodies. It's a shame Phil doesn't sing more of the album—rather than just growling—but on the whole these are some of the finest songs the band ever recorded.

Released on March 21, 2000, the album debuted at Number 4 on the *Billboard* 200. It fared rather well abroad, too, hitting Number 8 in Canada, Number 33 in the U.K., and the Top 20s in Germany, New Zealand, Finland, and Norway. It was also a Top 10 hit in Australia, where the band released a two-disc version of the album, the second disc of which comprised an unofficial (and now very rare) greatest hits collection. To promote the album, the band took porn stars, including Kira Kener, out on the road with them to in-store signings, while the official listening party took place at Vinnie Paul's strip joint, the Clubhouse.

Reinventing the Steel spawned two singles, the first of which, "Revolution Is My Name," hit Number 28 on the *Billboard* Mainstream Rock Tracks chart. It also earned the band their fourth Grammy nomination, for "Best Metal Performance," while the accompanying video, directed by Jim Van Bebber, makes reference to the band's musical heroes Black Sabbath and Kiss, as well as Led Zeppelin and ZZ Top.

The second single taken from the album was "I'll Cast a Shadow," which peaked at Number 37 on the Mainstream Rock Tracks listing. It would be the last single the band ever released, and, fittingly, the lyrics are about Pantera's influence on heavy metal, the genre they loved so much.

Reviews of the album were largely positive, with the wide variety of publications covering the record showing just how popular the band had become. *Alternative Press* called it "an undiluted, unvarnished slab of riffs paying distinct homage to Judas Priest's *British Steel*, and not just in a titular sense, but in basic song construction," while *Rolling Stone* found it "brutal enough to please underground purists and familiar enough for weekend head-bangers."

Historical reviews of the album would remain positive, although *Reinventing the Steel* does have its skeptics. In its "Where to Start" guide to metal, *Kerrang!* concluded: "The riffs were there but the spirit and invention wasn't." Writing in *Classic Rock*, Malcolm Dome was similarly apprehensive. "The problem? The production for the most part. Overseen by drummer Vinnie Paul, it is comfortable, rarely stretching the band's resources or showing signs of creative impact."

Although the album was generally well received, like *Far Beyond Driven* and *The Great Southern Trendkill*, it would ultimately be overshadowed by the past glories of *Cowboys from Hell* and *Vulgar Display of Power*. Perhaps at some point in the future, *Reinventing the Steel* will be spoken about with the same passion and respect as Pantera's first two major-label albums, but for now it remains sadly underrated.

15

IMMORTALLY INSANE: PANTERA ON TOUR

We are one of the only bands in the last ten years that are still around doing exactly what we fuckin' started out to do in the first place.

—Rex Brown to Tony Bonyata of ConcertLivewire, 2000

PANTERA'S TOURING SCHEDULE FOR 2000 began on February 1 with a two-month trek around the U.S. After that they headed to Europe for another couple of months of shows, this time with Satyricon and Powerman 5000 in support, followed by four dates in Japan. The band's April 28 show at Barrowlands in Glasgow was reviewed by the U.K. music weekly *NME*, which concluded:

"In the face of sports metal's lame irony filings, it's a ferociously intense, refreshingly simple thing to behold; a monosyllabic, slavering beast that has no agenda beyond the redemptive pursuit of noise. . . . 'GRRAARRGGHHRRURRR!' howls Anselmo during cast-iron closer 'Cowboys from Hell.' The zeitgeist may have gone thataway, but Pantera's righteously dumb voice is as eloquent as ever."

Pantera then joined the summer Ozzfest tour for the third time as part of a lineup that included Ozzy Osbourne, Godsmack, Static-X, Incubus, Methods of Mayhem, P.O.D., and Queens of the Stone Age on the main stage, and Soulfly, Kittie, Disturbed, Taproot, Slaves on Dope, Reveille, Shuvel, Primer 55, the Deadlights, Pitchshifter, Crazy Town, Pumpjack, Black Label Society, and Apartment 26 on the second stage.

"We had the opportunity to do our own tour or do the Ozzfest, and there is no way you can turn the Ozzfest down," Vinnie Paul explained to *KAOS2000 Magazine*'s David Lee Wilson. "You play a day, get a day off, and play with all of the new bands that are out, and you make a lot of good friends and a lot of fans."

Touring with Ozzy was an offer Pantera couldn't—and didn't want to—refuse. The tour wouldn't go down without a spot of trouble, however. When they played Dallas on August 18, the Abbotts were reacquainted with an old friend and employee, security guard Big Val. He and the band had parted ways after it was alleged that he had been selling Pantera merchandise online without the band's consent. He was now working for Ozzy. Vinnie later described the reunion to *KNAC*'s Jeff Kerby:

"I was going to the front of the house to watch Ozzy. I hadn't seen Big Val all day long or anything. I was walking along, and I had my girlfriend with me at the time, and I saw him and went to wave at him—then the dude just leveled me with one shove. I was there on my ass in front of 20,000 people walking out to see Ozzy."

Fortunately, Phil was able to resolve the situation and nothing further occurred. Overall, taking part in Ozzfest was once again a great experience for Pantera, particularly when it came to hanging out with and checking out the other bands. "That's why I like this Ozzfest so much," Rex told Debbie Seagle at *antiMusic*. "It's just real relaxed and calm, and . . . it just brings this whole metal thing together."

There was only one downside, as Vinnie explained to *Electronic Musician*'s Jeff Perlah: "The only bind on this tour is that we only get to play an hour: Coming down the home stretch, we really have to keep an eye on the clock and keep things moving."

Fortunately, the band had a very solid crew behind them. Guitar tech Grady Champion was adept at handling Dimebag's seven guitar changes (down from the usual ten at the band's own headlining shows) and knew exactly how to fix any problems that might come up. Aaron "Crank Wires" Barnes, the band's sound engineer, was likewise a trusted friend and ally. The same could be said for all of Pantera's road crew—they were one big family. Inside the band, however, the same underlying tensions continued to fester. L.A.-based photographer Neil Zlozower has worked with some of the biggest rock bands of our times, notably Van Halen and Mötley Crüe. He has seen firsthand how bands can be one big happy family, living in the same apartment, eating junk food every day, and even sharing girlfriends . . . and then they make it big and the bubble bursts: The drummer wants to get his girlfriend bigger breast implants than the singer's girlfriend; the guitarist wants a more expensive sports car than the bassist's new ride. There's an abundance of animosity and ego, and everything gets out of hand. The same was becoming true of Pantera, as Zlozower recalls:

"The last time that I probably worked with [Pantera] was when they were playing live in Ozzfest, but you could see something wasn't right when they were onstage. I guess Phil and Rex were teaming up in their own little scheme, and then you had Vinnie and Dimebag doing their thing—the two brothers. You can kind of tell something wasn't quite as family-orientated as they were back in 1993 when I first started working with them. They were a bunch of happy-go-lucky-guys. You can see when they were onstage that things weren't going peachy clean in the

Pantera camp. They played great [but] there wasn't much interaction [that] I remember...."

Even after all the time they had spent together on the road, in the studio, and at home, Vinnie and Darrell Abbott remained the best of friends. They both had roles to play, and they were completely in sync. Vinnie was the business guy; Darrell was the creative one. They rarely—if ever—disagreed on anything, and they had been through a lot together. They always sided with each other, and there was a lot of mutual trust. When it came to Phil, they both knew he was a strong personality and gave him an increasingly wide berth.

Pantera had acquired a reputation for their hedonistic behavior over the years, especially when it came to alcohol, so much so that they acquired an official drink, called a Black Tooth Grin, which was a combination of Crown Royal and/or Seagram's Seven Crown whiskey and Coca-Cola. The name came from a line in the Megadeth song "Sweating Bullets"; Dimebag used Pedialyte, an oral electrolyte solution, to rehydrate. Asked about life in Pantera by *Vox* magazine, Rex Brown replied: "I can't even describe it.... I'm so fuckin' hungover I can barely hold the fuckin' phone, man."

Pantera gave new meaning to the word *party*. As manager Walter O'Brien recalls, they were the only band on his roster that got upset if he didn't want to get drunk with them every night. Dimebag and Co. were dedicated to putting on the best show possible, playing every one like it could be their last—and then partying as hard as humanly possible afterward. They truly lived for the moment. Darrell's home in the small, exclusive town of Dalworthington Gardens, Texas, was often in such a state that he needed to call in a caretaker, while in 1997, he had had to reshoot photographs taken for *Guitar World* magazine, which had just named him their "Most Valuable Player," because of the huge bags under his eyes.

"You've just got to get in a rock 'n' roll mode," he told *Electronic Musician*'s Jeff Perlah. "What's tonight? It's Monday night? Fuck that, it's Friday night all of a sudden! Know what I mean? It's Friday night every goddamn night and it's going to burn."

As the years passed, however, the sex, drugs, and rock 'n' roll lifestyle began to lose a little of its edge and more prosaic activities slowly started to take its place. "I don't do drugs," Vinnie Paul told Spence D of *IGN*. "I like to drink, I love to play golf, I love hockey, football—that kind of stuff."

Darrell, meanwhile, was a born-and-bred Texan at heart and would never stray too far from home. He'd always be home for Christmas, and whenever he was off on tour he would send postcards to his buddies back home: "Man, I can't wait to get home and drink some cold beers with you."

The road would soon come calling again, however. After playing their final Ozzfest date on September 2, 2000, Pantera had a short break before a planned U.S. tour of their own with support from Morbid Angel and Kittie. The tour was due to begin at the Mississippi Coast Coliseum in Biloxi, Mississippi, on November 7, but was canceled after Phil fell from a balcony at House of Shock, a yearly Halloween event he had hosted in Jefferson, Louisiana, since 1992. Vinnie later described the accident to *Metal Rules* scribe Keith McDonald:

"He has always been an actor in it and apparently he jumped out to scare some people as he always does, tripped, fell down and landed on something that jabbed him pretty hard in the back. He was sore but thought he was going to be okay. He got up the next morning and was pissing blood."

Phil went to the doctor and was told that he had two broken ribs and a punctured kidney, and that he would have to take two months off to heal. It was an accident; there was nothing they could do about it, but it meant that the rest of the band had to sit tight during the lucrative touring season.

REINVENTING METAL

The tour was rescheduled to begin February 1, 2001, in Albuquerque. It had also been reorganized as a package tour with Nothingface, Soulfly, and Morbid Angel also on the bill. At some shows, according to *Metal Rules* writer Michael De Los Muertos, Phil would pick out fans wearing Slipknot T-shirts and tell them they should go back to old-school metal. Meanwhile, some fans, including De Los Muertos, were unhappy that the band neglected to perform songs like "Mouth for War" or "5 Minutes Alone." "Pantera's emphasis at this show was clearly on giving the crowd a good time, and they succeeded," he wrote. "My only real complaint is the lack of certain older songs."

Even after all these years, Pantera looked forward to getting back on the road. It was where they belonged. "A lot of bands, they don't realize how much touring is going to be the basis for their success," Vinnie Paul explained to *Metal Rules* writer Keith McDonald. "A lot don't tour that much and aren't that good live. For Pantera and any band that wants to be around for any length of time, touring is the ultimate."

Rock and metal had recently undergone a resurgence of popularity after facing something of a drought in the '90s. It may not have been as popular as it was in its '80s heyday, but the dark days were over, even if the kinds of bands that were now at the forefront—Linkin Park, Deftones, Limp Bizkit, and so on—bore no real relation to Pantera. The Texan group felt that some of these bands had neglected the music in favor of over-the-top stage productions. Sure, Pantera had the big amps, the flames, and the giant backdrop, but they continued to balance all of that with strong performances.

In May, Pantera made one of the most surprising guest appearances of their career when they showed up on the wacky kids cartoon series *SpongeBob Square Pants* in an episode entitled "Prehibernation Week." They also went back out on the road for dates in Alaska, South Korea, New Zealand, and Australia, with support from Corrosion of Conformity (C.O.C.) and the Australian band Segression. Then, on June 20, they began a U.S. tour they called "Extreme Steel," on which they were joined by Morbid Angel, Slayer, Static-X, and Skrape.

The following night's show at the Nassau Coliseum in Uniondale, New York, was reviewed by *Blistering*'s Scott Olivenbaum, who noted that Phil seemed "much more coherent" than he had during the band's recent shows at the Hammerstein Ballroom:

"[He] took time to talk between most every song in the set. Mentioning those shows, and the turnout this night, he thanked New York for all of the support that the fans have always given the band. He also said that this would be the last time, for a long time, that Pantera would be coming around. After three tours they are going to take some time off."

The tour was not without its critics, however. At a July 19 show at the Long Beach Arena in Southern California, *Kerrang!*'s reviewer concluded: "Pantera have a lot to follow, and in truth they don't really manage it." He felt that for all the flames and explosions, there was still something missing—a sense of momentum, perhaps.

In July the band ventured up to Canada, where their performance at the Northlands Agricom in Edmonton was reviewed by Mike Ross of the *Edmonton Sun*:

"It was a kick-ass heavy metal show of the highest caliber, tapping into ancient male aggression made obsolete with the invention of agriculture, when man didn't have to hunt the mammoth anymore. . . . Enhanced by blinding lights, explosions, and up to six columns of fire, the sound was pure catharsis. The crowd responded with flailing heads and pumping fists."

The cracks in the machine were widening, however, and they were becoming more obvious to those outside the band. Jeff Waters, whose band Annihilator had toured with Pantera back in 1991, was invited backstage at the band's show in Vancouver in July 2001. He quickly noted that while Rex Brown and the

Abbotts still hung around together, Anselmo had his own dressing room down the hall:

"He [Anselmo] was the type of guy where one minute you would see him being the craziest freaked out punk-metal front man type of guy, and the next minute I'd go to the front of the bus to see the driver and Phil would be sitting there reading a book with his glasses on. . . . He had a couple of different personalities and one of them was in a subtle sense this guy's sitting there reading a book with glasses on."

The tour concluded at the Winnipeg Arena on August 1, after which the band traveled to Japan. The plan then was to begin a European tour called "Tattoo the Planet" featuring Slayer, Biohazard, Vision of Disorder, and Static-X. Just as the tour was about to start, however, the band's plans were thrown into confusion by the terrorist attacks of September 11, 2001, as Walter O'Brien recalls:

"That was momentous in a number of ways. We had all gathered a few days early, on Sunday [September 9], for my assistant Kimberly's wedding in New Jersey. [Pantera] left for Ireland to begin a big European tour, and Kim prepared for a honeymoon in Europe. They arrived in Ireland and went to sleep just about when the buildings were attacked on Tuesday morning. Kim, who could see the buildings from the roof of her NYC apartment building, had to cancel her trip since planes didn't fly for about a week. Pantera were freaked out about being such obviously blatant 'Americans' and Texans during a time [when] it [didn't] feel . . . too safe to be traveling through Europe as a sitting-duck target. They wanted to come home, but were stranded until planes started flying back in the U.S.A. again."

The tour was due to begin at the Point Theatre in Dublin on September 13, but Pantera had no intention of carrying on. O'Brien continues:

"They had me cancel the tour, causing a world of problems with the European booking agent and promoters that we never recovered from, especially when Slayer, our opening act, decided to continue with the tour, making Pantera look pretty bad in the eyes of the promoters."

Nobody knew it at the time, but the band's decision not to tour meant that they had already played their very last show together, at the Beast Feast Festival in Yokohama, Japan, on August 26. For the record, they played "Hellbound," "5 Minutes Alone," "Goddamn Electric," "War Nerve," "Mouth for War," "Becoming"/"Throes of Rejection," "Revolution Is My Name," "Fucking Hostile," "This Love," and "Cowboys from Hell," before finishing with an encore of "Walk."

When they eventually made it home to the U.S., Pantera planned to record a new studio album and release a new video collection, but things would end up taking a very different turn. Tensions were rife within the band; they'd lost the fun, the humor, and the mischief of the old days. Pantera now felt like a very different band, as Vinnie Paul explained to *musicOMH*'s Vik Bansal:

"Without a doubt it makes a huge difference. . . . With Pantera, at the end, it was a lot of 'me, myself, and I.' It didn't have that fuckin' bond, that fuckin' power, that four people together can have."

16

WE'LL GRIND THAT AXE FOR A LONG TIME: THE INEVITABLE BREAKUP OF THE BAND

Over [the] last couple of years, it really went downhill to a level that I wasn't happy with, and Dime wasn't happy with.
—Vinnie Paul to Vik Bansal of musicOMH, 2005

PANTERA MADE SEVERAL ATTEMPTS at starting work on a new studio album, but while Vinnie, Darrell, and Rex were keen to move forward, Phil could never commit to the project. Tensions had already been high during the making of *Reinventing the Steel*, for which the band recorded the music at Dimebag's home studio and then sent the tapes to New Orleans for Phil to add vocals. Once again, Phil refused to go to Dallas to be a part of the writing and recording of a new album, and so the whole idea became a dead end.

Initially, Anselmo had said that he wanted to take a year off of touring after the September 11 terrorist attacks, but it soon transpired that that was not the case at all. He jumped right back into his side project, Down, releasing a second album, *Down II: A Bustle in Your Hedgerow*, in March of 2002. He also recorded an album called *Use Once and Destroy* as Superjoint Ritual, and formed an acoustic band called Southern Isolation with his then wife Stephanie Opal on vocals plus Christ Inversion keyboardist Ross Karpelman, Crowbar/Christ Inversion bassist Kevin Bond (who also played in Superjoint Ritual), and drummer Sid Montz.

It was obvious that Anselmo was shifting his focus away from Pantera and onto projects that he could control. His apparent lack of interest in Pantera, and the amount of time he was spending on other projects, came as a huge source of frustration to Vinnie and Darrell, as photographer Stuart Taylor, a longtime friend of the Abbotts, recalls:

"It was that second Down record that killed [Pantera]. The first Down record they did, they did like a two-week tour or something . . . and then they did that second record and they toured and it went on and on and on. It was a sad day. I remember when me and Darrell talked about it, when he realized Phil wasn't coming back. . . . He said, 'I thought I was gonna be in Pantera my whole life.'

"'Dude,' I said, 'you're Darrell, you're still you.' I didn't know what to say to him, you know. It was a big blow to Darrell. These guys were playing to 10,000 people a night, and then all of a sudden they start over. They had to go to these little radio stations and do all this stuff that they had done years before . . . playing to near 800 people or something. It's a blow to your ego."

There were rumors that the Abbott Brothers were considering working with Jerry Cantrell of Alice in Chains, Chad Kroeger of Nickelback, and Default front man Dallas Smith.

We'll Grind That Axe for a Long Time: The Inevitable Breakup of the Band

In December 2002, Dimebag hooked up with Kroeger and Kid Rock for a cover of the Elton John classic "Saturday Night's Alright (for Fighting)." The following month, the Abbott brothers announced that they were starting a new band called New Found Power with former Halford guitarist Pat Lachman on vocals and Sean Matthews on guitar. By October, Matthews was no longer a part of the band, which by now had the more menacing name Damageplan.

By 2003 it was clear that Pantera were no more. Phil Anselmo had always been a source of massive frustration to the Abbott brothers; now he had simply shut himself off from them. "We tried everything we could to communicate with him ourselves, through our management, and through our record company," Vinnie later told *KNAC*'s Jeff Kerby. "He just blew us off."

The Abbotts did not know what Phil's intentions were, but what they did know was that he had begun making derogatory remarks about Pantera and the band's legacy in the media. He was still going through a number of physical and emotional problems, and it seemed that whenever he went near a tape recorder, he would hit out angrily at someone, which would generally end up reflecting badly on him and no doubt helped bring the band closer to the end. (Eventually he made the wise decision to shut himself off from the press completely.)

The final straw came when the Abbotts learned that Rex Brown had chosen to join Anselmo in Down. What really pissed them off was the way Phil handled the situation. Rex may just have wanted to keep playing to make a living, but the way it all went down felt like a total loss of loyalty, and the Abbotts took it very personally, as Vinnie subsequently explained to Jeff Kerby of *KNAC*:

"The next thing you know, I'm getting a phone call that Phil has quit the band and he's doing Down now. This was the start of it all . . . [and then] there was a phone call from Rex that he made to Dime one night completely lambasting everything I did for Pantera, everything Dime did for Pantera, and everything we did as a band."

The Abbotts could not figure out what had happened. They would have preferred a call from Phil saying that he was going to take some time out to work on a another project and do some shows around the country, and perhaps in a few years' time come back to Pantera and make a new album. After all, the band's label wanted a new Pantera album. By now they had sold millions of albums, and their back catalogue was extremely lucrative. By handling the situation more amicably, Pantera might have been able to reunite at some point. The Abbotts lived and breathed Pantera, and would never have left the band. But clearly Anselmo felt otherwise.

Back in Texas, Vinnie and Darrell would sit down and try to figure out what had happened. They'd talk over past incidents and wonder whether they were the cause of the breakup. They just couldn't figure it out. This band was their life. All they knew was Pantera.

They were concerned for their fans, too—particularly because of the way things had ended. Pantera's fans had always been loyal to the band, and the band had been loyal in return. But now they simply ceased to exist. There was no official end point: no statement or press conference. There had not been a final argument; none of them had slept with one of the others' girlfriend or messed with the band's finances. The band had started out with an antiauthority spirit representative of the British punk bands of the '70s; it was Pantera against the world. The Abbotts had not for one moment considered that Pantera would be out of their lives, so the end came as a real shock to their systems. They were best friends with a common aim, and they'd been playing together for more than twenty years. It would take a long time to fill that void.

Dimebag's long-term girlfriend Rita Haney summed up the brothers' feelings when she spoke to *Guitar World*'s Chris Gill

We'll Grind That Axe for a Long Time: The Inevitable Breakup of the Band

in 2008. "I was there when they lost their mom, and I know how much that hurt them," she recalled. "But honestly, the breakup of Pantera was worse."

Anselmo blamed the split on the metal press, which he accused of twisting his words and thus driving a wedge between him and the Abbott brothers. The one seemingly neutral voice was Rex Brown, but in opting to join Down he had effectively chosen to side with Phil, and ultimately the Abbotts stopped speaking to him.

"Me and Dime realized that Pantera was finally over because with the other members there was no communication, and they didn't express an interest in working together anymore," Vinnie Paul later explained to Vik Bansal of *musicOMH*. "[Phil's] performance level was hit and miss, depending on what type of chemicals he was on. He would stand up and do thirty-minute ramblings onstage about nothing. It was difficult because the fans were there, and they still got into it, but I *know* we could have given them a whole lot more as a band."

Pantera had been a long marriage that ended in divorce, and even though communication broke down and certain members of the band had negative things to say about each other, playing together had been an experience that would live on in each of them forever, regardless of what they thought about each other as individuals. They had created some of the greatest American metal of all time, but they all had flaws and weaknesses, and it had become obvious that the band had come to its natural end.

The final curtain came down on the band on September 23, 2003, with the release of *The Best of Pantera: Far Beyond the Great Southern Cowboys' Vulgar Hits!*, its catchy if overzealous title making reference to the band's first four Atco albums. It hit Number 38 on the *Billboard* 200 and was certified platinum in January 2006. It also reached Number 32 in New Zealand and Number 44 in Ireland but stumbled to Number 116 in the U.K.

The album includes fifteen songs from all of the band's albums from *Cowboys from Hell* onward, presented in chronological order, as well as covers of Ted Nugent's "Cat Scratch Fever" (from the soundtrack to *Detroit Rock City*) and Black Sabbath's "Hole in the Sky" (originally released on the *Revolution Is My Name* EP). It was packaged with a DVD featuring twelve music videos (two of which were recorded live), while outside of America the set had a different track listing and was titled *Reinventing Hell: The Best of Pantera*. Recalling the circumstances of the album's release, Walter O'Brien says:

"After nearly a year of trying to get the post–*Reinventing the Steel* studio album together, we got the label to put out a greatest hits just to make some money for everyone to live on. But then I couldn't maintain the office and overhead, and it was becoming more and more obvious that Phil was just not coming around, and that Dime and Vinnie were going toward Damageplan. I didn't want to manage Damageplan, so I asked for a release and closed down the office, retiring from the music biz after thirty-two years. It had just become too frustrating and sad to keep going."

There was some cause for celebration when in July 2004 when *Vulgar Display of Power* and *The Great Southern Trendkill* went platinum. Pantera, it seemed, were still a force to be reckoned with in the metal world. To say the split was bitter, however, would be an understatement, as O'Brien recalls:

"Near the end communications just got terrible. Phil and Dime started developing a real feud. Phil wanted control, but so did Dime. Phil had moved back to his hometown of New Orleans and hung out with his old friends, while Dime, Rex, and Vinnie stayed in Dallas. They got further and further apart geographically, but also the heroin got hold of Phil and he withdrew more and more, to the point that, after the *Reinventing the Steel* album, none of us could get him on the phone or fax. We'd have to call one of the Crowbar guys or other New Orleans friends and have him go out to Phil's house. He just became noncommunicative. We were told the phone and fax was unplugged, or the fax paper was just falling behind the machine unread . . . .

"To the best of my knowledge, there was never a real breakup. They just stopped talking. Phil started doing all his side bands, like Down and Superjoint Ritual, and eventually Dime and Vinnie started Damageplan just to get back into playing again. . . . I love Vinnie and Rex. Still talk [to] or at least e-mail them fairly regularly, have talked to Rex on the phone and seen Vinnie play with [his new band] Hellyeah, along with another former client, Tom Maxwell from Nothingface. I would love to see Rex play again, but I won't go to a Down show or any show with Phil. I doubt seriously that Phil and I will ever speak again."

EPILOGUE

A Decade of Domination: The Tragic Death of Dimebag Darrell and the Enduring Legacy of the Panther

I think [Dimebag]'s the best. There's none better before him or after. None better might not be fair, but it's the truth.

—Phil Anselmo to Kenny Herzog of MMN, 2010

IN 1994, *Kerrang!* journalist Mörat asked Dimebag Darrell if he thought people would still be listening to *Far Beyond Driven* ten years down the line. The guitarist replied: "It's gonna be how it's gonna be, but I think it could fall into that category. I think people will be listening to us. It's gonna sound hokey, but I don't give a shit."

Dimebag was aware of Pantera's legacy and of their massive contributions to the development of American metal. He wasn't being arrogant—he was being honest. He'd worked hard to get there. All those years slaving away in sweaty clubs playing to dozens of people helped define him as a guitarist, and thus helped define Pantera as a band.

Epilogue

Fast-forward to the summer of 2004: Pantera had split up, while Darrell and Vinnie had recently released their first album as Damageplan. In August, Vinnie showed up at a gig former Pantera front man Terry Glaze was playing in Dallas. They hung out for a while, and Glaze started to get his hopes up that maybe there was a window of opportunity for him to start making music again with Darrell and Vinnie.

Alas, it was not to be. By the end of the year, people would still be listening to Pantera, but for very different reasons than those Dimebag had envisioned when he spoke to Mörat ten years earlier. The lure of one last payday often brings bands back together despite the obvious acrimony lingering between the musicians, but any notion of a possible reunion vanished in an instant when Dimebag Darrell was shot and killed by a mentally disturbed fan named Nathan Gale during a Damageplan show at the Alrosa Villa in Columbus, Ohio. The date was December 8, 2004: twenty-four years to the day since John Lennon was murdered by another crazed fan, Mark David Chapman, outside his New York apartment. Walter O'Brien—who in another grim twist had covered Lennon's murder live on air for a radio show in Toronto—got a call from booking agent John Dittmar minutes after Dimebag was shot. He couldn't believe what he was hearing.

Gale had tried to get into the club before the show but was told he had to buy a ticket like everyone else. He hung around and attempted to talk to the band but was asked to leave. He then jumped an eight-foot fence to get inside the club and made his way toward the stage with security guards, who had seen him enter, trailing. The band hadn't even made it to the end of their first song, "New Found Power," when Gale climbed onstage and shot Dimebag Darrell several times at close range with a Beretta 9mm semiautomatic handgun. His third shot killed the guitarist instantly. (The audience included a twenty-eight-year-old nurse, Mindy Reece, but sadly, she could do nothing to revive him.)

Epilogue

Gale continued firing after shooting Dimebag, killing fan Nathan Bray (age twenty-three), club worker Erin Halk (twenty-nine), and former Pantera security guard Jeff "Mayhem" Thompson (forty), who had raced onto the stage to try to stop the gunman. Drum tech John "Kat" Brooks, who also tried to stop the shooter and was consequently held in a headlock onstage as hostage, was shot three times during the struggle but miraculously survived. Tour manager Chris Paluska and audience member Travis Burnett were also shot—Burnett having also jumped onstage to challenge Gale—but thankfully recovered from their injuries after being sent to nearby Riverside Hospital.

As soon as the 911 call was made, seven police officers led by Officer Rick Crum entered the club via the front entrance; Officer James D. Niggemeyer came in through the back entrance and killed Gale with a single shot from his twelve-gauge Remington 870 shotgun. (Niggemeyer's actions were later found to be wholly justified during a routine investigation into the shooting; he was subsequently given a commendation from the Ohio Peace Officer Training Commission and named "Law Enforcement Officer of the Year" by the National Rifle Association.) Gale, meanwhile, had remained silent throughout his rampage of terror, and was found to have thirty-five rounds of ammunition left in his gun.

According to *Rolling Stone* magazine, Gale was a former Marine who was discharged in November 2003 after serving about two years of his four-year service. He lived alone and had been taking medication for mental health issues. During the ensuing police investigation—which resulted in a 627-page case file containing 287 eyewitness reports—it was discovered that Gale's apartment was full of stacks of notebooks about how Pantera had stolen his songs, although strangely no audio recordings of the band were found on the premises. A Damageplan CD (presumably *New Found Power* or one of the singles from the album)

Epilogue

was however found in Gale's Pontiac Grand Am, which he had driven to the concert on the day of the shooting. Details were not released.

Inevitably, many theories have been put forward as to the motive behind Dimebag's murder. Many of them are covered in Chris Armold's insightful book on the subject, *A Vulgar Display of Power: Courage and Carnage at the Alrosa Villa*. What seems most likely is that Nathan Gale suffered from paranoid delusions that led him to believe that the members of Pantera could read his mind; that they were stealing his thoughts (and songs) and in doing so mocking him. But that has not stopped the spread of other theories, most notoriously that Gale shot Dimebag as a result of the very public, very bitter, and very angry war of words between Phil Anselmo and the other members of Pantera, even as Detective William Gillette made clear that "there is no evidence leading detectives to believe Nathan Gale was communicating with Phil Anselmo or any other individual ... in an effort to hurt Dimebag Darrell Abbott."

What is clear, however, is that Anselmo's conflict with his former bandmates had cast an ugly shadow over Pantera's legacy, and would continue to do so even after Dimebag's death, as Walter O'Brien recalls:

"As most people knew, Phil had a bad attitude about many things after the heroin took hold, and even after he had said he was off it. But just a week or so before Dime was murdered onstage, a big cover story ran in one of the U.K. metal magazines [the Christmas 2004 issue of *Metal Hammer*] where Phil badmouthed Dime mercilessly, calling him stupid, and blaming Dime for the breakup. But he went further and said something to the tune of: Dime needed to be punished, but he wasn't the guy to do it, but was sure someone else out there would. And less than a week later, some maniac jumped onstage and murdered Dime point-blank, saying that Dime broke up his favorite band. A lot of people felt it was Phil's comments that led directly to the

Epilogue

killing, even though, of course, it was the killer's choice [to do] it. But the coincidence and timing are hard to ignore."

Phil would take a rather more contrite tone in the wake of Dimebag's passing. "I'd give one of my fingers to fix everything somehow, go back in time, or to have been there," he told *Revolver*'s Brandon Geist. "This is a harsh thing to say, but if I saw some stupid son of a bitch coming at my guitar player with a gun, I would have knocked his block off, you know?" Later, in a video interview with *High Times* editor Bobby Black, he suggested that he could just as easily have ended up as Gale's target. "I said to this cop [Niggemeyer] . . . 'So, then, what you mean is had it been me playing with Superjoint [Ritual] or Down that night, this motherfucker would have come after me?' And he just said, 'Absolutely.'"

None of this would do much, however, to staunch the river of bad blood that ran between Anselmo and those closest to Dimebag. Vinnie Abbott reportedly called Phil to give him a tirade shortly after Dimebag's passing, while the late guitarist's former girlfriend Rita Haney left no doubt as whether she held Phil to blame for what had happened. "If Phil Anselmo hadn't quit Pantera," she told *Guitar World*'s Chris Gill in 2008, "Darrell wouldn't have been playing in that shithole where that guy could get to him." (It was subsequently reported that the Alrosa Villa had been the scene of a parking lot shooting in January 2004, less than a year before Dimebag's murder.)

Anselmo was not invited to Dimebag's funeral, which took place at the Arlington Convention Center. It was a very rock 'n' roll affair. Jerry Cantrell and Mike Inez of Alice in Chains played a short acoustic set with former Halford guitarist Pat Lachman, while Black Label Society also performed. Ozzy Osbourne guitarist Zakk Wylde, Anthrax drummer Charlie Benante, and Eddie Van Halen gave speeches.

Dimebag loved rock music and his funeral represented his undying passion. The general tone of the funeral (and its lack of

Epilogue

religious ceremony) did not go down well with everybody, however, while some found it odd that Jerry Abbott was not asked to speak, as photographer Stuart Taylor, who got the first ever Pantera tattoo back in 1985, recalls:

"Rita or whomever was in charge didn't want anybody there that wasn't a rock star.... It was a nightmare, really, if you think about it in hindsight. I spoke to [former Pantera roadie] Randy Bell last night, and Rita told him not to come.... I don't remember seeing anybody, because I was so freaked out. They had all these people there. I didn't know half of them, man. They didn't even have a pastor at the funeral or anything. There wasn't anything about God.... All it was was like Charlie Benante from Anthrax, Eddie Van Halen, Zakk Wylde.... He was rude. He comes barging through, pushes me aside or whatever. I'm thinking, Who is this fucking guy? He didn't know fucking Darrell for as long as I did. Then you're gonna come in here and act badass or whatever. And then that Eddie Van Halen, he was so drunk ... he couldn't even tell the difference between a microphone and a cell phone."

Dimebag was famously buried in a Kiss Kasket, as donated for the purpose by Gene Simmons. Walter Trachsler describes the circumstances of how the casket was delivered to the home Dimebag shared with Rita Haney shortly after the guitarist's death:

"This big truck pulled up out front with a big delivery like UPS. The guy says he's got a delivery for what-the-fuck-ever and he comes in the house and we just left the front door open. He came in and he's like, 'Hey, I've got a delivery here. I just need somebody to sign for it and I can drop this off.' We're all like, 'Okay, cool.' We looked out front and it's this big parcel and we're like, 'What the fuck you got?' It's just a big fucking box. Okay, so we go out there and we help unload this big fucker, he takes off and we bring it up to the porch. It had no return address. It's just a box. We don't know where the fuck it came from. We're thinking, I wonder what this is? We're thinking its some guitars or some shit. We open this fuckin' thing up. And it was Gene Simmons's Kiss Kasket—his personal casket, which came from that Kiss movie *Kiss Meets the Phantom of the Park*. They made this movie in the '70s, and in that movie they had these caskets for each member of the band . . . so the guys decided that when they die we're going to be buried in our own fucking caskets from that movie. Gene Simmons in his fucking house had a Plexiglas room with a wax figure of him in his fucking casket in his house. That motherfucker went and took it all apart, had that casket boxed up, and sent it to the fucking house, and not one word was ever said. Nobody knew this. He never said one fucking word."

The Kiss Kasket was filled with rock memorabilia from friends and fellow bands, including a black-and-yellow-striped Charvel guitar (often dubbed the bumblebee) donated by Eddie Van Halen, having famously featured on the back cover of *Van Halen II*. The story of its arrival is just as interesting and wacky as the saga of the Kiss Kasket.

If there was one person that Dimebag ever wanted to meet in his life it was Eddie Van Halen. Before his death, Dimebag was working on a deal with Jim Dunlop's son to buy Dunlop Manufacturing, and Jim was a good friend of Eddie Van Halen. He introduced Dimebag to his guitar hero on Van Halen's 2004 summer tour with Sammy Hagar. They got on so well that it was suggested they make an album together with drums by Eddie's brother, Alex, and Dimebag's brother, Vinnie. According to Walter Trachsler, they had even a date set for when they were due to start work on what would have been the first full album that Eddie and Alex made outside of Van Halen.

In the meantime, Dimebag learned that Eddie had been taking a guitar, stripping and repainting it, and then putting it on eBay after playing it during the encore at each of the 2004 Van Halen shows. Dimebag was not particularly computer literate,

Epilogue

but he asked his friends to watch out for the one with yellow stripes from *Van Halen II*. Nothing more came of this until, on the day the Kiss Kasket turned up at Darrell's house, the phone rang, as Trachsler recalls:

"[Rita] had caller ID and it was Eddie Van Halen. It's Eddie Van Halen! You don't fucking not answer the phone. She answers the phone and I'm sitting right next to her on the couch, and she's holding the phone where I can hear everything.... He would call back, just asking general questions about Darrell. He was freaking the fuck out. If a question would pop in his head about Darrell—like: What was Darrell's first album? What was the first show he ever went to? What was the color of his first guitar?—as soon as the guy would think of something he would call. We're talking and the guy keeps ringing. One of the phone calls, he goes, 'I heard Darrell wanted a guitar.... What's the significance of that guitar?' This was just total curiosity. She was like, 'That's cool, I'm glad you brought it up.... We were wondering if you could take one of his guitars and paint it up and shit and we'll buy it from you. We will pay three times—cos Darrell's favorite number was three—three times the amount that the most expensive guitar sold for.' He's like, 'So you wanna buy this guitar? For what?' And she's like, 'So we can bury him with it. If he'd wanna be buried with anything it'd be one of those guitars, man.'"

Eddie agreed to paint a guitar for Dimebag to be buried with, but he didn't want Haney or the Abbott family to pay for it. Haney insisted, however, and in the end Eddie agreed to her request. She told him that Dimebag wanted the exact guitar from *Van Halen II*—the black one with yellow stripes. Eddie would ask, "Are you sure it's this one? Well, why do you think it's this one? What about this one? Why not that one?" They went back and forth on it, with Eddie repeatedly calling back to make sure that he had the right information. In the end, once Eddie was satisfied they were talking about the same guitar, he told Haney

Epilogue

he was going to mail it to them in time for the burial. And that was the end of that—or so they thought. Trachsler picks up the story:

"Well, two days later, we're at the funeral home with the family and it's dark outside; it's raining a little bit and it's kinda misty and I'm standing at the door. . . . It's open to the general public, so there had been a fucking line with all kinds of people comin', bringing stuff, and wanting to leave it in the coffin. We're standing there, shooting the shit, and here comes somebody walkin' up out of the dark literally carrying a guitar case. Why is some motherfucker coming up here with a fucking guitar? . . . This guy walks into the fucking light smoking a cigarette carrying this old guitar case and I recognize him instantly. It's Eddie Van Halen! All by himself, nobody with him. That motherfucker flew to Dallas on a commercial flight, got a cab, and came to the funeral by himself with this old guitar case in his hand. He's like, 'Hey guys, what's goin' on man?' He comes with us into this back room and . . . there's Rita, the drum tech, Vince, and The Eld'n [Jerry Abbott] all sitting there at this table. Eddie Van Halen walks into the room and all these people are fucked up, cos they're dealing with it. He just walks in—'Hey guys, what's up?'—and they're all sittin' at one side of the table. . . . He gets the guitar case and parks it down on the table . . . opens it up and it's the original black guitar with the yellow stripes. Eddie Van Halen walks into the room, puts this guitar case on the table, opens it and it's his fucking guitar! That's a piece of history. That's hard-core. That dude had met Darrell Abbott one time in his entire fucking life."

Hundreds of people attended the funeral, while thousands more attended the public viewing that followed. Among those who came to pay his respects was onetime Pantera guitarist Terry Glaze, whose parents were buried at the same memorial home, and who recalls:

"He just looked like he was asleep. There's this kid with all this great hair wearing shorts and flip-flops and laying in his casket. I guess since he got shot in the back [sic] that nothing came through. It wasn't an upsetting look. There wasn't all this trauma that was visible. He just looked like he was asleep . . ."

Glaze attended the funeral with his childhood buddy Tommy Bradford, Pantera's first bass player. There were a lot of hangers-on in attendance, but Vinnie went up to Glaze and Bradford and hugged them both. He knew they were there for the right reasons, but he felt less warmly toward some of the other people present, as Glaze recalls:

"When Pantera didn't get back together, Vince and Darrell held Phil and Rex responsible . . . Rex showed up [at the funeral] but there was no love for [him]. He wanted to get up and speak but they were not gonna let him. Those three had been together since high school, that rhythm section. I remember Rex looked like hell at the funeral. There was no love. There was no people going up and hugging him. He was treated as an outsider, and the hatred for Phil just was growing exponentially. Everybody at that funeral had some feeling that this is somehow connected with Phil saying something; all the stuff you've seen and heard . . . .

"The funeral, with his body lying there—like I say, it didn't look bad. He just looked like he was asleep. It wasn't until the next day, [when] I went back to the cemetery and I went to the gravesite . . . it wasn't until I saw the dirt that it sunk in. It was at that moment, when I'm by myself standing there, that it started sinking in. The other thing is you remember people how they were when you were with them. When I think of Darrell, I think of this skinny little kid. . . . At that time he was bigger than Vince, and when we were in the band Vince was the biggest one . . . Darrell, he was a big boy by that time. When I knew him he weighted 125 pounds. By that time, he's bigger than me . . . but I don't think of it that way."

In the weeks following Dimebag's death, tributes pored in from some of the biggest names in metal. Scott Ian from Anthrax,

Epilogue

Megadeth's Dave Mustaine, Ozzy guitarist Zakk Wyle, and Jonathan Davis of Korn all spoke to *Rolling Stone* about Dimebag and his senseless murder.

Exhorder's Kyle Thomas has many fond memories of Dimebag from back when they jammed together at parties playing Kiss, Black Sabbath, and Judas Priest songs. He remembers some of Darrell's famous pranks, such as when they threw sausages at the tubas of a passing marching band one Mardi Gras on St. Charles Avenue in New Orleans. Or there was the time Anselmo hosted a party at his house and Darrell turned up with a bottle of grape Mad Dog 20/20 and a video camera. He filmed Thomas doing shots—and promptly throwing up. Thomas last saw Darrell a few months before his death at a Black Label Society show in Houston:

"My friends and I went and hung out backstage with my ex-brother-in-law, Craig Nunenmacher of Black Label Society. After the show, Darrell was there, and he was kind of hot and bitching about some things to Craig. It was about Phil and people from New Orleans that are Phil's friends. This was after Phil said some ugly things about Darrell in a magazine. . . . Darrell thought that maybe most people from New Orleans were right behind Phil on that one, and Craig was telling him that he never felt anything badly toward him. He then looked at me and said, 'Kyle's not about all that shit either.' Darrell spun toward me and then looked at Craig and said, 'Is that who I think it is?' I replied, 'It's Kyle Thomas.' This was the first time I had seen him in almost ten years. He got a little excited [and] los[t] for words, then looked me in the eye and stammered, 'Dude, I wrote my own songs . . .' I stopped him and said, 'Darrell, I know this. I'm okay with everything.'

"At this point Zakk Wylde stuck his head out of the tour bus and bellowed, 'Dime, when are we going to the fucking bar?' Darrell blasted out, 'Shut the fuck up! I need to have this conversation!' He turned back to me almost with an imploring look,

Epilogue

and I just smiled. I told him that I never had a problem with him, that he was always righteous toward me, and I appreciated that. I let him know that if anything ugly toward him came from New Orleans that I was not party to it. We both loosened up, and by the time we were done it was suggested that he, Craig, and I maybe get together and do something musical together. I think that would have been an amazing project."

Dimebag was buried at Moore Memorial Gardens Cemetery in Arlington, alongside his mother, Carolyn, who passed away in 1999. After his death his finances were disclosed, and it transpired that despite the millions of albums sold and all the years of touring, he had only left a reported $250,000, plus his home in Dalworthington Gardens, which was worth some $450,000. Rock stars rarely have to buy anything because they're given almost everything they want; they get fed on tour, they get a place to sleep, and whatever else they want is put on the rider. Dimebag was never into hard drugs, although he did enjoy booze and marijuana. One of his only other excesses was buying stickers from his old friend Stuart Taylor's sign shop, which he would then stick all over the cars of anybody who visited him when they were not paying attention. It was just another one of his infamous pranks, as another old friend, Lenise Lopez, recalls:

"Darrell's entire life consisted of funny stories, and the cool thing about that is that he videotaped everything. Jerry Cantrell left his brand-new truck at Darrell's house while he left town—for safekeeping. Darrell took it down and had flames painted down the side and 'Cain Trail' printed in giant letters across the back window, and Jerry had to drive it all the way home like that...."

* * *

On January 5, 2005, some of Finland's most well-known metal musicians got together to celebrate Pantera's music at Helsinki's Rock 'n' Roll Station in a one-off tribute band called Dimen

Nimeen, which translates to In Dime's Name, in what would be the first of many public tributes to the guitarist's life and career. Then, on February 23, a benefit show was held at Chicago's Aragon Ballroom to help cover the medical expenses of the family of Damageplan security guard Jeffrey "Mayhem" Thompson and crew members John "Kat" Brooks and Chris Paluska. The show featured some of modern metal's most respected bands, including Soil, who covered Damageplan's "Save Me," and Drowning Pool, who played Pantera's "Message in Blood" during their set. Anthrax played "Fucking Hostile" and "A New Level" with Vinnie Paul and Pat Lachman, while Vinnie also joined Disturbed for a version of "Walk."

Further tributes would follow over the course of the year, with Vinnie often in attendance. He attended a show by Black Label Society at the WAAF Indoor Beach Party in the Tsongas Arena in Lowell, Massachusetts, on April 9, and joined the band for a rendition of "Suicide Messiah" at the House of Blues in Orlando on April 17. Perhaps the biggest surprise, however, came on October 4, 2005, with the release of Nickelback's *All the Right Reasons*, and in particular the song "Side of a Bullet," which made use of unused guitar recordings by Dimebag donated to the band by Vinnie Paul and Rita Haney, and became a Top 10 hit in the U.S. Nickelback front man Chad Kroeger was a friend of Dimebag's, and in the song he imagines an alternate universe where Dimebag's killer is still alive and Kroeger is on his tail, planning revenge. (He had also asked Vinnie to play on the track, but Vinnie felt Nickelback drummer Daniel Adair was more than up to the job.)

Nickelback were far from the only band to dedicate tribute songs to Dimebag. Former Guns N' Roses guitarist Buckethead wrote "Dime," while Machine Head dedicated "Aesthetics of Hate" to him. Numerous other bands—including Creed, Alter Bridge, Shinedown, Evile, 24-7 Spyz, Trivium, Disturbed, C.O.C., Static-X, Avenged Sevenfold, Cross Canadian Ragweed,

Crowbar, Carajo, Slayer, Black Label Society, Brides of Destruction, Dream Theater, Type O Negative, Anthrax, Evanescence, Brian Welch (formally of Korn), Ace Frehley, Krisiun, Ripper, and Between the Buried and Me—have also paid tribute to Dimebag in some way. In the fall of 2005, meanwhile, a selection of Italian musicians got together to record an album called *This Love: A Tribute to Dimebag*.

On May 11, 2006, VH1 broadcast an episode of *Behind the Music* on Pantera. Needless to say, much of it was dominated by the continuing feud between the Abbott Brothers and Phil Anselmo, but the fact that the episode aired at all was proof of Pantera's continuing appeal. With typically grim irony, it seemed that morbid curiosity about Dimebag's murder had made the band even more popular than before. As Rex Brown put it in an interview with James Zahn at *Kik Axe Music*: "I'd never thought of that before, and then I started seeing all these new tattoos from kids that couldn't be more than sixteen or so, and I was like, 'Shit, you weren't even alive when we were doing this.'"

In the meantime, the remaining members of the band continued to stay busy. A week before the VH1 special aired, Vinnie Paul launched his own Big Van label with *Rebel Meets Rebel*, the album he and Dimebag had recorded several years earlier with country singer David Allan Coe. Then, in August, he unveiled his new band, Hellyeah, which he formed with members of Mudvayne and Nothingface. The band's self-titled debut was released the following year. Vinnie's decision to form a new band so soon after his brother's death may have come as a shock to some Pantera fans, but keeping busy was Vinnie's way of healing. He needed to do it. Rex, meanwhile, stayed busy with various local projects, as well as working with Alice in Chains front man Jerry Cantrell, while Phil Anselmo continued to tour and record with Down.

Epilogue

On Saturday August 9, 2008, some of the biggest names in metal paid an all-star tribute to Dimebag Darrell at an Ozzfest event at Pizza Hut Park in Dallas. The super-jam featured Kerry King of Slayer, Scott Ian from Anthrax, Max Cavalera of Sepultura/Soulfly, King Diamond, Hatebreed's Jamey Jasta, Jerry Cantrell from Alice in Chains, Hellyeah/Mudvayne singer Chad Gray, and Metallica's Lars Ulrich. Perhaps the most memorable part of the tribute was a cover of Pink Floyd's "Wish You Were Here."

On May 3, 2010, Rhino Records released a compilation album titled *1990–2000: A Decade of Domination*, which covered all of the band's Atco releases, while *Cowboys from Hell* gained a twentieth-anniversary rerelease later in the year. As Rex Brown told James Zahn:

"We're just gonna put these things back into stores so that they have some shelf life again. [Iron Maiden bassist] Steve Harris once said when someone asked why they kept rereleasing all of their stuff, that 'it's the best thing to do to keep your music on shelves and get it restocked to keep yourself out there.'"

It was a welcome reissue for a landmark album in the band's career—the one that marked the point of their transition from glam metal to groove metal. "We knew from a band's sense . . . that the four of us were trying to make a great record," Rex Brown told *Sonic Excess*'s Brandon Marshall. "We didn't know what it would do. Looking back now, production-wise, it was a heavy record that still has the hooks."

The reissue came with a bonus CD featuring the *Alive and Hostile E.P.* as well as seven previously unreleased live tracks recorded in 1990 at the Foundations Forum in Los Angeles, while the deluxe version of the package also features a third CD comprising *Cowboys from Hell: The Demos*. Some of the tracks have different guitar parts and lyrics, while the running order differs from the original album, and "Primal Concrete Sledge" and "Clash with Reality" are not included.

It was around this time that false rumors began to spread of a Pantera reunion with Zakk Wylde on guitar. Such is the continuing level of conflict among the remaining band members, however, that the *Cowboys from Hell* reissue was put together without direct contact between the three of them, as Phil explained to *L.A. Music Blog*'s Shannon Joy:

"There is one common person that still works for the band [presumably manager Kim Davis], and Rex, Vinnie, and I will go through her. She will take [questions to the others], whether it be 'Is this photo okay? Is this okay? Is that okay?' . . . We all make a decision. We all have communicative input, she filters it, and that's how we work."

In early 2012, Phil told *Metal Hammer*'s Dave Everley that he hadn't spoken to Vinnie Paul since "probably 2001." He remains open to the idea of reconciliation; Vinnie, it seems, is not. "Fear controls him," Phil claimed when asked about his former bandmate by Bobby Black of *High Times*. "It's a shame, but it always has. Fear controls Vince, and I don't know why, but he fears me." Black then put it to Anselmo that had lost a brother, and had every right to be angry. "But he has pinned the guilt on the wrong guy," Phil replied. "And I'll tell you what: I resent it."

Rex Brown, too, has had little to do with Vinnie in the years since Dimebag's passing. "There's really not anything there to speak of," he told *Revolver*'s Christopher Krovatin in 2010. "He shut the door, you know? He's got a real problem with Philip, and that's something they gotta deal with. I really try to stay out of it."

In 2009, Brown was diagnosed with pancreatitis, reportedly as a result of the alleged alcohol abuse that led to him being ousted from Down. "He's not gonna die on my time," Anselmo told *High Times*, "because he ain't drinking around 'The Kid.' Straight up. And that means he can't be around right now, 'cause he's fucking drinking . . . ."

Epilogue

For his part, Anselmo had been through a lot during the intervening years. In mid-December 2004, he had released a video statement in which he said he loved Dimebag "like a brother loves a brother. I'm so sorry to his family and everyone else who was senselessly killed in Columbus, Ohio. . . . I never got a chance to say goodbye in the right way, and it kills me, and I'm so sorry. This has changed the entire world, and this is the last you'll be seeing of me for a long time."

Like everyone who knew Dimebag, Phil was heartbroken. After releasing the video, he closed himself off to the media for the second time in a decade, perhaps wary of how his words had been misconstrued in the past. He had made a lot of enemies—many of whom he had never actually met—and right now he just wanted to be alone. For a while he was like the Howard Hughes of the metal world, hidden away in his Louisiana mansion. He spent some of that time watching Pantera videos and listened to the band's music, and it made him appreciate just how vital they had been to the worldwide metal scene—and how much he missed his former bandmate.

"I miss him [Dimebag] more than I can even begin to say," he told *Revolver*'s Brandon Geist. I think of him every single waking day—every thirty minutes, if not every five minutes. . . . We had so much chemistry together. I miss it so goddamn much."

He eventually came out of hibernation on August 15, 2005, when he made a surprise guest appearance on guitar at a CBGB's show by Eyehategod, the band led by his old school friend Mike Williams. The show marked the dawn of a new Phil Anselmo. He had finally kicked his drug addiction, and had also undergone surgery to repair the back problems that had troubled him for years. Now, after months of rehabilitation, he had a more regimented lifestyle, built around yoga, boxing, and physical therapy. He was seeing a therapist regularly for the first time in his life, although he refused to take antidepressants—he didn't want any drugs in his system anymore.

In 2008, rumors began to circulate that he had slipped back into drug addiction, but he was adamant that was not the case. "That's fuckin' ridiculous," he told *Antiquiet* in 2008. "I'm on one drug, and it's called Lyrica . . . it's an anti-seizure medicine. A lot of people are on this drug who have sciatic pain, or pain like I have—which is sciatic, but it's from after the surgery. Sometimes when the nerves reconnect, they reconnect wrong."

On the whole, however, Anselmo had made his peace with the various issues that had dogged him over the years and had learned not to get wound up by the media. He has come to terms with who is and what he is here for. "I choose to use my gift," he told *Kerrang!*'s Joshua Sindell in 2002. "I know why I'm fucking here on this Earth, and that's to be one of the baddest-ass motherfucking heavy metal singers."

He has also become an inspiration not just to other musicians but also to other addicts. " I wish I could do more," he told *Metal Army* in 2010. "I feel humbled. I feel proud, but humbled at the same time. Honestly, the way I like to put it is: Without the people like that who love my music and what I do; who love one band I'm in, but hate all the rest, but give me that bit of love for that one band . . . the accomplishment is bigger than me."

Over the years he has learned how to deal with the chronic pain and treat his body with respect, while keeping himself busy with his various bands and other projects such as his Housecore Records label. "I really had some dark days, desperate days," he told *Hellbound*'s Jason Wellwood in 2010. "It's kind of baffling to me now . . . not really baffling because I understand where I was. . . . I've been clean six years now and I look back and even before back injuries, bone breakage, painkillers, and all that shit came into my life, there was always some sort of hovering doubt in my life."

He continues to mourn Dimebag's tragic passing. "All I can do is love him and cherish these memories and know that no matter what is said, no matter what has been believed, or no matter what the conception is in anyone's little mind out there, I was there," he told *Noisecreep*'s Amy Sciarretto. He echoed those sentiments in an interview with heavymetal.about.com's Justin M. Norton on December 8, 2009—the fifth anniversary of Dimebag's death:

"Each year gets harder. This was a very tough year and a very tough December. When an artist dies that means so much to people, he doesn't go away. You still hear about Elvis. We hear about Jim Morrison, Janis Joplin, Layne Staley. The list is long and it's a sad one. Is it hard for me? I respect the love. I know I will never have another person like this in my life. . . . To know that there is no tomorrow with him in it is crushing. He was a man of the world and a man of the people. He was very real, very vibrant."

Although seems unlikely that he and Vinnie will ever speak again, Phil has since made peace with Dimebag's girlfriend Rita Haney. "It's been well over a year now, maybe two almost three years since we've been cool," he told *Examiner*'s Elliot Levin in 2010. "I don't think that's anything that either one of us are going to go out and boast or brag about or anything like that, it's just between us, and that's fine."

"Everybody still has resentment toward each other about things in the past," Haney subsequently explained to *Marshall of Rock*. "It's easy to direct your anger at the wrong people. Philip didn't murder Darrell and [he] would never have wanted that. . . . Yeah, I resent Philip for becoming a jackass and a drug addict, and I'm a little sketchy about trusting him all the way yet. But some of the things he's e-mailed and some of the thing he's said—that's the Philip I know, the 'stronger than all.'" As for Vinnie Paul, she said: "I just hope someday he sees the light that I know Darrell is about, which is forgiving."

Epilogue

As it stands, the prospect of new Pantera music remains highly unlikely. During the writing of this book, a track called "Piss," dating back to the *Vulgar Display of Power* sessions, was unearthed by Vinnie Paul. It received its debut, with an accompanying music video, at the *Revolver* magazine "Golden God Awards" on April 11, 2012. Anyone expecting it to the be the first of many lost classics to see the light of day would be disappointed, however, since "Piss" was reportedly the only previously unreleased track in the band's vaults.

Had Dimebag not been murdered, would Pantera have gotten back together? Dimebag's friends knew him as a friendly, gregarious, and forgiving person, keen to make peace and move on. "I believe that the band would have reunited at this point if he was alive," says booking agent John Dittmar. Phil Anselmo agrees. "If Dimebag was alive we would have buried the hatchet a long time ago," he told *MMN*'s Kenny Herzog. "I know this. And we'd be playing out today, maybe even making new music." Speaking to *The Culture Shock*'s Patrick E. Douglas, he added: "I see bands out there—Slayer, Anthrax, all good friends of mine—still together, still touring. I think, Goddamn, if we were still together we'd still be humping it, man."

For all the convoluted personal dynamics, Pantera were as important to the metal scene in the '90s as Black Sabbath were in the '70s and Metallica were in the '80s. They argued like cats and dogs, but it was always to get the best out of the band, to create something new and unique. Metal was practically dead as far as mainstream audiences were concerned in the early '90s, but Pantera were determined to bring it back into the limelight without committing themselves to any short-term trend. They did things their own way, with a collective vision and a unique chemistry that will never be repeated. And in Diamond Darrell they had a guitarist whose complex, intricate, and powerful riffs have influenced virtually ever U.S. metal player since—a guitarist who genuinely changed the face of metal.

Epilogue

There have been many great metal bands over the years, but Pantera were up there with the best of them. "There was a lot of *hunger* there," Rex Brown recalled to *Kik Axe Music*'s James Zahn, "a lot of *fire* there." Pantera's unrelenting attitude, aggression, integrity, and fierce independence have inspired countless bands over the course of the past two decades, among them Tool, Korn, Slipknot, Killswitch Engage, Trivium, Limp Bizkit, Disturbed, White Zombie, and Hatebreed. Pantera's legacy is assured.

"Mark my words," Phil Anselmo told *MMN*'s Kenny Herzog, "and this is kind of empty of me to say, but if Dimebag Darrell was alive today, I would guarantee with all my heart that we would have already been back together, and then this entire talk of upper-echelon metal bands would be a moot point."

On December 14, 2011, the first of what is hoped to be an annual series of events, Dimebash, was held at the Key Club on the Sunset Strip in Los Angeles, with proceeds going to the Stand Up and Shout Cancer Fund set up Wendy Dio (widow of Ronnie James Dio). Just six hundred fans were able to witness the special event, which was hosted by Eddie Trunk, Jim Florentine, and Don Jamieson from VH1's *That Metal Show*. Among the musicians who showed up to pay tribute to Dimebag were members of Anthrax, Black Sabbath, Guns N' Roses, Alice in Chains, Megadeth, Anthrax, Rage Against the Machine, Deep Purple, and Machine Head, while songs played included the Pantera classics "Mouth for War," "War Inside My Head," "Fucking Hostile," "This Love," and "A New Level" as well as a selection of well-known covers songs such as Iron Maiden's "The Trooper," AC/DC's "Girl's Got Rhythm," Metallica's "Seek and Destroy," and Van Halen's "Ain't Talkin' 'Bout Love."

Despite the awards, accolades, and reverence that have been bestowed upon Pantera, however, it is hard not to view their story as a tragedy, as booking agent John Dittmar recalls:

Epilogue

"While each surviving member of the band is currently doing well, the Pantera story, overall, is a sad one. Pantera was a band that now grows every day in legend, but at the same time was a band that only scratched the mountain of its full potential. They could have had it all, but were brought down by the perfect storm of drug and alcohol additions, ego, poor communication, and, ultimately, tragedy. If it was not for Darrell's murderer, those internal issues would have been mended with a regrouping, for what I know would have been their ultimate triumph."

Dimebag Darrell's murder—onstage, in front of his brother—was a tragedy; so too was Phil Anselmo's descent into drug addiction, and the fact that he and Dimebag did not make amends before the guitarist was killed. Yet the band's legacy stands apart from that, and they will continue to be known, rightly, as one of the most important hard rock and heavy metal bands of the twentieth century.

Pantera's first three albums for Atco are among the finest metal albums ever made. They put their own spin on the genre, adding grooves and guitar chugs and taking ideas from everything from the blues to hardcore punk. They were emphatically not contrived. The band took influence from everything they heard: from Kiss and Van Halen to Lynyrd Skynyrd and Elmore James. They knew what came before them, what came before that, and what came before that. But while they were very much a product of what they listened to, they knew the importance of not sounding like anything else. If you're going to be a successful band, you have to make your sound your own.

"Pantera revolutionized the sound and the approach to heavy metal," Anselmo told Steven Rosen at *Ultimate Guitar*. "Once you up the production on a product—and not just the playing but the actual production—then it's going to up the ante."

What greater achievement is there for a band than to gain the respect of its members' heroes? One night, during an Ozzfest performance, a source who has asked not to be named remembers watching Pantera play "Respect." Standing at the side of the stage was Ozzy Osbourne, singing along to the song with a smile on his face like the biggest Pantera fan in the world.

It was a perfect, beautiful moment. Pantera had made an incredible, indelible mark, and continue to be revered as one of the greatest metal bands of all time. They reinvented metal. Period.

AFTERWORD

PANTERA WAS A TRULY VERY IMPORTANT PART of heavy metal history—one of the most important, in fact.

When everyone was saying metal was dead in the mid-'90s, Pantera was proudly holding up the flag for metal and selling tons of records and concert tickets. This was so important because without them, who knows if metal might have died at that point? Sure, there were underground bands like Cannibal Corpse out there, but Pantera was mainstream. For those of us around at that time it was a bit of a struggle, and to be able to have a band like them out there did help things along. Pantera was truly the bridge from old-school metal to the new school we have seen grow the last ten years.

Musically, of course, they also defined that time with a crossover of traditional metal with some new thoughts and heavier vocals, surely paving the way for many of today's bands. They also are such great guys and true metalheads. Dime was always talking metal—he was a true fan, as were the other guys as well. This was important at a time when the word *metal* was not looked at in the best of lights.

Afterword

So I tip my hat and raise a shot of Black Tooth for Dime and his mates in Pantera. They had a huge role in the resurgence of the music we all love.

Brian Slagel
Metal Blade Records
metalblade.com

DISCOGRAPHY

The following discography details the complete time line of Pantera releases.

THE GLAM YEARS

Metal Magic
Released 1983
Metal Magic Records
"Ride My Rocket" / "I'll Be Alright" / "Tell Me if You Want It" / "Latest Lover" / "Biggest Part of Me"/ "Metal Magic" / "Widowmaker" / "Nothin' on (But the Radio)" / "Sad Lover" / "Rock Out"

Projects in the Jungle
Released 1984
Metal Magic Records
"All Over Tonight" / "Out for Blood" / "Blue Light Turnin' Red" / "Like Fire" / "In Over My Head" / "Projects in the Jungle" / "Heavy Metal Rules" / "Only a Heartbeat Away" / "Killers" / "Takin' My Life"

I Am the Night
Released 1985
Metal Magic Records

Discography

"Hot and Heavy" / "I Am the Night" / "Onward We Rock!" / "D*G*T*T*M (Darrell Goes to the Movies)" / "Daughters of the Queen" / "Down Below" / "Come-on Eyes" / "Right on the Edge" / "Valhalla" / "Forever Tonight"

Power Metal
Release 1986
Metal Magic Records
"Rock the World" / "Power Metal" / "We'll Meet Again" / "Over and Out" / "Proud to Be Loud" / "Down Below" / "Death Trap" / "Hard Ride" / "Burnnn!" / "P*S*T*88"

THE GROOVE METAL YEARS

Cowboys from Hell
Released 1990
Atco Records
"Cowboys from Hell" / "Primal Concrete Sledge" / "Psycho Holiday" / "Heresy" / "Cemetery Gates" / "Domination" / "Shattered" / "Clash with Reality" / "Medicine Man" / "Message in Blood" / "The Sleep" / "The Art of Shredding"

Vulgar Display of Power
Released 1992
Atco Records
"Mouth for War" / "A New Level" / "Walk" / "Fucking Hostile" / "This Love" / "Rise" / "No Good (Attack the Radical)" / "Live in a Hole" / "Regular People (Conceit)" / "By Demons Be Driven" / "Hollow"

Far Beyond Driven
Released 1994
EastWest Records
"Strength Beyond Strength" / "Becoming" / "5 Minutes Alone" / "I'm Broken" / "Good Friends and a Bottle of Pills" / "Hard Lines, Sunken

Discography

Cheeks" / "Slaughtered" / "25 Years" / "Shedding Skin" / "Use My Third Arm" / "Throes of Rejection" / "Planet Caravan" / "The Badge"*
*Bonus track on rerelease

The Great Southern Trendkill
Released 1996
EastWest Records
"The Great Southern Trendkill" / "War Nerve" / "Drag the Waters" / "10's" / "13 Steps to Nowhere" / "Suicide Note Pt.1" / "Suicide Note Pt. II" / "Living Through Me (Hell's Wrath)" / "Floods" / "The Underground in America" / "(Reprise) Sandblasted Skin"

Reinventing the Steel
Released 2000
EastWest Records
"Hellbound" / "Goddamn Electric" / "Yesterday Don't Mean Shit" / "You've Got to Belong to It" / "Revolution Is My Name" / "Death Rattle" / "We'll Grind That Axe for a Long Time" / "Uplift" / "It Makes Them Disappear" / "I'll Cast a Shadow"

LIVE ALBUMS

Official Live: 101 Proof
Released 1997
EastWest Records
"A New Level" / "Walk" / "Becoming" / "5 Minutes Alone" / "(Reprise) Sandblasted Skin" / "Suicide Note Pt. II" / "War Nerve" / "Strength Beyond Strength" / "Dom/Hollow" / "This Love" / "I'm Broken" / "Cowboys from Hell" / "Cemetery Gates" / "Fucking Hostile" / "Where You Come From" / "I Can't Hide"

Discography

COMPILATIONS

The Best of Pantera: Far Beyond the Great Southern Cowboys' Vulgar Hits!
Released 2003 (U.S. release)
Elektra/Rhino
"Cowboys from Hell" / "Cemetery Gates" / "Mouth for War" / "Walk" / "This Love" / "I'm Broken" / "Becoming" / "5 Minutes Alone" / "Planet Caravan" / "Drag the Waters" / "Where You Come From" / "Cat Scratch Fever" / "Revolution Is My Name" / "I'll Cast a Shadow" / "Goddamn Electric" / "Hole in the Sky"

Reinventing Hell: The Best of Pantera
Released 2003 (International release)
Elektra/Rhino
"Cowboys from Hell" / "Domination" / "Cemetery Gates" / "Mouth for War" / "Walk" / "This Love" / "Fucking Hostile" / "Becoming" / "I'm Broken" / "5 Minutes Alone" / "Planet "Caravan" / "Drag the Waters" / "Where You Come From" / "Revolution Is My Name" / "Immortally Insane" / "The Badge"

1990–2000: A Decade of Domination
Released 2010
Rhino
"Cowboys from Hell" / "Psycho Holiday" / "Cemetery Gates" / "Mouth for War" / "Walk" / "This Love" / "5 Minutes Alone" / "I'm Broken" / "Drag the Waters" / "Revolution Is My Name"

BOX SETS

Driven Downunder Tour '94: Souvenir Collection
Released 1994
WEA

Discography

Far Beyond Drive: "Strength Beyond Strength" / "Becoming" / "5 Minutes Alone" / "I'm Broken" / "Good Friends and a Bottle of Pills" / "Hard Lines, Sunken Cheeks" / "Slaughtered" / "25 Years" / "Shedding Skin" / "Use My Third Arm" / "Throes of Rejection" / "Planet Caravan" / "The Badge"
Alive and Hostile E.P.: "Domination (Live)" / "Primal Concrete Sledge (Live)" / "Cowboys from Hell (Live)" / "Heresy (Live)" / "Psycho Holiday (Live)"
Walk: "Walk (Cervical Edit)" / "Fucking Hostile (Biochemical Mix)" / "By Demons Be Driven (Biomechanical Mix)" / "Walk (Cervical Dub Extended)" / "Cowboys from Hell (Live)" / "Heresy (Live)"

The Singles 1991–1996
Released 1996
WEA
CD 1: "I'm Broken" / "Slaughtered" / "Domination (Live)" / "Primal Concrete Sledge (Live)"
CD 2: "5 Minutes Alone" / "The Badge" / "Cemetery Gates"
CD 3: "Mouth for War" / "Rise" / "Cowboys from Hell (Live)" / "Heresy (Live)"
CD 4: "Walk" / "A New Level" / "Walk (Cervical Dub Extended)" / "Walk (Cervical Edit)"
CD 5: "Planet Caravan" / "The Badge" / "A New Level (Live)" / "Becoming (Live)"
CD 6: "Planet Caravan" / "The Badge" / "Domination (Live)" / "Hollow (Live)"

SINGLES

"Cowboys from Hell" (1990)
"Cemetery Gates" (1990)
"Psycho Holiday" (1990)
"Mouth for War" (1992)

"This Love" (1992)
"Hollow" (1992)
"Walk" (1993)
"I'm Broken" (1994)
"Planet Caravan" (1994)
"5 Minutes Alone" (1994)
"Becoming" (1994)
"Drag the Waters" (1996)
"Suicide Note Pt.1" (1996)
"Floods" (1996)
"Where You Come From" (1997)
"Catch Scratch Fever" (1999)
"Revolution Is My Name" (2000)
"Goddamn Electric" (2000)
"I'll Cast a Shadow" (2000)
"Piss" (2012)

VIDEO COLLECTIONS

Cowboys from Hell: The Videos
Released 1991
Atlantic Records

Vulgar Video
Released 1993
Atlantic Records

3 Watch It Go
Released 1997
Elektra

3 Vulgar Videos from Hell
Released 1999
Elektra

Discography

MUSIC VIDEOS

"Cowboys from Hell" (1990; directed by Paul Rachman)
"Psycho Holiday" (1990; directed by Paul Rachman)
"Cemetery Gates" (1990; directed by Paul Rachman)
"Mouth for War" (1992; directed by Paul Rachman)
"This Love" (1992; directed by Kevin Kerslake)
"Walk" (1992; directed by Paul Anderson)
"Planet Caravan" (1994; directed by Michael Boydstun)
"I'm Broken" (1994; directed by Wayne Isham)
"5 Minutes Alone" (1994; directed by Wayne Isham)
"Drag the Waters" (1996; directed by Dimebag Darrell)
"Revolution Is My Name" (2000; directed by Jim Van Bebber)
"Piss" (2012; directed by Zach Merck)

* * *

The following (selective) discography details albums released by the bands associated with Pantera.

DAMAGEPLAN

New Found Power
Released 2004
Elektra
"Wake Up" / "Breathing New Life" / "New Found Power" / "Pride" / "Fuck You" / "Reborn" / "Explode" / "Save Me" / "Cold Blooded" / "Crawl" / "Blink of an Eye" / "Blunt Force Trauma" / "Moment of Truth" / "Soul Bleed"

DOWN

NOLA
Released 1995

Elektra

"Temptation's Wings" / "Lifer" / "Pillars of Eternity" / "Rehab" / "Hail the Leaf" / "Underneath Everything" / "Eyes of the South" / "Jail" / "Losing All" / "Stone the Crow" / "Pray for the Locust" / "Swan Song" / "Bury Me in Smoke"

Down II: A Bustle in Your Hedgerow
Released 2002
Elektra
"Lysergik Funeral Procession" / "There's Something on My Side" / "The Man That Follows Hell" / "Stained Glass Cross" / "Ghosts Along the Mississippi" / "Learn from This Mistake" / "Beautifully Depressed" / "Where I'm Going" / "Doob Interlude" / "New Orleans Is a Dying Whore" / "The Seed" / "Lies, I Don't Know What They Say But . . ." / "Flambeaux's Jamming with St. Augustine" / "Dog Tired" / "Landing on the Mountains of Meggido"

Down III: Over the Under
Released 2007
Elektra
"Three Suns and One Star" / "The Path" / "N.O.D." / "I Scream" / "On March the Saints" / "Never Try" / "Mourn" / "Beneath the Tides" / "His Majesty the Desert" / "Pillamyd" / "In the Thrall of It All" / "Nothing in Return (Walk Away)" / "Invest in Fear"*
*Bonus track on the European and Japanese releases

Diary of a Mad Band: Europe in the Year of VI (Live)
Released 2010
Elektra
CD 1: "Losing All" / "Lifer" / "Lysergik Funeral Procession" / "Rehab" / "Temptations Wings" / "Ghosts Along the Mississippi" / "Learn from This Mistake" / "Hail the Leaf" / "New Orleans Is a Dying Whore"

Discography

CD 2: "Lies, I Don't Know What They Say But . . ." / "Underneath Everything" / "The Seed" / "Eyes of the South" / "Jail" / "Stone the Crow" / "Bury Me in Smoke"

SUPERJOINT RITUAL

Use Once and Destroy
Released 2002
Sanctuary
"Oblivious Maximus" / "It Takes No Guts" / "Everyone Hates Everyone" / "The Introvert" / "The Alcoholik" / "Fuck Your Enemy" / "4 Songs" / "Messages" / "All of Our Lives Will Get Tried" / "Antifaith" / "Ozena" / "Drug Your Love" / "Haunted Hated" / "Stupid, Stupid Man" / "Creepy Crawl" / "Superjoint Ritual" / "Starvation Trip"* / "Little H"*
Bonus tracks on the first 10,000 copies sold

A Lethal Dose of American Hatred
Released 2003
Sanctuary
"Sickness" / "Waiting for the Turning Point" / "Dress Like a Target" / "The Destruction of a Person" / "Personal Insult" / "Never to Sit or Stand Again" / "Death Threat" / "Permanently" / "Stealing a Page or Two from Armed & Radical Pagans" / "Symbol of Nevermore" / "The Knife Rises" / "The Horror" / "Absorbed"

HELLYEAH

Hellyeah
Released 2007
Epic
"Hellyeah" / "You Wouldn't Know" / "Matter of Time" / "Waging War" / "Alcohaulin' Ass" / "Goddamn" / "In the Mood" / "Star" / "Rotten to the Core" / "Thank You" / "Nausea" / "One Thing"

Discography

Stampede
Released 2010
Epic
"Cowboy Way" / "Debt That All Men Pay" / "Hell of a Time" / "Stampede" / "Better Man" / "It's On!" / "Pole Rider" / "Cold as a Stone" / "Stand or Walk Away" / "Alive and Well" / "Order the Sun"

SOURCES

The following publications and websites were integral in making this book possible. A special thanks goes to *Guitar World* and *Kerrang!*.

REFERENCE TEXTS

Betts, Graham. *Complete U.K. Hit Singles 1952–2005*. London: Collins, 2005.

Betts, Graham. *Complete U.K. Hit Albums: 1956–2005*. London: Collins, 2005.

Larkin, Colin. *The Virgin Encyclopaedia of Rock*. London: Virgin Books, 1999.

Roberts, David, ed. *British Hit Singles & Albums*. 19th ed. London: Guinness World Records Ltd., 2006.

Strong, Martin C. *The Great Rock Discography*. 6th ed. London: Canongate, 2002.

BOOKS ON METAL

Christe, Ian. *Sound of the Beast: The Complete Headbanging History of Heavy Metal*. London: Allison & Busby Limited, 2004.

Konow, David. *Bang Your Head: The Rise and Fall of Heavy Metal*. London: Plexus, 2004.

Popoff, Martin. *The Collector's Guide to Heavy Metal—Volume 2: The Eighties*. Collector's Guide Publishing: Toronto, 2005.

Popoff, Martin. *The Collector's Guide to Heavy Metal—Volume 3: The Nineties*. Collector's Guide Publishing: Toronto, 2007.

Popoff, Martin and Perri, David. *The Collector's Guide to Heavy Metal—Volume 4: The '00s*. Collector's Guide Publishing: Toronto, 2011.

Sharpe-Young, Gary. *Thrash Metal*. London: Zonda Books, 2007.

BIOGRAPHIES/AUTOBIOGRAPHIES

McIver, Joel. *Metallica: And Justice for All*. 3rd ed. London: Omnibus Press, 2009.

McIver, Joel. *The Bloody Reign of Slayer*. London: Omnibus Press, 2008.

Mustaine, Dave. *A Life in Metal*. New York: HarperCollins, 2010.

BOOKS ON PANTERA

Armold, Chris. *A Vulgar Display of Power: Courage and Carnage at the Alrosa Villa*. MJS Music & Entertainment LLC: Florida, 2007.

Crain, Zak. *Black Tooth Grin: The High Life, Good Times and Tragic End of Dimebag Darrell Abbott*. New York: DaCapo Press, 2009.

Doll, Susan and Morrow, David. *He Came to Rock*. Texas: Big Vin Records, 2008.

MAGAZINES

Alternative Press
Classic Rock
Guitar World
Kerrang!
Melody Maker
Metal Edge
Metal Hammer

Sources

NME
Q
Revolver
Rolling Stone

ARTICLES

Akin, Chris. "Celebrating 20 Years of Cowboys from Hell: A Conversation with Philip Anselmo." *Addicted to Vinyl*, August 28, 2010. http://addictedtovinyl.com/blog/2010/08/28/philip-anselmo-pantera-2010-interview/.

Arnopp, Jason. "American Psycho." *Kerrang!* 517 (October 22, 1994): 59–62.

Arnopp, Jason. "Beer! Money! Dope! Black Metal!" *Kerrang!* 512 (September 17, 1994): 38–42.

Bonyata, Tony. "Exclusive Interview with Pantera's Bassist Rex Brown." *ConcertLivewire*, July 21, 2000. http://www.concertlivewire.com/interviews/pantera.htm.

Bowcott, Nick. "Dimebag Darrell Discusses Pantera's 1996 Album, *The Great Southern Trendkill*." *Guitar World*, February 1996. Posted on GuitarWorld.com January 22, 2013. http://www.guitarworld.com/archive-dimebag-darrell-discusses-panteras-1996-album-great-southern-trendkill.

D, Spence. "Pantera Interview." *IGN Formen*, September 5, 2002. Reposted on *IGN* December 13, 2004. http://www.ign.com/articles/2004/12/14/pantera-interview.

Devenish, Colin. "Anselmo Mourns Dimebag." *Rolling Stone*, December 16, 2004. http://www.rollingstone.com/music/news/anselmo-mourns-dimebag-20041216.

Doreian, Robyn. "Clash of the Titans." *Kerrang!* 418 (November 14, 1992): 46–49.

Sources

Douglas, E. Patrick. "Pantera/Down—Philip Anselmo." *The Culture Shock*, September 27, 2010. http://www.thecultureshock.com/index.php?option=com_content&task=view&id=961&Itemid=49.

Edney, Cameron. "Interview with Vinnie Paul of Hellyeah, Pantera, Damageplan." SoundwaveTouring.com, June 2010. http://www.soundwavetouring.com/artists/hellyeah/.

Everley, Dave. "Bustle Their Hedgerow." *Metal Hammer* 227 (February 2012): 44–53.

Ferris, D. X. "Workaholic from Hell." *Alternative Press* (August 2002).

Firecloud, Johnny. "Phil Anselmo of Arson Anthem." *Crave Online*, January 23, 2011. http://www.craveonline.com/music/interviews/130190-phil-anselmo-of-arson-anthem-down.

Florino, Rick. "Interview: Philip Anselmo." *ArtistDirect*, September 13, 2012. http://www.artistdirect.com/nad/news/article/0,,10230311,00.html.

Garza, Janiss. "They Love It Loud." *Yahoo! Music*, April 24, 2000. http://music.uk.launch.yahoo.com/read/interview/12052754.

Geist, Brandon. "By Demons Be Driven." *Revolver* (February 2005).

Gill, Chris. "Dimebag's Ex Blames Phil Anselmo for His Murder." *Guitar World*, March 2008. Posted on GuitarWorld.com January 7, 2008. http://www.guitarworld.com/dimebag-s-ex-blames-phil-anselmo-his-murder.

Gitter, Mike. "New Metal Gods . . ." *Kerrang!* 483 (February 23, 1993): 40–44.

Gropp, Joshua. "Dimebag Darrell Interview." *Guitar World*, March 2004. Posted on GuitarWorld.com December 8, 2009. http://www.guitarworld.com/dimebag-darrell-regular-people.

Herzog, Kenny. "Pantera's Phil Anselmo Talks Demons and the Legacy of Dimebag Darrell." *MMN*, September 19, 2010. http://mogmusicnetwork.com/mmn-exclusive-interview-pantera-s-phil-anselmo-talks-demons-and-the-legacy-of-dimebag-darrell-11703. (Dead link.)

Sources

Joy, Shannon. "Interview with Phil Anselmo of Down." *L.A. Music Blog*, July 8, 2010. http://lamusicblog.com/2010/07/interview/interview-with-phil-anselmo-of-down/.

Kerby, Jeff. "New Found Power: From the Fall—Vinnie Paul Interview." *KNAC*, December 9, 2004. http://www.knac.com/article.asp?ArticleID=3056.

Krovatin, Christopher. "Interview: Former Pantera and Down Bassist Rex Brown on His New Band, Kill Devil Hill, and Upcoming Book." *Revolver*, November 15, 2011. http://www.revolvermag.com/news/exclusive-interview-rex-brown-on-his-new-band-and-upcoming-book.html.

Levin, Elliot. "Pantera's *Cowboys from Hell* Turns 20: An Interview with Philip Anselmo." *Examiner*, November 16, 2010. http://www.examiner.com/article/pantera-s-cowboys-from-hell-turns-20-an-interview-with-philip-anselmo-part-2.

Marshall, Brandon. "*Sonic Excess* Interviews Rex Brown of Down." *Sonic Excess*, March 12, 2013. http://www.sonicexcess.com/rex_brown_interview_2013.html/Rex_int.html.

McDonald, Keith. "Interview with Pantera's Vinnie Paul." *Metal Rules*, January 26, 2001. http://www.metal-rules.com/interviews/Pantera_VinniePaul.htm.

McKeon, Therese. "Pantera: Reinventing the Metal." *Shoutweb*, 2000. Reposted to Melissa's Page on Angelfire.com. http://www.angelfire.com/art/My333/interview7.html.

Metal Odyssey. "Phil Anselmo—The Hard Rock Hideout Interview." *Hard Rock Hideout*, September 20, 2010. http://hardrockhideout.com/2010/09/20/phil-anselmo-the-hard-rock-hideout-interviewl/.

Miller, Gerri. "Vinnie Paul on the Line." *Metal Edge* (November 1995): 12–13, 79.

Mörat. "Attitude Adjustment." *Kerrang!* 412 (October 3, 1992): 36–39.

Mörat. "F_king Hostile." *Kerrang!* 430 (February 13, 1993): 42–45.

Mörat. "Beyond Hostile!." *Kerrang!* 484 (March 5, 1994): 38–41.

Newquist, H. P. "Dimebag Darrell: A Cowboy from Hell." *Guitar Magazine* (1995). Posted on GuitarInternational.com

August 20, 2010. http://guitarinternational.com/2010/08/20/diamond-dimebag-darrell-the-pantera-interview/.

Norton, M. Justin. "Phil Anselmo Interview: A Conversation with the Housecore Records Founder and Down Singer." HeavyMetalAbout.com, last modified March 25, 2010. http://heavymetal.about.com/od/interviews/a/philanselmointerview.htm.

Pacheco, George. "Phil Anselmo Talks Housecore, Horror, the Media and More . . ." *Metal Army America*, March 24, 2010. http://www.metalarmyamerica.com/?p=1828.

Perlah, Jeff. "Hell Onstage." *Electronic Musician*, January 10, 2008. http://www.emusician.com/features-interviews/0777/hell-on-stage/140379.

Previ, Dave. "Vinnie Paul: Exclusive ModernDrummer.com Interview." *Modern Drummer*, July 15, 2010. http://www.moderndrummer.com/site/2010/07/vinnie-paul-2/.

Rafi, "Interview with Phil Anselmo." VampireFreaks.com, March 15, 2010. http://vampirefreaks.com/content/comment.php?entry=455.

Ramirez, Ramsey. "Hell Yeah: Vinnie Paul Interview." *Magx Online* (2010).

Rosen, Steven. "Phil Anselmo: 'Extreme Music Has Been Kind to Me: Give It Back." *Ultimate Guitar*, December 20, 2010. http://www.ultimate-guitar.com/interviews/interviews/phil_anselmo_extreme_music_has_been_kind_to_me_give_back.html?no_takeover.

Salamon, Jeff. "Vinnie Paul Abbott." *Texas Monthly*, 2010. Accessed April 23, 2013. http://www.texasmonthly.com/story/vinnie-paul-abbott.

Sciarretto, Amy. "Phil Anselmo Interview: Pantera Singer Relaunches Label, Celebrates Cowboys from Hell." *Noisecreep*, March 3, 2010. http://www.noisecreep.com/2010/03/03/phil-anselmo-interview-pantera-singer-relaunches-label-celebra/.

Scott, Roger. "Interview with Vinnie Paul of Pantera." *NYRock*, October 1997. Accessed April 24, 2013. http://www.nyrock.com/pantera_int.htm.

Seagle, Debbie. "Pantera Interview." *antiMusic*, 2000. Accessed April 24, 2013. http://www.antimusic.com/reviews/11/Flashback-_Pantera_Interview.shtml.

Sharken, Lisa. "Dimebag Darrell: Reinventing the Steel with the SH-13 Dimebucker." SeymourDuncan.com, February 9, 2007. http://www.seymourduncan.com/blog/artist-interview/dimebag-darrell-of-pantera/.

Sindell, Joshua. "Ritual Slaughter." *Kerrang!* (June 29, 2002).

Skwerl. "On Marches Philip Anselmo." *Antiquiet*, November 24, 2008. http://www.antiquiet.com/interviews/2008/11/phil-anselmo-interview/.

Stander, Tazz. "Vinnie Paul—Hellyeah—Interview Exclusive." *Über Röck*, July 13, 2010. http://www.uberrock.co.uk/interviews/58-july-interviews/1088-vinnie-paul-hellyeah-interview-exclusive.html.

Steinle, Cindy. "Interview: Hellyeah's Tom Maxwell and Vinnie Paul." *Club Kingsnake*, July 25, 2007. http://club.kingsnake.com/index.php?/archives/498-Interview-Hellyeahs-Tom-Maxwell-and-Vinnie-Paul.html.

Tolinski, Brad. "Dimebag Darrell Discusses His Roots, Gear and Pantera in 1994 Guitar Interview." *Guitar World* (April 1994). Posted on GuitarWorld.com November 1, 2011. http://www.guitarworld.com/dimebag-darrell-discusses-his-roots-gear-and-pantera-1994-guitar-world-interview.

Wellwood, Jason. "Phil Anselmo: The Hellbound Interview." *Hellbound*, November 12, 2010. http://www.hellbound.ca/2010/11/phil-anselmo-the-hellbound-interview/.

Wilson, David Lee. "Interview with Vinnie Paul of Pantera." *KAOS2000 Magazine*, 2000. Accessed April 24, 2013. http://www.kaos2000.net/interviews/pantera/.

Winwood, Ian. "Hard for Life!" *Metal Hammer* (September 1994): 19–22.

Vox. "Interviews—Pantera." *Vox*, 2001.

Zahn, James. "Exclusive: Rex Brown Talks 20 Years of Cowboys from Hell and the Legacy of Pantera." *Kik Axe Music*, September 15, 2010.

Reposted on Down-Nola.com. Accessed April 24, 2013. http://www.down-nola.com/index.cfm/pk/view/cd/naa/cdid/440022/pid/400042.

WEBSITES

addictedtovinyl.com
antimusic.com
artistdirect.com
bbc.co.uk/music
classicrockmusicblog.com
club.kingsnake.com
concertlivewire.com
cmj.com
craveonline.com
thecultureshock.com
emusician.com
ew.com
examiner.com
heavymetal.about.com
hellbound.ca
kaos2000.net
kerrang.com
kikaxemusic.com
lamusicblog.com
marshallofrock.com
magxonline.com
metal-army.com
metal-rules.com
mogmusicnetwork.com
nme.com
noisecreep.com
nyrock.com
seymourduncan.com

Sources

sonicexcess.com
soundwavetouring.com
uberrock.co.uk
uk.music.ign.com
ultimate-guitar.com
vampirefreaks.com
voxonline.com

INDEX

Abbott, Carolyn, 4, 11, 20, 24, 161, 198
Abbott, Darrell, 3–13, 15–21, 23–27, 31–51, 55, 57, 58–59, 62, 63–65, 67, 69, 73–79, 82–88, 91–92, 94–95, 98–100, 104–108, 111–112, 116–117, 123–125, 135, 150, 155, 157–158, 162, 172–173, 179–180, 182, 187–188, 190–192, 194–198, 201, 205–208, 214, 219, 224–229
Abbott, Jerry, 4–7, 12, 17–20, 23, 25, 31, 35, 41, 48, 50, 61, 77, 85–86, 116, 192, 195
Abbott, Vinnie, 3, 4, 10–13, 15–19, 23, 26, 31, 34, 36, 43–44, 47, 49, 53–54, 57, 59, 63, 65, 70, 74–77, 87, 91, 96–98, 100, 104, 105, 107, 115, 117, 120, 123–125, 127, 136, 138–139, 141, 145, 147, 149, 150, 156–163, 166, 170–171, 173–174, 177, 179–185, 188, 191, 193, 196, 199–200, 202, 205–206, 226–229
Accept, 44, 46
AC/DC, 6, 12, 46, 76, 101, 118, 141, 152, 207
Ace of Base, 120
"Ace of Spades," 109
Adair, Daniel, 199
Adams, Eric, 108
Addicted to Vinyl, 73, 112, 225

Aerosmith, 27, 124
"Aesthetics of Hate," 199
Agnostic Front, 93
"Ain't Talkin' 'Bout Love," 207
Akin, Chris, 73, 112
Alice Cooper, 33
Alice in Chains, 103, 138, 157, 180, 191, 200–201, 207
Aldridge, Tommy, 10
Alive!, 55, 152
Alive II, 152
Alive/Worldwide (tour), 150
Alive and Hostile E.P., 120, 201, 217
All Music, 32, 63
"All Over Tonight," 26, 36, 41, 213
All the Right Reasons, 199
Alter Bridge, 199
Alternative Press, 154, 166, 224, 226
Anal Cunt, 137
And Justice for All, 86
Andrews, Jayne, 100
Angelo, Michael Batio, 89
Angelus Apatrida, 89
Annhilator, 95–96, 98, 99, 175
Anselmo, Phil, 3, 53–55, 58–59, 61, 73, 75, 82, 85, 97, 103–105, 107, 109, 112, 115–116, 122, 125–127, 138, 140, 142, 146, 154–155, 160, 163, 181, 187, 190–191, 200, 203, 206–208, 226–229

233

Index

Anthrax, 27, 40–41, 44, 66, 93, 153–154, 191–192, 196, 199–201, 206–207
AntiMusic, 51, 150, 160, 171, 229, 230
Antiquiet, 204, 229
Apartment 26, 170
Apocalyptica, 89
April Wine, 12, 26
Armold, Chris, 190, 224
Arnopp, Jason, 90, 104, 106–107, 118, 123, 125, 128, 225
"Art of Shredding, The," 55, 89, 94, 101, 214
Arlington Convention Center, 191
Asterix, 124
Atco Records, 74–75, 83, 104, 142, 214
Atlantic Records, 218
Avenged Sevenfold, 199
Azra Records, 28

Bach, Sebastian, 154
"Badge, The," 120, 215–217
"Bang Your Head," 26
Banished Rhythmic Hate, 155
Bansal, Vik, 177, 179, 183
Barnes, Aaron, 171
Basement, the, 74, 76, 88
Battye, Andy, 99
BBC Music, 89
Bear Creek, 77
Beatles, the, 40, 54
"Becoming," 118, 120, 152, 177, 214–218
Behind the Music, 200
Bell, Randy, 34, 192
Benante, Charlie, 191, 192
"Best Metal Performance," 120, 154, 166
Best of Pantera: Far Beyond the Great Southern Cowboys' Vulgar Hits!, The, 183, 216

Between the Buried and Me, 89, 200
"Big Dumb Sex," 104
Big Val, 110, 142–143, 170
Big Vin Records, 224
Big Wheel Skating Rink, 34
"Biggest Part of Me," 18, 213
Billboard, 88, 108, 120–122, 139, 165–166, 183
Biohazard, 93, 126, 146, 176
Black, Bobby, 191, 202
Black Album, The, 86
Black Crowes, the, 101
"Black Diamond," 19
Black Flag, 90
Black Label Society, 170, 191, 197, 199–200
Black Metal, 55
Black 'N Blue, 33
Black Sabbath, 5, 15, 40–42, 44, 54, 57, 86, 110, 117, 119, 151, 154, 159–162, 165–166, 184, 197, 206–207
Black Tooth Grin, 172
Blaze, Buddy, 7, 8, 18
Blaze, Steve, 56
"Blind in Texas," 44
Blistering, 175
Blizzard of Ozz, 6
Blowphish, 107
"Blue Light Turnin'," 25, 213
Bon Jovi, 33, 40, 64, 74, 76
Bond, Kevin, 180
Bonded by Blood, 28
Bonham John, 10
Bono, 57
Bonyata, Tony, 169
Boss Tweed, 28–29
Boston, 11
Bowcott, Nick, 135, 137, 155
Boydstun, Michael, 219
Bradford, Tommy, 3, 12–14, 196

234

Index

Bray, Nathan, 189
Brides of Destruction, 200
British Steel, 166
Broadrick, Justin K., 109
Bronco Bowl, 34, 37
Brown, Rex, 15, 20, 38, 45, 47, 51, 75, 81, 83–84, 111, 119, 139, 145, 150, 156, 160, 169, 172, 175, 181, 183, 200–202, 207, 225, 227, 229
Buckethead, 199
Buffy the Vampire Slayer, 99
Bullet for My Valentine, 89
Bulldozer, 60
Buras, Will, 53
"Burn," 41
Burnett, Travis, 189
"Burnnn!," 214
Butler, Geezer, 151
"By Demons Be Driven," 107, 152, 214, 217

Cale, J. J., 6
Campbell, Vivian, 8
Cantrell, Jerry, 138, 180, 191, 198, 200–201
Captain D's, 21
Carajo, 200
Carbonneau, Guy, 161
Carriage House, the, 85
Cat Daiquiri, 78
"Cat Scratch Fever," 161, 184, 216
Cavalera, Max, 126, 201
"Cemetery Gates," 73, 84–86, 88–89, 94, 96, 101, 109, 152, 154, 216–217, 219
Ceravolo, Jay, 92
Champion, Grady, 78, 93, 101, 171
Chapman, Mark David, 188
Chasin Jason Studios, 136, 152, 162
Cheap Trick, 33, 40

"Children of the Sea," 42
Christ Inversion, 180
Cinderella, 33, 68, 76
Circle and the Square, 54
Clapton, Eric, 6, 9
"Clash with Reality," 85, 101, 201, 214
Classic Rock Music Blog, 121
Classic Rock, 166, 224
Clutch, 149
Coal Chamber, 151, 153–154
Coe, Allen David, 6, 156, 200
"Cold Gin," 113
"Come-on Eyes," 32, 214
ConcertLivewire, 169, 225
Concrete Management, 76
Coors Light, 47
Cornell, Chris, 84
Corrosion of Conformity, 174
Countdown to Extinction, 110
Counter, David, 29
Cowboys & Idiots (tour), 101
Cowboys from Hell, 74, 76, 81, 83, 85–91, 93, 102, 107–108, 120–122, 137, 140, 153, 162, 163, 169, 184, 201–202, 214, 225, 227–229
"Cowboys from Hell," 82–83, 88, 94, 96, 101, 109, 151, 152, 169, 177, 214–217
Cowboys from Hell: The Demos, 101, 201
Cowboys from Hell: The Videos, 89, 157, 218–219
Criss, Peter, 10, 95
Cross Canadian Ragweed, 199
Crown Royal, 125, 172
Crow, The, 120
Crowbar, 53, 123, 180, 184, 200
Crowley, Aleister, 155
Crowley, Anton, 155
"Crushing Day," 65

Index

D, Spence, 146, 161, 173, 225
"D*G*T*T*M (Darrell Goes to the Movies)," 214
Dallas Stars: Greatest Hits, 161
Dalworthington Gardens, 172, 198
"Damage, Inc.," 38
Damageplan, 181, 184–185, 188–189, 199, 226
Dangerous Toys, 50
Danzig, Glenn, 55
Darkthrone, 155
Darin, Bobby, 75
Date, Terry, 83, 84, 86, 105, 116, 122, 136, 162
"Daughters of the Queen," 32, 214
Davis, Jonathan, 197
Davis, Kim, 202
Day on the Green, 39
"Dazed and Confused," 41
Dead Green Mummies, the, 63
Deadlights, the, 170
Deaf Gods of Babylon, 42, 74
Dean ML, 7–9, 137
"Dean from Hell," 8, 9
"Death Rattle," 165, 215
"Death Trap," 59, 63, 65, 214
Deep Purple, 5, 41, 207
Def Leppard, 5, 41, 207
Default, 180
Deftones, 142, 159, 162, 174
Destroyer, 57
Detroit Rock City, 161, 184
Dez Fefara, 93
Diamond Head, 27, 28
Dickinson, Bruce, 25, 43, 57
Dio, Ronnie James, 42, 57, 207
Dio, Wendy, 207
Dirkschneider, Udo, 44
Disturbed, 170, 199, 207
Dittmar, John, 101, 160, 188, 206–207
Divine Intervention, 126

Dokken, 15, 33, 64
"Dom/Hollow," 152, 215
Dome, Malcolm, 166
"Domination," 85, 89, 96, 100, 101, 109, 11, 113, 151, 152, 214–215
Doreian, Robyn, 56, 111, 116, 140, 225
Douglas, Patrick E., 61, 206, 226
Down, 136, 139, 146, 155, 159, 180, 181, 183, 185, 191, 200, 202, 219, 220
"Down Below," 32, 61, 214
Down II: A Bustle in Your Hedgerow
Down II: A Bustle in Your Hedgerow, 180, 220, 226
Downing, K. K., 99
Downset, 127, 151
"Drag the Waters," 138, 139, 154, 215–216, 218–219
Drain STH, 151
Dream Theater, 84, 89, 200
Driven Downunder Tour '94—Souvenir Collection, 120, 216
Drowning Pool, 156, 199
Drop-D Magazine, 144
Duperre, Damon, 28

EastWest Records, 139, 162, 214–215
Edmonton Sun, 175
Edney, Cameron, 120, 145
Eld'n, The, 17, 195
"Electric Eye," 51
"Electric Funeral," 161
Electronic Musician, 26, 150, 173, 228
Elektra Records, 76, 162
Elliott, Joe, 25
"Enema," 154
Entertainment Weekly, 109
Entombed, 154
"Eruption," 25, 41

Index

Esquibell, Ambrose, 35–36, 77–78, 94
Evanescence, 200
Everley, Dave, 105, 202
Evile, 89, 199
Examiner, 89, 94, 109, 164, 205, 227
Exhorder, 60, 90–93, 197
Exodus, 93–94, 157
Exorcist, The, 105
Extreme, 124
Extreme Steel (tour), 175
EyeHateGod, 142, 203

Facebook, 82
Fall from Grace, 53
Fastway, 24
Fear Factory, 137, 151, 154
Fenriz, 155
Ferrari, Marc, 60, 63
Ferris, D.X., 154–155
Fight, 97
"Fight Fire with Fire," 41
Firebird, 7, 9
"5 Minutes Alone," 118, 120, 142, 151, 152, 154, 174, 177, 214–218
"Floods," 137–140, 215, 218
Florentine, Jim, 207
Floyd Rose, 8
Foetus, 109
Foo Fighters, 154
Forced Entry, 47
"Forever Tonight," 32, 214
Frampton, Peter, 27, 57
Frampton Comes Alive, 57
Frehley, Ace, 5, 6, 10, 13, 19, 32, 74, 95, 200
Friedman, Marty, 74, 116
"Fucking Hostile," 107, 109, 126, 151–152, 177, 199, 207, 214–217

Gale, Nathan, 188, 190
Gammacide, 29, 38, 59, 68, 69
Gasoline, 156
Gazzarri's, 42
Geist, Brandon, 130, 191, 203
Gentle Giant, 76
"Get Drunk Now," 156
Get Rude, 90
Gibbons, Billy, 6, 139
Gill, Chris, 182, 191
Gillette, William, 190
"Girls Got Rhythm," 207
Giron, Joe, 36, 101, 129
Gitter, Mike, 77, 101
Glaze, Terry, 3, 12, 13, 15–16, 25–27, 31, 40, 43, 47, 50–51, 58, 61, 68, 74, 107, 188, 195
Glória, 89
"Goddamn Electric," 165, 177, 215–216, 218
Godflesh, 109
Gods of Metal, 154
Godsmack, 170
Gold Mountain Records, 60, 61
"Golden God Awards," 206
"Good Friends and a Bottle of Pills," 117, 119, 214, 217
"Good Friends and a Bottle of Wine," 117
"Goodbye to Romance," 65
Grace King High School, 54
Grammy, 120, 138, 154, 166
Great Southern Trendkill, The, 136, 137, 138, 139, 140, 142, 147, 161, 163, 164, 165, 167, 184, 215, 225
"Green Manalishi," 69
"Grinder," 95, 105
Gromaskas, Thomas, 54
Gropp, Joshua, 15, 226
Guitar Magazine, 88, 123, 227
Guitar World, 109, 116, 135, 137, 140, 145, 155, 172, 182, 191, 223–226, 229
Guns 'N Roses, 66, 199, 207

Index

Hagar, Sammy, 26, 149, 193
Haggard, Merle, 6
Halford, Rob, 25, 44, 57, 61, 83, 85, 87, 95–97, 108, 112–113, 157, 181, 191
Halk, Erin, 189
Haney, Rita, 5, 37–38, 182, 191–192, 199, 205
"Hard Lines, Sunken Cheeks," 119, 153, 214, 217
"Hard Ride," 65, 214
Hard Rock Hideout, 103, 115, 127, 227
Harris, Steve, 201
Harris, Thomas, 116
Hart, Donny, 3, 4 12, 13, 20, 49
Hatebreed, 201, 207
Heavy Medows, 28, 34
"Heavy Metal Rules," 41, 213
Hed PE, 154
"Hell Bound," 165, 177
Hellbound, 204, 215, 229
Hellhammer, 55, 56
Hellyeah, 185, 200–201, 221, 226, 229
"Hellion, The," 51
Henderson, Bugs, 6
Hendrix, Jimi, 9
"Heresy," 85, 94, 101, 109, 214, 217
Herzog, Kenny, 68, 142, 187, 206–207, 226
Hetfield, James, 26–27, 38, 40, 62, 82, 99
Hetrick, Gary, 5, 10, 36–37, 47, 51, 58, 77
High Times, 191, 202
Hobbs Angel, 60
"Hole in the Sky," 184, 216
"Hollow," 107–109, 151, 152, 214–218
Hollywood Palladium, 147
Holmes, Chris, 39

Holocausto de la Morte, 155
Hostile Mixes, 109
"Hot and Heavy," 214, 36, 65
House of Blues, 199
Housecore Records, 204, 228
Hughes, Howard, 203
Human Waste Project, 154
Hurricane Hugo, 74
Hurricane Katrina, 54

I Am the Night, 31, 32–33, 35, 37, 44, 64, 87, 213
"I Am the Night," 214
"I Can't Hide," 153, 215
"I Don't Know," 65
Ian, Scott, 196, 201
If You Want Blood ... You've Got It, 152
IGN, 161, 173, 225
"I'll Be Alright," 18–19, 213
"I'll Cast a Shadow," 164–166, 215–216, 218
"I'm Broken," 116, 119–120, 152, 154, 214–219
"In Over My Head," 213
Incubus, 159, 170
Inez, Mike, 191
Innocence from Hell, 155
Iommi, Tony, 86, 98, 151
Iron Maiden, 27, 28, 44, 57, 110, 201, 207
Iron Tyrants, 28
Isham, Wayne, 219
"It Makes Them Disappear," 165, 215

James Bowie High, 4
James, Elmore, 208
James, Jimmy, 34, 36
Jamieson, Don, 207
Jasta, Jamey, 201
Joel, Mitch, 127

Index

Joe's Garage, 46, 69
John, Elton, 181
Joplin, Janis, 205
Jose Cuervo, 47
Joy, Shannon, 202
Judas Priest, 12, 26–27, 37, 44, 46, 51, 55, 57, 61, 63–64, 67, 87, 95–97, 101, 109, 110, 113, 119, 166, 197

Karpelman, Ross, 139, 180
Keel, 60, 63–64
Kerby, Jeff, 23, 31, 156, 170, 181
Kerrang!, 29, 54, 56, 67, 77, 90, 101, 104, 106, 110–111, 116–118, 121, 123–125, 128, 144–147, 166, 175, 197, 204, 225–227, 229
Kerslake, Kevin, 219
Kid Rock, 181
Kik Axe Music, 200, 207, 229
Kill 'Em All, 39
"Killers," 25, 213
Killjoy, 155
Killswitch Engage, 207
King Crimson, 54
King, Kenny, 24, 35, 49, 59, 77
King, Kerry, 40, 66, 67, 113, 116, 157, 165, 201
King's X, 6, 86
Kittie, 170, 173
Kiss, 3, 5, 10, 12, 13, 15, 18–19, 26–27, 33, 37, 40, 44, 55, 57, 74, 95, 113, 137, 150–152, 166, 192–194, 197, 208
Kiss Kasket, 192–194
KISS Meets the Phantom of the Park, 193
Kleinberg, Steve, 76, 101
KNAC, 23, 31, 156, 170, 181, 227
Korn, 197, 200, 207
Kramer, 8, 84
Krisiun, 200

Kroeger, Chad, 180, 199
Krovatin, Christopher, 202, 227
Kurz, Jules, 74

L'Amour, Matt, 42–43, 49
L.A. Guns, 76
L.A. Music Blog, 202, 227
Lachman, Pat, 181, 191, 199
Larrabee Sound Studios, 136
"Latest Lover," 18, 213
LaVey, Anton, 155
Law, The, 92–93
"Law Enforcement Officer of the Year Award," 189
Lawless, Blackie, 39
"Lay It Down," 51
Led Zeppelin, 4, 41, 92, 166
Lennon, John, 188
Les Paul, 5
Life of Agony, 154
"Lifer," 220
"Light Comes out of Black," 97
"Like Fire," 213
Lillian Axe, 56–57
Limp Bizkit, 174, 207
Linkin Park, 174
"Live in a Hole," 107, 214
"Living Through Me (Hell's Wrath)," 138, 215
Lizzy Borden, 63
Lombardo, Dave, 66
Lopez, Lenise, 37–39, 198
Lord, Tracy, 42, 74, 107
Lost Cities (tour), 150
Lynch, George, 64

Machine Head, 137, 151, 153, 199, 207
"Mack the Knife," 75
"Madhouse," 41, 44
Magx Online, 3, 149, 228
Mama's Boys, 36

Index

Maniac, 155
Manowar, 108
Manson, Marilyn, 151
Marshall, Brandon, 201, 227
Marshall of Rock, 205
Master of Puppets, 39, 86
Masterdisk, 85, 105, 162
Matthews, Sean, 181
Matley's Phase II, 46
Maxwell, Tom, 185, 225
Mayhem (band), 155
McDonald, Keith, 54, 70, 139, 162, 173, 174
McKeon, Theresa, 159, 160, 163, 227
McMaster, Jason, 50
"Medicine Man," 85, 214
Megadeth, 27, 39–40, 66, 74, 83, 110–111, 116, 159, 172, 197, 207
Melody Maker, 121, 140
Menza, Nick, 74
Mercyful Fate, 57
"Message in Blood," 85, 94, 101, 199, 214
Metal Army, 204, 228
Metal Asylum, 81, 83, 84
Metal Blade Records, 28, 212
Metal Church, 76, 84,
Metal Circus, 44
Metal Edge, 138, 141, 227
Metal Forces, 29, 33, 60, 67, 145
"Metal Gods," 69, 95, 109
Metal Hammer, 105, 127, 140, 190, 202, 226, 229
Metal Health, 26
"Metal Magic," 18
Metal Magic, 17, 18, 25, 32, 213
Metal Magic Records, 25, 213–214
Metal Maniacs, 92
Metal Odyssey, 103, 115, 127, 227
Metal-Rules, 54, 70, 139, 162, 173–174, 227
Metal Works, 69

Metallica, 26–28, 32, 37–40, 44, 47, 49, 57, 62, 65–66, 79, 82, 86, 99, 101, 103, 109, 113, 147, 160, 201, 206–207
Metallica, 86
Methods of Mayhem, 170
Miller, Gerri, 138, 141, 227
Milton Keynes Bowl, 154
Mind Over Four, 93
Minority, 142, 144
"Mob Rules, The," 41
Moffitt, Greg, 89
Molly Maguire's, 34
Monster Magnet, 160
Monsters in Moscow, 157
Monsters of Rock, 101, 110, 124
Montz, Sid, 180
Moon, Keith, 10
Moorcock, Michael, 19
Moore Memorial Gardens Cemetary, 198
Mörat, 54, 110–111, 121, 124–125, 128, 144, 146, 161, 187–188, 227
Morbid Angel, 173–175
"More Than a Feeling," 11
Morrison, Jim, 205
"Most Valuable Player," 172
Motörhead, 109, 117, 126, 152
"Mouth for War," 106–107, 109, 113, 153, 174, 177, 207, 214, 216–218
Mötley Crüe, 26, 33, 101, 171
MMN, 68, 142, 187, 206–207, 226
MTV, 77, 88, 92, 121–122, 127, 145
Mudvayne, 200, 201
Muertos, Michael de los, 174
MusicOMH, 177, 179, 183
Mustaine, Dave, 74, 111, 197
Mythiasan, Rick, 43–46, 49

Nail, Chris, 91
National Rifle Association, 189

Index

Nativity in Black II, 161
Necrophagia, 155
Neil, Vince, 25
Neurosis, 146, 149, 151
Nevermind, 103
New Found Power, 181
New Found Power, 189, 219
"New Found Power," 188, 219
New Heavy Metal Revue, The, 28
"New Level, A," 106, 151, 199, 207, 214, 215, 217
New Wave of British Heavy Metal (NWOBHM), 27, 29
New York Dolls, 33
Newquist, HP, 88, 123, 227
Nickelback, 180, 199
Niggemeyer, John D., 189, 191
Night at the Opera, A, 55
Night Ranger, 33
Nine Inch Nails (NIN) 136
1984 (Van Halen), 26
1990–2000: A Decade of Domination, 201, 216
Nirvana, 103, 142
NME, 169
"No Good (Attack the Radical)," 107, 214
"No Remorse," 65
No Sleep 'Till Hammersmith, 152
Noisecreep, 105, 205, 228
NOLA, 136, 146, 155, 219
Norman, Max, 83
Norton, Justin M., 205, 228
"Nothin' On (But the Radio)," 18, 213
Nothing Studios, 136
Nothingface, 174, 185, 200
Nugent, Ted, 27, 117, 156, 161, 184
"Number of the Beast, The," 28, 44
Nunenmacher, Craig, 197
NYRock, 17, 117, 150, 228

O'Brien, Walter, 76, 83, 98, 101, 122, 136, 143, 157, 172, 184, 188, 190
Official Live: 101 Proof, 152–154, 162, 215
Ojeda, Eddie, 8
Olivenbaum, Scott, 175
Oliver, Derek, 101
On Through the Night, 6, 12
1001 Albums You Must Hear Before You Die, 109
"Onward We Rock!," 32, 214
Osbourne, Dusty, 23, 34–35
Osbourne, Ozzy, 57, 65, 83, 150–151, 154, 159, 170, 191, 197, 209
Osbourne, Sharon, 159, 160
"Out for Blood," 25, 213
Out of the Cellar, 26
"Over and Out," 63, 214
Overkill, 84
Ozzfest, 130, 150, 152, 154, 160, 165, 170–171, 173, 201, 208

"P*S*T*88," 63, 214
Painkiller, 95
Paluska, Chris, 189, 199
Pantego Sound, 7, 12, 17, 48, 59, 81–83, 85, 105, 136
Pantera's Metal Magic, 3, 4, 11, 12
Paranoid, 55
Patchin, Craig, 8
Peace Sells ... But Who's Buying?, 40
Peacock, Dave, 46–49, 60
Pearl Jam, 103
Peart, Neil, 10
Perlah, Jeff, 26, 150, 171, 173
Perry, Jennifer, 160
Perry, Rick, 29, 38, 59, 68–69
Pink Floyd, 201
"Piss," 206, 218
Pitchshifter, 154, 170
"Planet Caravan," 117, 119, 210, 142, 154, 218–219

241

Index

P.O.D., 170
Poison, 33, 64, 68
Poison Idea, 120
PolyGram Records, 74, 76
Polzin, Mark, 121
Popoff, Martin, 26, 153
Power Metal, 48, 61–64, 66–67, 70, 83, 86, 140, 214
"Power Metal," 214
Powerman 500, 151, 169
"Prehibernation Week," 74
Presley, Elvis, 205
Pride and Glory, 124
"Primal Concrete Sledge," 85, 91, 94, 96, 101, 109, 113, 142, 201, 214, 217
Primer 55, 170
Projects in the Jungle, 25, 27, 42, 44, 213
"Projects in the Jungle," 41, 213
Prong, 93, 126
"Proud to Be Loud," 63, 214
"Puck Off," 161
Pumpjack, 170
Puncture, 69
Putnam, Seth, 136
"Psycho Holiday," 85, 88, 94, 101, 214, 216–217, 219

Q, 109, 125
Queen, 27, 33, 55
Queens of the Stone Age, 170
Queensrÿche, 101
Quiet Riot, 6, 15, 26, 32–33, 70

Rachman, Paul, 108, 219
Rafi, 55, 66, 131, 228
Rage Against the Machine, 207
Rainbow, The, 39, 147
Raitt, Bonnie, 120
Ram It Down, 64
Ramirez, Ramsey, 3, 149, 228

Randall Amplifier, 24, 65, 69, 137
Ranch, The, 42
Ratt, 18, 26, 29, 33, 51, 63, 70
Razor White, 53, 55–57
Razor's Edge, The, 76
Red Dragon, 116
Red Velvet, 33
Reece, Mindy, 188
Rees, Paul, 124–125
"Regular People (Conceit)," 107, 214
Reign in Blood, 40, 59
"Reign in Blood," 66–67
Reinventing Hell: The Best of Pantera, 184, 216
Reinventing the Steel, 162–167, 179, 184, 215, 229
Rebel Meets Rebel, 156
Rebel Meets Rebel, 200
"(Reprise) Sandblasted Skin," 138, 215
Reveille, 170
Revolver, 130, 191, 202–203, 206, 226–227
"Revolution Is My Name," 165–166, 177, 215–216, 218–219
Revolution Is My Name, 184
Reznor, Trent, 136
Rhoads, Randy, 6, 64, 86
"Ride My Rocket," 18–19, 213
Ride the Lightning, 37, 39
"Right on the Edge," 32, 65, 214
Rigor Mortis, 29, 60, 68
Ripper, 200
"Rise," 107, 214, 217
Ritz, The, 93
Rivadavia, Eduardo, 19, 32, 63
Roadrunner Records, 122
Rock City, 124
Rock 'n' Roll Station, 198
"Rock Out," 18–19, 213
"Rock the World," 63, 214
Rolling Stone, 121, 166, 189, 197, 225

Rollins, Henry, 90, 108
Rosen, Steven, 58, 106, 208, 228
Ross, Mark, 74–76, 81
Ross, Mike, 175
Roth, David Lee, 42, 57
Rotting Corpse, 29, 57, 69, 82
"Run to the Hills," 44
Rush, 10

Sacred Reich, 110, 157
"Sad Lover," 18, 213
Samhain, 53, 55
Saso's Bar and Grill, 43
Satriani, Joe, 65
Satterfield, Sonny, 94
"Saturday Night's Alright (for Fighting)," 181
Satyricon, 155, 169
"Save Me," 199, 219
Savvy's, 34, 36, 38, 46, 58
Saxon, 27–29, 89
Scarsdale, 94
Schenker, Peter, 6
Sciarretto, Amy, 105, 205, 228
Scorpions, 6, 44, 57
Scott, Roger, 17, 117, 150
Seagle, Debbie, 51, 150, 151, 160, 170, 229
"Seek and Destroy," 207
Sepultura, 93, 124, 126, 137, 157, 201
Seymour Duncan, 164
Sharken, Lisa, 164, 229
"Shattered," 85, 214
"Shedding Skin," 119, 215, 217
Shinedown, 119
Shout at the Devil, 26
Shoutweb, 159, 160, 163, 227
Shulman, Derek, 74–77, 83, 90, 101, 104, 122
Shuvel, 170
Sick of It All, 93

"Side of a Bullet," 199
Simmons, Gene, 95, 150, 192–193
Sindell, Joshua, 204, 229
Singles 1991–1996, The, 140, 217
Sixteen, 5
Sixx, Nikki, 40
Skid Row, 110, 113, 157
Skrape, 175
Skwerl, 229
Slade, 22
Slagel, Brian, 28, 212
Slaughter in the Vatican, 90–91
"Slaughter in the Vatican," 92
"Slaughtered," 119, 215, 217
Slaves on Dope, 170
Slayer, 39–40, 55, 57–59, 66–68, 79, 93, 107, 113, 116, 141, 147, 154, 159, 165, 175, 176–177, 200–201, 206
"Sleep, The," 85, 214
Slipknot, 174, 207
Slo Burn, 151
Smith, Dallas, 180
"Smoke on the Water," 5, 11
Soil, 199
Solitude, 29
Sonic Excess, 201, 227
Soulfly, 154, 159, 170, 174, 201
Soundgarden, 84, 103–104, 110
Soundwave Touring, 120, 145, 226
South of Heaven, 66
"South of Heaven," 67
Spin, 140
SpongeBob Square Pants, 174
Springsteen, Bruce, 6
"Stairway to Heaven," 4
Stand Up and Shout Cancer Fund, 207
Stander, Tazz, 229
Stanley Cup, 161
Stanley, Paul, 57, 95
Starwood, 53, 153

Index

Static-X, 170, 175–176, 199
Staley, Layne, 205
Steel Prophet, 46
Steele, Pete, 128
Sterling Sound, 136
"Strength Beyond Strength," 118, 214–215, 217
Stryper, 15, 33, 70
Suicidal Tendencies, 93, 157
"Suicide Messiah," 199
"Suicide Note Pt. I," 138–139, 215, 218
"Suicide Note Pt. II," 137, 215
Sunken Gardens, 50
Superjoint Ritual, 180, 185, 191, 221
Surfing with the Alien, 65
"Sweating Bullets," 172
Sweet Savage, 51
Sykes, Guy, 93, 98, 101

T-Rex, 33
Tabor, Ty, 86
"Takin' My Life," 213
Tales from the Crypt Presents Demon Knight, 88
Taproot, 170
"Tattoo the Planet," 176
Taylor, Stuart, 12, 33–34, 42, 180, 192, 198
"Tell Me If You Want It," 18, 213
Templeton, Kevin, 144
Ten, 103
"10's," 138, 215
Testament, 110
Texxas Jam, 64
That Metal Show, 207
Therapy?, 124, 154
Thirlwell, J. G., 109
"13 Steps to Nowhere," 137–138, 215
"This Ain't a Beer Belly, It's a Gas Tank for My Love Machine," 156

"This Love," 107–109, 113, 151, 177, 207, 214–216, 218–219
This Love—A Tribute to Dimebag, 200
Thomas, Kyle, 90, 92, 197
Thomas, Matt, 53
3 Vulgar Videos from Hell, 156, 218
3 Watch It Go, 154, 157, 218
"Throes of Rejection," 119, 151–152, 177, 215, 217
Tolinski, Brad, 5, 7, 10, 18, 116, 145, 229
Tongs, Bobby, 34
Tool, 154, 207
Trachsler, Walter, 7, 20, 23, 29, 35, 37, 57, 77, 79, 82, 111, 158, 192–193
Travers, Pat, 156
Trip, the, 33
Trivium, 199, 207
"Trooper, The," 207
Troubadour, 42
Trunk, Eddie, 207
Turbo, 64
"25 Years," 116–117, 119, 215–217
24-7 Spyz, 199
Twisted Sister, 8, 33
Tygers of Pan Tang, 28, 29
Type O Negative, 50, 128, 151, 200

Uberrock, 229
UFO, 6
Ulrich, Lars, 27, 37–38, 201
Ultimate Guitar, 58, 106, 208, 228
Uncle Sam, 147
"Underground in America, The," 38, 215
Unorthodox Steps of Ritual, 155
"Up Lift," 165
Uriah Heep, 70
"Use My Third Arm," 119, 215, 217

Use Once and Destroy, 180, 221
U2, 57

"Valhalla," 214
VampireFreaks, 55, 66, 131, 228
Van Halen II, 194
Van Halen, 5, 7, 9–10, 13, 15–16, 18, 25–27, 40–41, 56–57, 64, 106–107, 157, 171, 191–195, 207–208
Van Halen, Alex, 10
Van Halen, Eddie, 5, 7, 9, 25, 64, 106, 191–195
Vapid Phase, 56
Venom, 27, 29, 55, 57
Verdun Auditorium, 127
VH1, 200, 207
Viking Crown, 155
Vision of Disorder, 151, 176
Vulgar Display of Power, 90, 104–109, 112, 119–122, 137, 140, 147, 153, 167, 184, 206, 214
Vulgar Display of Power: Courage and Carnage at the Alonsa Villa, A, 190
Vulgar Video, 98, 112, 157, 218

"Walk," 105, 107–108, 113, 142, 151, 177, 199, 214–219
Walk, 120
Wallis, Jimmy, 6
"War Nerve," 137–138, 152, 177, 215
Ward, Bill, 151
Warden, Jerry, 20, 27, 62
Warlock, 29, 47
Warrant, 110, 125
W.A.S.P., 39, 44
Watchtower, 50
Waters, Jeff, 96, 175
Watts, Charlie, 3
Weekend Warriors, 117

"We'll Grind That Axe for a Long Time," 164–165, 215
"We'll Meet Again," 63, 214
Wellwood, Jason, 204
Weinberg, Howie, 85, 105, 162
Weinstein, Stephanie Opal, 155, 180
Welch, Brian, 200
"Where to Start," 166
"Where You Come From," 153, 215–216, 218
Whisky a Go Go, 33, 42
White Zombie, 110, 142, 144, 157, 207
Whitesnake, 8, 47
"Widowmaker," 18–19, 213
"Will to Survive, The," 83
Williams, Mike, 203
Wilson, David Lee, 53, 141, 161–162, 170, 229
Winfield, Sterling, 152, 162
Winwood, Ian, 127
"Wish You Where Here," 201
Women and Children First, 59
Wongraven, Satyr, 155
Woodstock, 24
Wylde, Zakk, 191–192, 197, 202

"Yesterday Don't Mean Shit," 161, 165, 215
YouTube, 20
Young, Angus, 6, 13
Young, Malcolm, 13
"You've Got to Belong to It," 165, 215

Zahn, James, 200–201, 207
Zelinsky, Dean, 7
Zlozower, Neil, 147, 171
ZZ Top, 6, 87, 139, 166